BLACK
DIPLOMACY

BLACK DIPLOMACY

African Americans and the
State Department
1945-1969

Michael L. Krenn

M.E. Sharpe
Armonk, New York
London, England

Library of Congress Cataloging-in-Publication Data

Krenn, Michael L., 1957–
Black diplomacy : African Americans and the State Department, 1945–1969 /
Michael L. Krenn.
p.   cm.
Includes bibliographical references and index.
ISBN 0-7656-0380-2 (alk. paper)   ISBN 0-7656-0381-0 (pbk. : alk. paper)
1. United States—Foreign relations administration—History—20th century.
2. Afro-American diplomats—History—20th century. 3. Afro-Americans—Politics and
government. 4. Race discrimination—United States—History—20th century.
5. United States—Foreign relations—1945–1989. I. Title.
JZ1480.K74   1999
353.1′3′0973—dc21
98-29529
CIP

Printed in the United States of America

The paper used in this publication meets the minimum requirements of
American National Standard for Information Sciences—
Permanence of Paper for Printed Library Materials,
ANSI Z 39.48-1984.

BM (c)   10   9   8   7   6   5
BM (p)   10   9   8   7   6   5   4   3   2

Contents

Acknowledgments

Eight years ago I published a research note dealing with African-American ambassadors after World War II. At the time, I was immersed in research on my second book dealing with U.S. policy toward Central America in the postwar years, and so I suggested at the end of the note that this was a subject worthy of further study. I soon decided that it was time to put my money (and research) where my mouth was and I embarked on the present project. It was a daunting prospect. I had spent the first dozen years of my career focused on U.S.-Latin American relations. My knowledge of African-Americans and U.S. foreign policy was slight. It was obvious that I would need the help of a good many people. Fortunately, I found that help in abundance. I would like to take this opportunity to thank the people and institutions who assisted me with such vigor and interest.

A small army of archivists made the research for this project a pleasure. The staffs of the Amistad Research Center, the Moorland-Spingarn Research Center, the Special Collections at the Mugar Memorial Library, the Schomburg Center for Research in Black Culture, the Seeley G. Mudd Manuscript Library, the Department of Special Collections of the University Research Libraries at UCLA, the John F. Kennedy Library, the Richard B. Russell Memorial Library, the National Archives, and the Yale University Library, were all incredibly helpful in ferreting out the needles of this gigantic research haystack. At the Library of Congress Manuscript Division, Michael Womack, Brian McGwire, and Michael Spangler provided valuable assistance, and allowed me access to a number of collections not fully archived. Regina Greenwell at the Lyndon Baines Johnson Library pointed me to several collections I might have overlooked and never blinked an eye at my hundreds of declassification requests. The Harry S. Truman Library staff, particularly Dennis Bilger, Sam Rushay, and Randy Sowell, helped me sift through boxes of records. David Haight of the Dwight D. Eisenhower Library turned me on to several avenues of exploration, including the "Unfinished Business" exhibit at the 1958 World's Fair. Thomas Jefferson Jr. and Gloria Jackson from the Department of State's Office of Equal Employment Opportunity and Civil Rights were thorough and friendly in answering my requests for information. At the USIA Historical Collection, Martin Manning pointed out some fascinating material. Unable to arrange a trip to the Institute and Special Collections at the MIT Libraries, I nevertheless managed to get all the information I needed due to the efforts of Elizabeth Andrews. Charles Kennedy of the Foreign Affairs Oral History Program at Georgetown University was very forthcoming with help and provided funds for my interview of Terence A. Todman.

Several colleagues undertook the task of reading through chapter after chapter of the draft manuscript. David Schmitz, Carol Anderson, Brenda Gayle Plummer, Gerald Horne, Cary Fraser, and John Rossi all gave up immense amounts of time to offer their expertise and criticisms. The readers selected by M.E. Sharpe, Walter Hixson and Thomas Borstelmann, offered very helpful suggestions and criticisms, as well as identifying a number of problems and errors. Any problems remaining, therefore, must be attributed to my failure to heed some of their suggestions.

I would also like to thank the Office of Research and Sponsored Programs at the University of Miami for providing research and travel money for this project. Funding was also provided by the Lyndon Baines Johnson Foundation and the Harry S. Truman Library Institute.

Peter Coveney of M.E. Sharpe showed consistent and real interest in this project almost from the beginning. He offered much needed encouragement many times during the publication process.

BLACK
DIPLOMACY

Introduction

Thinking About Race

As World War II drew to a close, the annual report of the Smithsonian Institution of 1945 chose to include a reprint of a 1944 article by S.L. Washburn entitled, "Thinking About Race." The basic thrust of the article was that "race" was a strictly anatomical concept, having "nothing to do with language, religion, nationality, or social habits." It was specious, Washburn continued, to try and relate intelligence and race. More untenable was the idea of a "pure race," and he made this point with a biting conclusion: "Below is an analysis of one race. Race: Pure Nordic. Location: Nowhere. Method: Imagination. Result: Nonsense." The article was, as its author noted, quite timely, since, "Recently the subject of race has been lifted from comparative obscurity to the headlines."[1]

Washburn's article, while informative and entertaining, was unintentionally misleading on at least two major points. First, the racial issue had never existed in "comparative obscurity" for millions of African-Americans. Face to face with the problem from the day the first African slaves were brought to the American colonies, black Americans had, since the end of the Civil War, coped as best they could with an American society which consigned them to second-class citizenship. It was not until the 1930s, and the Italian invasion of Ethiopia, however, that a growing number of African-Americans began to equate their own struggle for civil rights with the worldwide battle of people of color against colonialism and racial discrimination. As the civil rights movement in America intensified during World War II and

3

the years afterward, so too did the interest in foreign affairs. The beliefs that color was an international issue; that colonialism, apartheid, and racist attitudes overseas could not be divorced from domestic issues of segregation, disenfranchisement, and racial inequality; that the United States, to have a truly representative foreign policy—one which would signify to the world, especially Africa and Asia, that America's talk of freedom, equality, and justice for all was something more than mere rhetoric—needed a black voice *and* presence in the Department of State and Foreign Service, all combined during the post-World War II period to force the African-American community into thinking about race in new and dynamic ways.

Second, while the struggle against racist thinking (of which Washburn's article was one small part) had become a headline issue in many ways—exposés of the horrors of Nazi racialism; the domestic civil rights struggle (which had occasionally exploded into violence, such as the Detroit race riot of 1943); and the rise of anticolonial movements in Africa and Asia—such an attitude had difficulty making much headway in the foreign policy making bureaucracy of the United States. The Department of State, and especially the elite Foreign Service, had for decades been bastions of privileged white males. The "race problem" in America was considered a purely domestic issue, and so the Department never really addressed the matter in any comprehensive way. On the international level, many officials in the Department of State continued the long-held tradition, as historian Michael Hunt explains, of locating "race at the center of their world view."[2] During the post–World War II period, however, the Department of State—faced with an aggressive civil rights movement at home and equally aggressive anticolonialist movements abroad—was pressured to begin thinking about race in new and different ways.

The focus of this book is on understanding what happened during the period 1945–1969 when African-American and Department of State thinking about race collided. It was not a particularly happy meeting. African-Americans launched heavy attacks against U.S. policies dealing with colonialism, charging that America was caving in to the demands of the white European colonial masters rather than siding with the struggles for independence being fought by indigenous—and colored—people. United States officials, they argued, did not understand the central importance of race in the postwar world; that in addition to the East-West struggle, there was a colored-white struggle also ongoing. Nor did they seem to grasp the terrible damage done to America's reputation around the world by racial discrimination and segregation in the United States. This, many African-Americans claimed, was hardly surprising, since the Department of State lacked any real sensitivity to the issue of race. The most concrete evidence of this was the nearly complete lack of a black presence in the Department and in the Foreign Service. Increasing that presence was imperative, not only to demonstrate that the Department was responsive to the domestic demand for equal employment opportunity, but also to indicate to the world—particularly the Third World—that America's foreign policy recognized that people of color must have a voice in mankind's future.

The Department of State only grudgingly accepted that it too had to be "thinking about race": economics and politics, treaties and tariffs, these were the stuff of diplomacy, not the messy and somewhat distasteful issue of racism, especially when that racism had so long been ingrained in what many referred to as the "lily-white" Department of State. But after World War II, the Department was buffeted by too many attacks to ignore the issue any longer. At home, African-Americans denounced the almost complete exclusion of a black voice from the foreign policy making apparatus of the United States. Abroad, both enemies and allies pointed with increasing regularity to America's "Achilles' heel" in terms of its international status and prestige: its inability and/or unwillingness to deal with its serious racial problems. This became a special concern as the United States found itself face to face with more and more nations that had finally been freed from colonial rule and were populated by peoples of color, many of whom were understandably suspicious about America's claims to be the leader of the "free world" when many of its own citizens could not enjoy even the most basic civil rights. That anti-American propaganda often targeted this contradiction was no surprise. United States diplomats could attempt to dismiss attacks on America's racial problems as mere communist propaganda, but this had little impact on the international audience which saw and read about acts of racial violence in Little Rock, Birmingham, and Watts. As for the hiring of more blacks for diplomatic service, any efforts in this direction ran into a stone wall made up of equal parts of disinterest, racism, and tradition. With so many "bigger" issues to tackle, few members of the Department of State gave much time or energy to the notion of equal opportunity employment. Racism, which permeated American society, also found its way into the "best and the brightest" in State and the Foreign Service. And decades of a "lily-white" tradition had built up innumerable obstacles to any efforts at more of a racial balance.

In short, African-Americans and officials in the Department of State and Foreign Service simply did not think about race in the same way. For African-Americans, race was a constant feature of their lives; it defined who they were and how they lived in American society. It also gave them a unique perspective on U.S. foreign policy, which allowed them to analyze problems in the underdeveloped world in a more sympathetic and dynamic fashion. Their demands for more blacks in the diplomatic service exemplified the view that America's foreign policy should represent *all* Americans. For U.S. foreign policy officials, race was, first and foremost, basically a domestic matter. They felt uncomfortable dealing with it at home, and, since America's record on the issue was not a particularly exemplary one, they felt even more uneasy dealing with it in the international arena. For most of them, the primary enemy in the world was communism, not racism. Arguments that the Department and Foreign Service needed to be more representative of the American population at large generally fell on deaf ears. Such action, it was argued, would dilute the "professionalism" of these elite institutions.

By examining what happened when these two ways of thinking about race collided in the postwar years, this study addresses a variety of issues, but three seem to stand out in importance. First, it examines how and why a specific interest group—African-Americans—tried, and generally failed, to influence U.S. foreign policy and State Department hiring practices. The focus of this particular study is on African-American individuals and groups that might be said to form the black mainstream. United States policymakers discounted, attacked, ignored, and tried to suppress what they perceived as more "radical" voices among African-Americans. Therefore, individuals such as Paul Robeson and W.E.B. Du Bois (especially after his break with the National Association for the Advancement of Colored People [NAACP]) and groups such as the Council on African Affairs were greeted with apathy or hostility. Walter White, Roy Wilkins, the NAACP, and the American Negro Leadership Conference on Africa—all seen as relatively "moderate" voices from the black community—were more acceptable to the foreign policy elite in Washington. The story of both the effort and the failure of even this latter group to have any substantial impact on U.S. foreign policy speaks directly to the issue of public opinion and pressure group politics, and the influence both have on American diplomacy.

Second, the book highlights the divergence between the Cold War rhetoric of United States foreign policy makers—which emphasized freedom, justice, and equality—and the reality: that they could barely comprehend, much less effectively address, the racial discrimination and inequities in their own society. This, in turn, leads to some rather troubling questions concerning exactly what the goals of the United States were in the Cold War. Was the rhetoric mere window dressing? Were U.S. officials unable to comprehend the contradictions between their words and the nation's actions at home? Likewise, this study suggests that the issue of race may have overridden hardline talk about "national security" and "power politics" during the Cold War. American officials were well aware that their nation's domestic racial problems were hurting U.S. diplomatic efforts. It was obvious that a stronger national stance for civil rights and more and better use of African-American personnel in the foreign policy bureaucracy would reap benefits for American diplomacy around the world. Even with the overwhelming pressures of the Cold War, however, few U.S. officials pushed for those goals with any intensity or consistency. Was maintaining the "color line" at home more important than breaking down Iron Curtains abroad?

Third, this study demonstrates how a particular bureaucracy—the Department of State—reacted to, perceived, and ultimately frustrated the calls for a more representative diplomatic service. That it was able to do so for so long (and, in many ways, still does) suggests that a deeply ingrained bureaucratic mindset is at work—one that maintains its hold through various presidents, secretaries of state, and personnel changes. Michael Hunt's arguments concerning the racial "ideology" of U.S. foreign policy, which has permeated America's diplomacy, are particularly applicable to this situation. The main thrust of Hunt's thesis is that ideas about race (particularly the superiority of the "Anglo-Saxon" race and, consequently, the inferiority of all other races) have formed an important part of a foreign-policy ideology that has guided U.S. diplomacy since the nation's independence. These ideas have been particularly in evidence when America has had to deal with people of color in Asia, Latin America, and Africa. Measuring the people of those regions using a "hierarchy of race," U.S. policy makers have consistently applied different standards and policies to those areas. Whether during the age of territorial expansion during the mid-1800s, overseas expansion and gunboat diplomacy during the late nineteenth and early twentieth centuries, or while confronting anti-colonial revolutions during the post–World War II period and fighting wars in Korea and Vietnam, the "long-established American views on race" continued to play an important role in the nation's foreign policy.[3] This study, by looking particularly at the personnel decisions of the Department of State and Foreign Service, confirms Hunt's basic assumptions. Yet, it also suggests that those very personal and social views on race were sustained on a bureaucratic level. Even when someone like Dean Rusk—who had relatively more liberal views on race than most of his fellow Americans—was in charge of the Department in the 1960s, and both President John F. Kennedy and President Lyndon B. Johnson pursued the issue of black employment in foreign service work more vigorously than their predecessors, only minor inroads were made into the predominantly white make-up of the Department of State and Foreign Service. All of this suggests that there is a "bureaucratic ideology" at work from generation to generation, administration to administration; one that has taken such a hold that it seems impervious to individual attempts to ameliorate the racial imbalances in employment. And, if this is true, what other kinds of bureaucratic ideologies are at work shaping U.S. foreign policy?

Finally, the story told here prompts a thought-provoking "what if" question (which, of course, historians are not supposed to ask, but always do). What if there *had* been a greater black voice in America's foreign policy during the 1940s, 1950s, and 1960s? Would the nation's policies, particularly in the Third World, have been any different? Would there have been new, and perhaps more helpful, insights into America's seemingly endless problems in Africa, Asia, and Latin America? We will, of course, never know: the black voice in foreign policy was decidedly muted. It is intriguing, nevertheless, to ponder the question. After all, no one can deny that African-Americans' efforts in forcing the United States to confront its domestic racial problems helped make for a fundamentally healthier society. Perhaps by bringing some new ways of thinking about race in the international arena, they could have helped make a better world as well.

~ 1 ~

Can Negroes Make Diplomats?

African-Americans and the Department of State, 1945–1952

During and after World War II, African-Americans turned their attention not only to the fight for civil rights at home but also to the struggle for racial equality on a worldwide basis. A number of African-American individuals and organizations came to the conclusion that the two fights were intimately connected and that victories (and losses) in one had repercussions on the other. This is not to argue that foreign policy became a more important issue than the domestic struggle for equality. Yet, during those years more and more African-Americans came to see race and racism as global issues. In this regard they were far ahead of most white Americans.

One specific aspect of that growing interest was the demand for greater numbers of blacks in the Department of State, particularly in the prestigious Foreign Service. As a domestic issue, this demand was part of the African-American campaign for equal employment opportunity. In terms of foreign policy, the desire for more of a black *presence* in the Department of State was a manifestation of the growing demand for a black *voice* in the making of that policy.

Before analyzing these matters, it is first necessary to understand why that department became such a focal point of African-American discontent. Why did African-Americans see the need for more black diplomats; what issues drove them to seek a more direct voice in U.S. foreign policy? And what factors pushed a number of African-Americans to consider careers in what was an almost exclusively white Department of State and Foreign Service?

For many African-Americans, World War II was a watershed in terms of drawing their attention to foreign policy issues. It was certainly not the first time that African-Americans had demonstrated interest in the subject. During the late nineteenth and early twentieth centuries, the U.S. intervention in the Philippines, the British war with the Boers, and the U.S. occupation of Haiti attracted serious attention from African-American observers.[1] During the 1910s and 1920s, the work of W.E.B. Du Bois in the 1919 Pan-African Congress and the success of Marcus Garvey's Universal Negro Improvement Association focused African-American attention on Africa.[2] As Brenda Gayle Plummer has noted, however, it was with the Italian invasion of Ethiopia in 1935 that one can see "the first great manifestation of Afro-American interest in foreign affairs." The spectacle of a white nation battering one of the only independent black nations in the world was quickly equated with the American government's forbearance of gross violations of African-American civil rights at home. African-Americans protested the Italian action and called for a more active response from the United States.[3]

During the next decade or so, African-Americans continued to develop an increasing interest in their nation's foreign policy, as well as the idea that race was an international issue. Books on the subject were written by Executive Secretary of the NAACP Walter White, W.E.B. Du Bois, and Howard University professor Rayford W. Logan. In addition, there were numerous articles on foreign policy in African-American newspapers. These were supplemented by pieces in *The Crisis,* the official organ of the NAACP, and in *New Africa,* the bulletin of the more radical Council on African Affairs, which had been founded during the 1930s by Paul Robeson and Max Yergan.[4]

This did not dissipate in the postwar years, and in a variety of ways African-Americans expressed their continuing concerns. Since their activities also brought them to question the hiring and employment practices of the Department of State, it may prove useful to briefly examine some of the basic foreign policy premises developed by African-Americans during the years 1945–1952. By building on the efforts of scholars such as Mary Dudziak, Thomas Borstelmann, Brenda Gayle Plummer, Penny M. Von Eschen, and Gerald Horne, among others, it will become clear that efforts to desegregate America's diplomatic corps were intimately connected with ongoing efforts to push American leaders into accepting what might be called a diplomacy of desegregation in its relations with the postwar world.[5]

W.E.B. Du Bois had once written that, "The problem of the twentieth century is the problem of the color line—the relation of the darker to the lighter races of men in Asia and Africa, in America and the islands of the sea."[6] Certainly by the end of World War II a growing number of African-Americans shared that prophetic vision, far outpacing most of their white counterparts who only dimly perceived the racial dynamics of the postwar world. In the years following the war, African-Americans made two interrelated points: first, that the United States could not ignore the issue of race, particularly the plight of millions of people of color around the world; and second, that to be an effective world leader in the coming years, the United States would need to more seriously address its domestic race problems. In short, the United States had to commit itself to breaking the "color line" both at home and abroad.

Du Bois was one of the most vocal proponents of these ideas. In a 1946 letter to former U.S. Minister to Liberia Lester Walton, Du Bois complained that at the upcoming meeting of the United Nations General Assembly the "Colonial peoples will, for the most part, be represented either by the nations owning or governing them or at best by representatives chosen by these master nations." It was a galling thought, but it might happen that "not a single person of Negro descent will have any voice save in the case of Ethiopia and Liberia, which are free nations." The result would be that millions of Africans would be "unrepresented and unheard."

Representatives of "the empires" (America included) would try and forestall this, but according to Du Bois "there is no reason that the elementary basis of democracy—the right of peoples to speak for themselves—should be entirely ignored in international consideration of African questions."[7] Less radical African-Americans concurred with Du Bois that the idea of a segregated world was an unacceptable situation. Walter White, in a 1951 letter to Howard University professor Rayford Logan, gave vent to his frustration: "I have been screaming my head off for the past eight or ten years ... that the United States had better wake up to the significance and the danger of this anti-white, anti-colonial revolt. . . . When, oh when will white Europe and America wake up?"[8]

Such ruminations also found expression in a number of publications during the years 1945–1952. An editorial from the April 1945 issue of *The African* was blunt in laying out the fundamental issue to be faced at an upcoming meeting to set up the framework for the United Nations. At the session, "all races, creeds, colors and nationalities" would be represented. The delegates would "speak for two-thirds of the world population which is not white, and other delegates will represent one-third, which is classified as white. Therefore, the so-called white races should, at least, come to the realization that they are a mere minority in a world which up to 1945 they dominated." A piece in a 1948 issue of *Race Relations* noted that, "Of the fifty-five nations now members of the UN, well over forty have either a majority of colored people or a colored minority so substantial as to make their presence an important factor in the foreign policy of the country."[9]

Speaking before a symposium organized by the United Negro College Fund, Edith Sampson, who served as a U.S. representative to the General Assembly during the Truman presidency, highlighted the same points by stressing the irony of her own situation: "I just happened by accident of birth to be identified with the two-thirds majority group of mankind, which is colored; again by accident of birth I am a citizen of a country where nine-tenths of the people are classed in the little one-third minority of mankind, which is white. Our country seeks security in a world in which two-thirds of the people are dark-skinned." And, in a much more sarcastic vein, the "Charley Cherokee" section of the monthly publication, *Negro Digest,* in October 1950 argued that, "the world is divided into three groups,—the pro-United States group, the pro-Russian group and those who for one reason or another don't give a damn or are undecided. What hasn't been said is that most of the folks in this large and powerful third group are colored folks, not exactly Negroes but something less than white according to our current standards."[10]

The most powerful expression of the African-American viewpoint came through their attacks on colonialism—the ultimate symbol of a world segregated into white masters and colored slaves and workers. A strong current of anticolonialism ran through the commentary of many African-Americans as World War II drew to a close and continued throughout the Truman period.[11]

The National Association for the Advancement of Colored People (NAACP) and the Council on African Affairs spearheaded the attack on colonialism. On 10 March 1945, the NAACP wrote to Secretary of State Edward Stettinius to ask whether the issue of colonies would be discussed at the upcoming conference in San Francisco and, if so, whether there were any plans for including "commissions or spokesmen from the colonial peoples themselves who can directly or indirectly speak for their aspirations and progress." A few months later, an editorial in *The Crisis* expressed extreme disappointment in the stand taken by the United States in San Francisco. America had aligned itself with the "imperial masters" on the issue of independence for colonized peoples. The best it could manage was support for a vague system of "trusteeship," which was a "bald compromise of basic American principle." As the Truman administration drew to a close, the national NAACP convention passed the following resolution: "It would still be our moral duty to relieve poverty and try to end exploitation and colonialism throughout the world."[12]

The Council on African Affairs (CAA), which had come into being in 1937, was also an important organization representing a black voice against colonialism. The CAA was more radical than the NAACP and somewhat narrower in its approach, since it focused exclusively on colonialism in Africa.[13] In November of 1937, the CAA asked the NAACP to join it in sending a letter to Franklin Roosevelt and Stetinnius urging the United States to work toward the advancement of all people in Africa and especially for "self-government" for those people held in colonies and mandates. A 1944 issue of the CAA's publication, *New Africa,* had a picture of Nigerian troops on its cover and pointed out that they were at that moment serving with Allied forces in Burma battling against Japan. An editorial asked the readers, "after hearing and seeing how other men live and what they think, after feeling in his marrow the meaning of a common struggle for a common purpose—will you ask this African to go back to the static, profitless, hopeless existence of a colonial subject?"[14]

In addition to criticisms of the U.S. policy toward colonialism, African-Americans also engaged in harsh denunciations of the colonizers, such as Great Britain. Shortly after a November 1945 address to the U.S. Congress by Prime Minister Clement Attlee, the NAACP fired off an angry telegram protesting the fact that while Attlee argued for "civilization" and "Christian principle . . . British troops bomb, strafe, and otherwise slaughter Indonesians and Palestinian youths." Would the loan he had asked for be used to "perpetuate empire and to suppress by force of arms or otherwise the legitimate demands of colonial peoples?" After former Prime Minister Winston Churchill's famous "Iron Curtain" address in March 1946, the NAACP commented that the speech was "beyond question one of the most dangerous and cynical made in contemporary history. . . . It calls for an Anglo-Saxon bloc" which would have "particularly disastrous effects upon the fate and fortunes of colored peoples." The pages of *The Crisis* were filled with articles denouncing British colonialism in the Sudan, Nigeria, the West Indies, and India.[15]

The French and Dutch also came under fire. A selection of titles from *The Crisis* suggests the breadth of African-American interest. Concentrating on the French holdings in West Africa, an article attacked the "French Terror in Negro Africa." "Madagascar Fights for Freedom" announced another. Even "The Vietnamese Struggle for Independence" attracted the magazine's attention. As with the articles dealing with British colonial rule, the French were excoriated for their brutal treatment of indigenous peoples and policies that held their colonies in a state of perpetual backwardness. An article in *Race Relations* called the Dutch attack on Indonesian nationalist forces in 1947 one of "the most depressing events in human relations in recent months."[16]

Even the United States did not escape criticism of its "colonial" policies.

An article in *The Crisis* attacked the discriminatory policies in the Panama Canal Zone, which amounted to a virtual Jim Crow system. Non-American workers in the Canal Zone were paid less, had less opportunities for promotion, and lived in segregated housing. "Southern racist attitudes transplanted to the Canal Zone" had made for a "double standard" that stood in stark contrast to "American ideals." The same situation, noted a 1946 editorial in *The Crisis,* held true for Guam, where Guamanians were given "inferior education in segregated schools," the native language had been banned, and native workers were paid less than imported American workers. Actions by the U.S. Navy in Guam indicated that the " 'Navy mind' on colored people is the Dixie mind, undiluted."[17]

While African-Americans sharply criticized America's role in creating and maintaining a segregated world through its toleration and even support of British, French, and Dutch imperialism and its actions in its own "semi-colonial" spheres of influence, they also warned that segregation and racism within America were adding fuel to what Walter White had called the "anti-white, anti-colonial" fires beginning to rage in Asia, Africa, and elsewhere. In short, America's race problem was hurting its standing abroad and was giving communist propagandists all the ammunition they needed to fire holes through American rhetoric about freedom, equality, and justice.

A favorite tactic for African-American spokespersons during the years immediately after World War II was to point out the inescapable contradictions between the Truman administration's public rhetoric about battling for freedom and democracy in its foreign policy, while at home millions of African-Americans suffered the indignities heaped upon them by official and unofficial acts of segregation and bias. A brief selection of editorials from *The Crisis* which appeared from 1945 through 1947 are good examples. In two separate pieces in December 1945, the journal's editors took aim at the situation. In one, the writer expressed his confusion over America's policies. America and Britain had just fought a war to defeat "the master race theory," and now warned the Soviets to stop "meddling" in Eastern Europe. Yet, "we continue to follow the race superiority line at home and abroad." "Politically," the writer concluded, "the citizens of seven states are thus little better off than the Indonesians or the Nigerians." And what of those Indonesians and Nigerians? Supplied with Lend-Lease weapons from the United States, Britain was restoring its colonial rule in Africa and helping the Dutch crush a rebellion in Indonesia. In the second piece, Secretary of State James Byrnes's concern for "democratic elections" in the Balkans was measured against his complete lack of interest in promoting " 'free democratic elections' in his home state"—South Carolina.[18]

By 1947, the tone was angrier. Taking note of President Truman's criticism of recent elections in Poland, an editorial remarked, "Mr. Truman and the American people can peer far beyond the seas, wring their hands, and choke with rage at an election in Poland, but they are strangely dumb at a similar election in South Carolina or Mississippi." The reason for Truman's action, of course, was clear: the United States was "wrapping herself in holy garments and uttering righteous words" in order to attack Soviet communism. In a full-page editorial in April 1947, a speech by Secretary of State George C. Marshall at the Moscow Council of Foreign Ministers meeting was dissected. Marshall had argued eloquently for the American conception of democracy. The Soviet representatives, the editorial suggested, must have had to stifle their amusement, since they knew "quite well that in the American states Negroes do not enjoy democracy as defined by Mr. Marshall." The editorial reached its bitter conclusion: "preaching about democracy before a world council of nations while practicing lynching is something else again. We have proved in the past that our hides are tough enough and our moral sense dull enough to stand this paradox without great shame. Whether the present struggle for power and survival will force us to do what shame could not remains to be seen."[19]

While many African-Americans remained skeptical as to whether the international pressures brought on by the Cold War *would* force the United States to confront its domestic racial problems, nearly all argued that it *should,* because they were convinced that America's treatment of its minority citizens was a foreign policy liability of the first degree. African-Americans attacked the idea that the United States could battle for freedom abroad while denying it at home. A 1949 editorial in *The Crisis* was typical. Commenting on a women's club meeting in Japan at which a paper complimenting the United States for helping to establish a democratic Japanese government was presented, the editorial noted some of the responses from the audience: "How can we trust those who proclaim in our constitution ideas which they do not practice in their own land? In the United States there is racial discrimination against the Negro. . . ." And, "I cannot applaud a speech which asks allegiance to the United States while they have a color line. That makes all words about equality a hypocrisy." "There you have it," the piece succinctly concluded. A year later, *The Crisis* recounted recent developments within the NAACP, including a report on the association's response to the Korean War. The NAACP had passed a resolution in support of U.S. actions in Korea and condemning communist aggression. Nevertheless, "guns alone" could not win the war against communism. Should the United States seek victory in regions such as Asia, "it will have to demonstrate that democracy is a living reality which knows no limitation of race, color or nationality."[20]

In the *Negro Digest,* "Charley Cherokee" confronted the issue with his usual sarcasm. Writing about the State Department's "concern over world opinion on racial discrimination within the United States," he suggested that the only response State could come up with was to air Voice of America pieces "which so emphasize the achievements of individual U.S. Negro citizens as to take them out of context and make it appear to persons not familiar with American life, that all is lovey-dovey." A few months later he revisited the topic, declaring that, "Race is the weak spot in the defense of our State Department and of the United Nations, against [the] spread of communism." The only response from the United States was to "beam a few beautiful little tear-jerker stories on Voice of America radio about how Booker T. Washington and George Carver and Mary Bethune made good."[21]

An article written by Fisk University President Charles S. Johnson in 1948 put the issue in somewhat more dramatic terms. "A vast and mighty sweep of forces that involves most of the world, has telescoped our national role into one of guardianship of a democratic civilization." In accepting this role that had been thrust upon the United States, it would have to be recognized that, "Race relations as race relations cannot be dealt with as if in a vacuum." Johnson concluded that, "Race, in short, has become far more than a domestic issue. It has become the scale on which democracy is being weighed in a world that is being relentlessly forced to choose between ideologies. If democracy is to prove its case on the world scene, there is need for more than words. The time of proof has come, and race is the touchstone."[22]

Johnson's warning was echoed by various members of the African-American community. In comments for a symposium on civil rights published in the *Harlem Quarterly,* President of the Brotherhood of Sleeping Car Porters A. Philip Randolph declared that "the elimination of jim-crow in all phases of American life . . . would remove the most damaging indictment to democracy as practiced in the United States of America." Using much the same terminology as Johnson, Randolph concluded that, "The American race problem represents the proving ground to the colored peoples of the world as to the sincerity of the United States in the democratic cause. Jim-crow is America's national disgrace. Its existence confuses and embarrasses our foreign policy."[23]

Even NAACP Executive Secretary Walter White, who usually tried to balance pessimism with equal doses of optimism, was vexed at the damage done to the nation's diplomacy by racial bias. In a "progress report" on civil rights published in 1951, White described his embarrassment when queried by foreigners about America's mistreatment of its black minority. He could only respond that change was taking place, but very slowly; nevertheless, as one of his foreign correspondents told him, "Colored people in Asia, Africa,

and South America read with horror and alarm" the stories of white brutality in America, all of which was "building up a terrible and terrifying
anti-white feeling all over the world." Despite slow progress in civil rights
since the beginning of World War II, White was forced to admit that, "We
are not yet able effectively to answer the barbed attacks on our practices
which increase in number from the critics of American democracy. There
are still wide gaps between what we profess and what we do to implement
our beliefs."[24]

Some of the most stinging indictments came from Ralph Bunche. Considered by many Americans, both black and white, to be *the* African-American
voice in international affairs, Bunche's public denunciations of his nation's
racial problems usually got wide coverage. As part of an official statement
put out by the Federal Council of the Churches of Christ in America in 1946,
Bunche declared that, "Segregation handicaps the nation in international
relations." Bunche elaborated on this point in a speech to the NAACP in
1950. Exhorting the nation to greater efforts in dealing with discrimination
and segregation, he argued that, "We cannot convert the vast masses of Asia
and Africa to a democracy qualified by color. Even Europe is no little baffled
by that type of democracy." The time for "gradualism" in working to solve
the nation's race problems was gone, for the contradictions between
America's public statements about freedom and its domestic practices of
racial discrimination had "already cost us prestige, good will, and more lives
than we have needed to lose on far-off battlefields. . . . We must exert an
extraordinary effort to put our interracial house in order."[25] In a speech in
1951, Bunche launched a bitter attack on South Carolina Governor James
Byrnes for Byrnes's support of segregated schools and other facilities. More
specifically, he noted the international damage done by the governor's
stance. Byrnes, as a former secretary of state, should "know how costly are
such undemocratic declarations and practices to our foreign relations, to our
international reputation for democracy, our prestige and our leadership."[26]

In these and other ways, African-Americans were implicitly calling for a
diplomacy of desegregation: an end to white colonialism over peoples of
color; a recognition by U.S. policymakers of the fact that American racial
problems contradicted much of what the nation was trumpeting overseas;
and a further recognition that those contradictions were coming home to
haunt the United States. The African-American struggle for civil rights was,
therefore, not simply a growing reminder of a national embarrassment, but
an increasingly important issue in terms of America's foreign relations. At
the same time, there was a call for the desegregation of U.S. diplomacy
through the increased integration of African-Americans into the Department
of State. The two efforts were intimately related: the desire for an African-

American *voice* in U.S. foreign policy could perhaps be most concretely met through a greater African-American *presence* in the foreign policy bureaucracy. In addition, the hiring or appointment of African-Americans by one of the most prestigious and visible agencies in the federal government could not help but provide a boost to the fight for equal employment opportunities.

In May 1949, an editorial entitled, "Can Negroes Make Diplomats?," appeared in *Ebony*. The piece attacked the miserable record of Franklin Roosevelt and Harry Truman in terms of the appointment of African-Americans to government positions. Very quickly, however, the author zeroed in on one department's terrible performance: "Ironically enough in these cold-war days when America trumpets loud and long to the rest of the world about her democracy, this happens to be the department which is the face and front the U.S. presents most often and most openly to foreign nations. It is the U.S. State Department." Calling specifically for the appointment of an African-American as ambassador to Haiti, the editorial ended by stating: "If America's self-assumed role as No. 1 champion of world democracy is to be accepted by other nations, it is time that America demonstrated in its foreign service that it practices what it preaches," and that President Truman "personally shook up the State Department and appointed outstanding Negroes as consuls, ministers and ambassadors to nations around the globe."[27]

Throughout the years 1945–1952, African-Americans criticized the Department of State and Foreign Service for their nearly all-white composition, pushed for the use of more African-Americans in the diplomatic field, celebrated and publicized the appointment of blacks to foreign affairs positions, and made suggestions as to other appointments that could be made. They were aided by a number of highly qualified and motivated African-Americans who were determined to make their careers in diplomacy.

In the forefront of the fight for getting more African-Americans in the Department of State was the NAACP. In early 1945, when the U.S. delegation to the upcoming San Francisco conference was being formed, the NAACP wrote to Secretary of State Stettinius to discover "if any provision will be made for the representation of American Negroes." They were needed to "advocate and advise measures for their own social progress and also be given opportunity to speak for other peoples of African descent whom they in a very real sense represent." Stettinius allowed the NAACP to send a team of "consultants" to the conference: Walter White, W.E.B. Du Bois, and Mary McLeod Bethune.[28]

In 1947, Walter White wrote directly to President Truman concerning the issue. White argued that the United States needed closer relations with India, and he hoped that Secretary of State George Marshall would be able to make a personal visit to that country. If he could not, then a "small but very distinguished economic mission" should go in his stead. It would be "exceedingly valuable if a member of such a mission ... were a distinguished American Negro whose skin color would clearly indicate his racial identity." This, he claimed, would help counter anti-U.S. propaganda which fed on the racial issue.[29]

In 1951, Roy Wilkins of the NAACP was invited to a State Department conference on foreign policy issues. He was particularly impressed by a presentation given by Assistant Secretary of State for Public Affairs Edward W. Barrett. Wilkins's most important suggestions was that the NAACP "should do whatever we can to get a qualified colored person or persons on Mr. Barrett's staff since the explanation of the functioning of American democracy in the area of colored minorities is such an important part of what they call 'The Campaign of Truth.' "[30]

Du Bois was a bit more skeptical when it came to topics such as the Department of State's willingness to bring more African-Americans into the fold. Writing to a young man seeking information about U.S. foreign policy toward Africa, he claimed that "Negroes have been pretty well weeded out of our consular service and the service of the State Department although there are a few left." Nevertheless, he saw some hope: "I think that if the interest of Negroes were aroused as to the particular problems of Africa," they might make some headway."[31]

Other voices were also heard. A. Philip Randolph, following a 1952 fact-finding tour that took him through East Asia, held a press conference in which he argued that "Negro officials and personnel should be sent to all Asian countries as representatives of the United States Government." And from the *Negro Digest,* "Charley Cherokee" tore into the "white folks" who "insist on treating Chinese, Koreans, Japanese, etc., as colored folks and hence inferior to white folks." He signed off, "BUY ANOTHER U.S. SAVINGS BOND, MISTER, but until our State Department has a 'Ralph Bunche' in every department, especially in its Voice of America program, KEEP 'EM SQUIRMING!"[32]

The most blistering attack on the lack of African-American representation in the Department of State came in a series of articles written by Howard University professor Rayford Logan, which appeared on the front pages of the prestigious *Pittsburgh Courier* in April–May 1950.[33] Logan skewered the Department's hiring policies, its use (and misuse) of the few African-Americans in the diplomatic service, and argued that such policies and practices were injuring the nation's international standing. The first article laid out the problem in detail: only thirty-three of the over 13,000 members of the U.S. Foreign Service were African-American, and twenty-eight of those were in the lower classifications. In looking for reasons, Logan first described the department "culture":

> It is not absolutely necessary for a high official of the Department of State to be a decendant [sic] of the Puritans, the Dutch Patroons, the Huguenots or the Cavaliers. No requirement stipulates he must have gone to Groton, Hill School, Harvard, Yale, Princeton or the University of Virginia. An independent income in the higher brackets and a knowledge of what wine to serve with filet mignon or lobster a la Newburg are not sine qua non. But in the top echelons these desiderata are not small change. As one cynic has remarked many State Department officials learn protocol before they know how to write a dispatch, an instruction, or even a memorandum.

In this setting it was not surprising to find that African-Americans largely served as "courtly servitors"—messengers.

This overall "culture" was not the only problem. Logan also noted that many of the "personnel men" in State came from the South. This might be circumstantial, but, "Unless evidence to the contrary is adduced ... The Courier is forced to conclude that there is more than [a] casual relationship between these Southern origins and the lamentably small number of Negro professional workers" in the Department of State.[34]

Logan followed up a week later with a devastating piece on the assignments given to African-Americans in the Foreign Service. He was particularly irate that African-Americans seemed to be assigned only to "colored countries." Of the thirty-three blacks in the Foreign Service, two-thirds were in Liberia. Most of the rest were spread among Ponta Delgada in the Azores, Madagascar, Haiti, Cuba, Egypt, Turkey, and Portugal: "all of which have a large population that is either colored or could easily 'pass' for colored." Only two African-Americans were assigned to posts in Europe. This was troubling enough since, "The Pittsburgh Courier does not accept the thesis that American Negroes should be assigned only to colored countries." But even here the Department of State seemed to demonstrate no consistency. If the department really was set on sending African-American diplomats to "colored countries," then why were they not serving in nations such as Brazil, Venezuela, or the Dominican Republic? Why were there none in Ethiopia? There were no blacks assigned to the Far East, the Middle East, the Near East, or India.

Not only were African-Americans in the diplomatic service segregated in terms of where they could serve, but they were also separated from their white counterparts in terms of positions held. Only one African-American, Edward Dudley, held the rank of ambassador (to Liberia). Five others held the rank of Foreign Service Officer, and Logan mentioned three others who were Foreign Service specialists. The vast majority of the African-Americans in the Foreign Service, however, held jobs at the bottom of the employment ladder: clerks, stenographers, and guards. "American Negroes are obviously being taxed without proportionate opportunities to represent their country abroad."[35]

In his next article, Logan turned his attention to the lack of African-Americans in high-level positions at the Department of State in Washington. Again, the numbers spoke for themselves: as of 1947, less than 200 of the 7,000 departmental employees were black, and "most of these were classified as custodial or minor clerical." Yet, Logan argued, there were jobs open at the Department that might be filled "if competent colored men and women are considered on their merits." Admittedly, not many African-Americans applied for positions with the Department of State, but this was due to the "notorious reputation of the reluctance of the State Department to appoint Negroes to the higher brackets." It was time for that attitude to change.[36]

Logan tempered his attacks in his next installment, instead focusing on the need for African-Americans to understand the stiff competition they would be facing in trying to secure diplomatic positions. In fact, Logan even complimented the Department for breaking down a few color barriers in Washington by inviting blacks to conferences and luncheons held at previously segregated restaurants and hotels. Yet, he once again complained about the "vicious circle which has led very few Negroes to prepare themselves for jobs [in the State Department] because they knew they would not be considered solely because of their race and are then chided because so few do apply." It was up to black universities and colleges to better prepare African-American applicants. Of course, "competent but 'undesirable' candidates can be ruthlessly eliminated" at the oral examination stage, but Logan argued that it "would be much more difficult to justify wholesale elimination of colored candidates than to explain the elimination of one or two."[37]

In the last article of the series dealing with African-Americans and the Department of State and Foreign Service, Logan targeted the School of Foreign Service at Georgetown University. Though the School denied that African-Americans were not welcome, Logan noted that a "policy of complete exclusion" had been the norm in the past. Although the School had been in operation since 1919, no more than half a dozen African-Americans had been admitted. The reasons seemed clear. First was the fact that few blacks had applied; the same reasoning that kept them from applying for positions with the Department of State also prevailed in their choices for higher education. But more than that was at work at Georgetown, which had "been adamant in its policy of excluding colored students." At the present time, there were four black students enrolled at the School, but this was out of a total enrollment of nearly 1,700. Graduation from the School of Foreign Service was not an automatic ticket to high-level foreign policy positions, but it did "prepare its graduates specifically for the examinations held for appointments in them. It is all the more necessary, then, that more colored students be admitted to the School of Foreign Service if the total diplomacy of the United States is to be conducted at home and abroad without distinction as to race or color."[38]

In addition to the criticisms of Logan and others concerning the lack of a black presence in the Department of State, further evidence of the African-American interest in having more blacks in the U.S. diplomatic service is to be found in the wide publicity given to the handful of African-Americans who *were* appointed during the Truman years. Whereas newspapers such as the *New York Times* usually gave but scant notice of all but the most high-level diplomatic appointments, black newspapers and journals celebrated the selections of African-Americans for positions from ambassador to clerk. Typical was a piece from the *Baltimore Afro-American* in 1948, which noted that five African-Americans had recently been appointed to the Foreign Service. Not only did it mention Giles Hubert and William George, both of whom had been appointed as Foreign Service Officers (FSO), but also John George (William's brother) and William Boswell (both appointed to administrative positions in Liberia), as well as Beatrice Carson, who had been made a clerk, also to Liberia. The latter three were pictured standing around a globe, and were characterized as "New appointees to Uncle Sam's Foreign Service."[39]

Groundbreaking appointments were always covered by the black press. For example, Giles Hubert, a professor of economics at Fisk University, was featured twice. In 1947, the *Baltimore Afro-American* noted his appointment as an FSO to Haiti, where he was to serve as agricultural attaché. Four years later, the *New York Amsterdam News* ran a feature photo of Hubert leaving the U.S. embassy in Haiti for his new job as consul and economic office in Bombay. And when Edward R. Dudley was named as the first black U.S. ambassador in 1949, *Ebony* ran a four-page spread.[40]

There were also frequent articles giving overviews of African-American appointess. Lester Walton, who had served as U.S. minister to Liberia from 1935 to 1946, wrote a piece for the *New York Amsterdam News* in 1949 that provided a brief history of black diplomatic appointments since the late 1800s. Walton went on to cite the achievements of more recent appointees (including himself). In a similar vein, Alice Dunnigan, in the *Baltimore Afro-American,* surveyed the careers of the forty African-Americans currently serving in the field of U.S. diplomacy.[41]

At the same time that they celebrated those African-Americans who were successfully pursuing careers in diplomacy, black individuals and publications also kept up pressure for more and higher profile appointments by pushing the Department of State to consider specific people, sometimes for specific jobs. Logan had berated the Department for limiting the areas of service for black diplomats, and argued that they should be sent to Latin America, Asia, the Middle East, and Europe. In the final article of his 1950 series, he had offered a short list of some of the most qualified black candidates: Professors E. Franklin Frazier and Merze Tate from Howard University; Horace Mann Bond, president of Lincoln University; Charles Johnson, president of Fisk University; and Edward Lawson Jr., who currently held a position in the United Nations. Seven months after his articles appeared, Logan and Stanley Roberts, who was the Washington editor for the *Pittsburgh Courier,* had a conference with Robert Oliver, executive assistant for the Economic Cooperation Administration. Following the meeting, Logan sent a detailed list of prospects to Oliver. These included Frazier and Tate, and others such as William H. Dean, who was with the United Nations, and Dr. Hugh Smythe and his wife, Dr. Mabel M. Smythe.[42] Elmer Henderson, director of the American Council on Human Rights, wrote to Secretary of State Dean Acheson in September 1950 with a list of twelve names he wished to have considered for appointment to the UN General Assembly meeting for 1951, including that of Rayford Logan. Henderson also listed Ralph Bunche; Channing Tobias, who was director of the Phelps-Stokes Fund; and Walter White.[43]

When talk turned to the subject of black appointees for prestigious jobs in the Department of State, however, one name dominated the discussions: Ralph Bunche. Bunche had first become directly involved in the U.S. foreign policy apparatus when he joined the Office of Strategic Services (OSS) in 1941, where he served as an expert on African issues. In 1944, he transferred to the Department of State, where he worked on the planning for the United Nations. In 1946, he was "loaned" to the U.S. delegation to the United Nations, where he served as director of the Trusteeship Division. By 1947, he had left the Department of State to serve full-time with the UN and began the most illustrious chapter of his career, culminating in his Nobel Peace Prize in 1950 for his work on the delicate issue of Palestine.[44]

As a result of Bunche's tremendous success in working for the United Nations, he was constantly promoted as a candidate for a high-level job in State. Walter White suggested to Secretary Dean Acheson in 1950 that Bunche be proposed by the U.S. delegation to the UN for secretary general. He argued that the "Soviet Union would find it exceedingly difficult [to] explain to Asia and Africa as well as to [the] world generally any opposition to him in light of Palestine and his winning of [the] Nobel Prize"; his nomination would help in "exploding Soviet appeal to non-white peoples of the world." A year later, White was pushing Bunche as U.S. ambassador to the Soviet Union. Not only was he a "superlative" diplomat, but the "sending of a distinguished Negro American to Moscow would be one of the most devastating answers possible to Soviet propaganda that all American Negroes are kept in the lowest stratum of society."[45]

Eventually, Bunche was asked to serve as an assistant secretary of state, but the incident turned out to be a public relations fiasco. Early in 1949, Bunche had been approached about taking the position of assistant secretary of state for Near Eastern, South Asian, and African affairs. He rejected the offer, but was pressured to meet with President Truman before he made a final decision. Bunche held his meeting with the President in late May, at which time he explained that he did not want to give up his duties with the United Nations. He also had another reason for his decision: his refusal to live in segregated Washington, D.C. Bunche gave an interview to the *Pittsburgh Courier* when he left Washington a few days later. With the gigantic headline, "Bunche Blasts D.C. Jim Crow," the article served as a sounding board for Bunche's frustrations with segregation in the nation's capital: "I have bucked segregation long enough in my own lifetime. I do not intend to inflict it unnecessarily on my children."[46]

While Bunche was the main focus of attention, there were other African-Americans who were trying to make careers in U.S. diplomacy, often in the face of what they perceived as subtle (and sometimes not so subtle) racial prejudice. Their efforts were additional ingredients in the pressure being exerted for better opportunities for African-Americans.

Lester Walton, who served as U.S. minister to Liberia from 1933 to 1945, wrote a scathing letter to Du Bois late in 1945 just prior to his replacement. While he congratulated the Department of State for standing "four-square at all times behind me," he also noted that, "There is a certain element here and in the United States which looks with some disfavor on my presence here as American Minister." Walton suspected that it was "the aim of certain Americans to bring about the appointment of a white man as chief of diplomatic mission in Liberia. . . . Either that or a Negro who is willing to do their bidding."[47]

Clifton Wharton Sr., who became the first African-American to pass the new Foreign Service examination in 1924, faced different difficulties than Walton, who was a political appointee. Wharton had earlier become the first black to hold a professional position in the Department of State when he had been hired as a law clerk. Despite this groundbreaking assignment, he found little encouragement among his colleagues in terms of taking the

Foreign Service examination. As he stated in an interview years later, "They couldn't care less; they didn't want me in the Department of State." When he passed the examination, he found himself confined to a narrow circle of overseas assignments: Liberia, the Azores, the Canary Islands, and Madagascar. These postings became known as the "Negro circuit." After serving twenty-one years circulating among these posts, Wharton seemed to be on the verge of breaking the cycle in 1946 when an opening occurred in Portugal. The assignment fell through, however, and Wharton was returned to the Azores. Meeting with an official from the Department's personnel office, Wharton explained that, "You're not only discriminating against us [African-Americans] in the Service, but you're exporting discrimination abroad in the Foreign Service." It was not until 1949 that Wharton finally broke free from the "Negro circuit."[48]

Terence Todman did not join the Department of State until 1952, but he faced some of the same problems. A native of the U.S. Virgin Islands, Todman had early become interested in foreign affairs and after serving in the occupation forces in Japan after World War II his fascination with international relations was cemented. In 1952, he joined the Department of State. His career (which would eventually include tours as U.S. ambassador to six nations and a stint as assistant secretary of state for Latin American affairs) was almost short-circuited when he was told by an official from Personnel that the Department wanted only those who were "one hundred percent identifiable as Americans"; thus, Todman's Virgin Islands accent would preclude him from diplomatic work. Given a second chance, Todman secured a position in the Office of South Asian Affairs. He quickly discovered, however, that his race was going to put some limits on his opportunities. Encouraged by one official to apply for work in the Latin American Division (Todman was fluent in Spanish), he was told, "Don't even dream of it." It was a frustrating experience, "But there was not a chance of doing that. The only thing they had blacks doing then was serving as messengers and secretaries." Even in his position in South Asian Affairs, he was daily reminded of the racial barrier: "I remember people coming to my office for meetings, and they'd come and say, 'We're here to see Mr. Todman.' And I'd say, 'Well, I'm Mr. Todman, come on in.' And it was, 'You've got to be kidding!' It took them a little while, several people, to accept the fact that I could be the person responsible for some activities. It was a different world."[49]

Even more bitter over his early experiences with the Department of State was Hugh Smythe who, during the 1940s, had worked with Du Bois on special projects for the NAACP. As soon as the first article in Logan's series had appeared in 1950, Smythe wrote to Logan detailing his own trials and tribulations. In 1947, Smythe had applied under special conditions: Public Law 488 had stipulated that highly qualified candidates could be admitted to higher classified grades in the Foreign Service, and the written examination would be waived. In accordance with the act, Smythe had presented himself before the examining committee for the oral examination. According to Smythe, there was "surprise when I walked into the room for the examination, for some of the committee members did not know that I was colored." This was matched by Smythe's surprise at the simple nature of the questions: "one could not help but give a correct reply." He quickly concluded that "this was not the purpose of the questions. The chairman's attitude indicated that so far as I was concerned he was going through the motions and the sooner it was over the better, for there was no chance of my being okayed." Smythe noted that some of "the committee members were Southern." His suspicions were confirmed when he received a letter of rejection a few days later. Immediately, Smythe wrote to Carl Wedell, who had chaired the examination committee, asking for an explanation. Since he had answered each of the questions satisfactorily, and since his qualifications for diplomatic work were excellent, Smythe could draw but one conclusion: "I had heard that the Department of State did not encourage, in fact did not want Negroes working in a professional capacity." He was aware that there were but a handful of African-Americans in the Foreign Service. This left him with "no other alternative than to assume that I was refused addmitance [sic] solely on the grounds of being an American of Negro descent." He also sent a copy of the letter to Joseph Green, who was executive director of the Board of Examiners for the Foreign Service. He received no reply from Wedell, but Green wrote a terse response, explaining that the committee, and not Smythe, had to be the "judge of his performance." "It is to be regretted," Green concluded, "that you have drawn the wholly unwarranted conclusion that personal feelings and racial prejudice governed the decision of the Panel." Smythe responded with a brief research paper on discrimination in the Department. First, he argued, numbers did not lie. Both State and the Foreign Service had been documented as employing just a few African-Americans, almost always in the lowest level jobs. Second, the "personal element" was always present in his interview. It became clear to Smythe that the Department was, as it was always rumored to be, a reserved club for the "sons of 'gentlemen,' alumni of Harvard, Yale, or Princeton." With all of the evidence, Smythe hoped that Green understood "why there was no other conclusion for me to reach, other than that the United States Department of State is racially prejudiced in its employment policy."[50]

It was a conclusion that many African-Americans had reached. For them, the biased hiring policies of the Department of State and Foreign Service were mirrored by the biased policies of the United States in terms of dealing with people of color in the underdeveloped and colonial world. In their view, the United States sided with the white colonizers against people of color. Though it was quite obvious to them that the U.S. stance on these issues, together with its highly publicized and disreputable civil rights record at home, was hurting the nation overseas, they were consistently frustrated in their attempts to have a voice in U.S. foreign policy deliberations.

The desire for more African-Americans in the Department of State and Foreign Service was one outgrowth of that frustration. Perhaps, the thinking went, a greater physical presence of African-Americans in the machinery of U.S. diplomacy would lead to a greater voice and, hopefully, influence. Achieving that greater presence would take some doing. The Department of State and Foreign Service were both nearly all-white institutions, and neither had demonstrated much interest in hiring or appointing African-Americans to positions of power or authority. African-Americans attacked the segregation existing in America's diplomatic corps as unrepresentative, undemocratic, and, ultimately, damaging to the nation's prestige in the world and its ability to function effectively when dealing with underdeveloped nations in Africa, Asia, and Latin America. To the question of "Can Negroes Make Diplomats?," African-Americans had answered resoundingly in the affirmative. The problem now remained to convince the Department of State.

~ 2 ~

Playing Catch-Up

The Department of State and the World of Race, 1945–1952

During the years 1945 to 1952, Department of State officials slowly came to the conclusion that race would play an important role in the postwar world and strained to define and understand the issue and develop policies to cope with it. In particular, they were confronted with the fact that America's domestic racial problem was now a foreign policy problem. That the realization of all this did not come as quickly for the Department as it did for African-Americans was no surprise. While the concept of race had never been completely absent from U.S. foreign policy during the nineteenth and early twentieth centuries, it had usually manifested itself in a very different manner. Diplomats, like the American public at large, carried with them certain preconceptions about inferior and superior races, and these often dovetailed nicely with official U.S. policies: the decimation of the Native American population to make way for white settlers; the stripping of territory from Mexico in order for white America to achieve its Manifest Destiny; the overseas expansion of the late nineteenth and early twentieth centuries, which could be justified, at least in part, by theories of the "white man's burden"; and, even as late as World War II, America's "war without mercy" (as John Dower has called it) against the Japanese. All had been charged with racial overtones.[1] In all of these cases, however, race had played the role of justifying American policies of aggression, expansion, exploitation, or, at best, paternalism. In the post–World War II period, the United States trumpeted its dedication to freedom, equality, and human rights, tirelessly endeavoring to draw unflattering comparisons with the oppressive and totalitarian rule of the Soviet Union. Both at home and abroad, the Department of State began to feel the pressure to confront the obvious contradiction posed by the nation's racial problems. Some readjustment in the official thinking about race would have to take place.

Just how difficult that readjustment was going to be was illustrated by the actions of the Department of State in 1947 in response to several requests from the President's Committee on Civil Rights (PCCR). In April of 1947 Robert K. Carr, who was executive secretary of the PCCR, requested of Acting Secretary of State Dean Acheson any information dealing with "our international obligations with respect to civil rights." A month later, Carr wrote Secretary of State George C. Marshall. The PCCR, he stated, was "disturbed by the oft-repeated suggestion that our country's bad record in the field of race relations is being used against us in other parts of the world." With that consideration in mind, he asked Secretary Marshall to provide information as to how the nation's foreign policy was "handicapped by our bad domestic record in the civil rights area." No responses were forthcoming from either Acheson or Marshall, and so in June Carr tried Marshall again. As tactfully as possible, Carr noted that perhaps the Secretary should delegate the duty to someone else in the State Department.[2]

Secretary Marshall took Carr's suggestion, and passed the request on to Dean Rusk, who was then director of the Office of Special Political Affairs. Rusk had contacted the Policy Planning Staff and the United Nations Liaison Committee. Both "agreed that the conduct of our foreign policy is handicapped by our record in the field of civil rights and racial discrimination." He then requested specific examples of this hurtful effect from several of the Department's geographic bureaus, and here he got a very different picture. These responses concluded that U.S. racial problems had "largely ceased to be of major significance"; therefore, they were reluctant to provide "illustrative examples" lest this "further serve the interests of communist propaganda." In his memorandum to Secretary Marshall, Rusk noted that he had talked with Carr assuring him of "the Department's desire to cooperate fully," but also pointing out "our difficulty in supplying useful background material." He also enclosed a draft letter to the committee, which the secretary sent on 28 July.[3]

The letter from Marshall to Chairman of the PCCR Charles Wilson was a cautious and somewhat backhanded response. It began by agreeing that America's racial problems hurt the nation's "moral influence." It pointed out that "isolated incidents" of discrimination against foreign nationals, as well as discrimination against domestic minorities had been "alluded to frequently in the foreign press." Marshall then proceeded to undercut everything that had just been said. First and foremost, he wanted the PCCR to know that "much of the adverse publicity abroad given to our civil rights record" was the work of followers of "a political philosophy" who cared little about civil rights. Indeed, it was the fact that the civil rights record in America "represents a truly remarkable political achievement" that caused "these elements to seize upon and exaggerate instances of violations and discrimination" in America. This "naturally creates embarrassment out of proportion to the actual instances of violation." In addition to this rather innocuous document, Rusk finally, in late July, sent Carr the "background material" the PCCR desired. This consisted of nine excerpts from foreign newspapers (about half of them from Soviet publications), with the caveat that "the sources which follow are either communist or acknowledged left-wing organs." Other requests for information from the PCCR to the Department of State's Office of Intelligence Research (OIR) brought similar excerpts from communist newspapers.[4]

It was evident from Marshall's letter and the materials provided by Rusk that the Department of State was unwilling to consider the international ramifications of America's racial problems as anything more than the work of communist propagandists. Carr became frustrated; dispensing with the tact he had used in his earlier letter to Secretary Marshall, he tried to explain the situation to Rusk. It was clear "that it would be a mistake to include the Secretary's letter in its present form in the committee's report." Perhaps, he suggested, he had been at fault for "not indicating more clearly the stand . . . we hoped to obtain from the Secretary." To clear matters up, he provided an "unequivocal" statement of the committee's position. While acknowledging that there was some "distortion in foreign propaganda," the committee believed that "the American record is in many ways a bad one" and did not want to "minimize this condition" in its report. In sum, the PCCR "is convinced that the way to bring an end to foreign criticism of our civil rights record is to take steps to improve that record rather than to argue with our critics about their motives or the honesty of their reporting." He suggested three options: use only certain portions of Marshall's letter, excising the sections dealing with communist propaganda on the race issue; prepare a new letter; or use a 1946 letter from Dean Acheson to the Fair Employment Practices Committee, which dealt with roughly the same issue. Carr preferred a new letter, and proceeded to suggest what that letter should contain. The United States, the PCCR believed, was strong due to the "vigor and appeal of our ideology." "Cleavages" within America weakened that position. "If we can establish the fact that our darker skinned citizens are truly first class citizens, it will create a reservoir of sympathy for us among all the dark skinned peoples of the world." That such "cleavages" were "exaggerated and misrepresented by foreign critics should be noted in passing as something we regret," but this should not divert America's attention from the very real problems at home.[5]

The reception given to Carr's letter is not detailed in the Department of State files, but the result was certainly not what he or the PCCR desired. When "To Secure These Rights," the 1947 report of the PCCR appeared, it contained a relatively lengthy section dealing with the diplomatic problems caused by America's racial problems. Yet, when it came time for a statement from the Department of State, there was no new or revised letter from Marshall; instead, the old 1946 letter from Acheson was used. Though not exactly hard hitting, the excerpt did acknowledge that "the existence of discrimination against minority groups in this country has an adverse effect upon our relations with other countries." In announcing the release of the report, President Truman issued a statement declaring the report to be "an American charter of human freedom in our time."[6] Perhaps it was, but the Department of State, seemingly of the opinion that any negative foreign implications arising from the nation's "race problem" were the work of communist propagandists, demonstrated indifference, at best, about making such declarations.

Despite this rather stumbling start, during the years of the Truman administration officials of the Department of State were made aware, through both official and unofficial reports, that America's racial problem was an international embarrassment and potentially harmful to the carrying out of the nation's diplomacy. Even in the nations of Western Europe, where America's most solid allies resided, there was persistent comment on U.S. civil rights issues. James W. Ivy, in an article for *The Crisis* in July 1950, summed up his findings after reviewing over five hundred pieces from European newspapers and journals: "This preoccupation of the European press with the American Negro and his problems is a postwar phenomenon, partly an outgrowth of our use of a jim-crow army to war on Third Reich Aryanism, and partly European resentment of what many of their intellectuals regard as pernicious meddling in Continental affairs. Even the European man in the street sensed the incongruity of a 'democratic equality' that condemned negroes to service battalions and segregated outfits."[7] American visitors to Europe came back with the same impressions. Frank M. Snowden Jr., chairman of the Howard University Department of Classics, visited Italy in 1949–1950 and came to the conclusion that while not all Italian press coverage dealing with the U.S. race situation was negative, much of it could not help but note the "existence of a gap between the profession and the practice of democracy." Another American visitor to several European nations in 1951 remarked in a letter to Representative Fred Marshall that questions about the "Negro problem" were "the most frequent," and that Europeans seemed to consider the race problem "a permanent blot on our character."[8]

The Department of State was hardly unaware of the problem. United States missions in Europe and around the world kept the Department apprised of foreign commentaries on America's racial situation. A 1947 report summarizing the coverage of U.S. racial discrimination contained excerpts from condemnatory articles in Swedish, Greek, and Danish newspapers. From the Netherlands, the U.S. public affairs officer claimed that the "treatment of the negro in the United States is the ever recurring theme of discussion in Holland." The contradiction between that treatment and U.S. demands for freedom for Indonesia was often noted.[9]

In Asia, the most consistent and worrisome criticisms came from India.[10] A June 1950 report from the U.S. representative in Madras reviewed recent South Indian press coverage of U.S. racial problems. While some of the articles examined noted the progress of African-Americans, on the whole they seemed to suggest that in America "segregation is a national practice." Such a conclusion could "not be lightly dismissed as the typical, exaggerated view of many Asians." It was a "serious judgment," and potent evidence that "what happens in the United States is still the most realistic measuring rod of democracy." When, early in 1951, seven African-Americans were executed in Virginia for the crime of rape, the American general consul in Calcutta reported that the newspapers there were nearly unanimous in their criticisms of American discrimination. Most were contemptuous of "America's claims to be the saviour of Asia" in the face of what they saw as the racially motivated killings of the seven prisoners.[11]

From Latin America, as well, came denunciations of racial discrimination in the United States. A 1950 State Department report examined a wide range of Latin American newspapers and found that "the most active criticism of the United States in the field of civil rights is criticism on the score of our race prejudice." The general tone of the writings was "frequently bitter, often sarcastic," and focused not only the treatment of African-Americans but also on "anti–Latin Americanism."[12]

That nations considered to be friendly to the United States could engage in such denunciations was troubling enough. The fact that communist propaganda feasted on America's racial problems was even more disturbing. A June 1947 summary of intercepted Russian radio broadcasts indicated that the Soviets were using the issue as a primary point of attack against the United States. "The lynchings in southern States afford a ready vehicle for several commentaries on the deprivation of the civil rights of Negro citizens." A later report noted a cartoon in *Pravda* that showed "Uncle Sam with pockets full of atom bombs strangling a chained negro on whose back he rides." Just a month later, another analysis of communist radio broadcasts dealing with U.S. civil rights took a somewhat more "scientific" approach, breaking the broadcasts down into three categories: "More or less accurate descriptions of civil rights limitations with adverse comments; Distortions of the civil rights situation with virulent, unfair attacks on us; Miscellaneous." In reality, it made little difference which category was consulted. The United States was uniformly condemned for its discrimination against African-American citizens, and the communist broadcasts often warned peoples of underdeveloped nations to beware the "impact of American race discrimination policy."[13]

A July 1947 report had tried to put the issue in perspective. The communist attack on U.S. civil rights problems was "more than merely one aspect of the general propaganda program." The aim was to systematically destroy the Free World's faith in U.S. professions of freedom and democracy and to inhibit the flow of such ideas to those people trapped in totalitarian states.

> Since the moral position of the United States in the world is based on respect for human rights, and since the continued existence of totalitarian regimes depends upon the suppression of human rights, this may be said to be the central issue of present-day world politics. The United States should not, therefore, take a passive attitude toward its own problems in the field of civil liberties. Even without aggressive use, this issue forms perhaps the greatest natural weapon in this contest, and should be recognized and used whenever the opportunity arises. Similarly, the free institutions of the United States should be improved and strengthened in every way possible.[14]

This message began to strike home among some Department of State personnel during the Truman years. Dean Rusk, who just a few years before had delivered George Marshall's tepid response to the PCCR, replied to a 1951 request for a statement on the subject of U.S. race discrimination from NAACP Secretary Walter White by stating that, "The greatest burden we Americans have to bear in working out satisfactory relations with the peoples of Asia is our minority problems in the United States. . . . We Americans are living in a goldfish bowl and cannot hide our own conduct. A billion people in Asia are sitting as a great jury."[15]

By far the most vocal of department insiders was Chester Bowles, who served as U.S. ambassador to India from 1951 to 1953.[16] As already noted, India was a particularly harsh critic of U.S. racial practices, and Bowles wasted no time in explaining the damage those practices were doing to U.S. relations with India. In letters to Walter White, he explained that India's interest in U.S. racial problems was immense; it was "a sure-fire question every time I speak." To one of his former colleagues in the Office of Price Administration, Frances Williams, he reiterated that point, claiming that when he spoke, "half of the question period will be on our mistreatment of the Negroes in the South." Something would have to be done about the situation, since it "represents without question the greatest triumph of Soviet propaganda in Asia." To colleagues in the department, he was even more emphatic. Writing to Howland Sargeant, deputy assistant for public affairs, he once again hammered home the Indian interest in and concern with America's racial practices, concluding that "honest and friendly Indians have become convinced that America as a nation is guilty of brutal practices towards her negro citizens. . . . that lynching is a daily occurence in America, that the Ku Klux Klan is a dominant factor in our political life, and that we are unwilling to do anything about it."[17]

The Department of State, faced with both domestic and international pressures to confront the issues of race, discrimination, and civil rights more forcefully, began two different approaches to the problems. First, it moved to quiet the complaints of African-Americans that the Department was not sympathetic to or understanding of their criticisms. This required a three-pronged approach, involving the solicitation of advice and input from African-American organizations such as the NAACP, a more public recognition of the U.S. government's sensitivity to the foreign policy concerns of African-Americans, and, in some cases, attempts at silencing the more vocal and radical African-American critics of U.S. foreign policy. Second, it acted to defuse the international criticisms concerning America's racial problems through the use of a sustained propaganda campaign. There was overlap between these approaches, but it will be more useful to consider them separately.

Whereas in 1945 the Department of State had rather grudgingly accepted the presence of three representatives from the NAACP—Walter White, W.E.B. Du Bois, and Mary McLeod Bethune—during the meetings establishing the United Nations, by 1947 the department was actively seeking input. In October 1947, Francis Russell of the department's Office of Public Affairs wrote to the NAACP asking for representatives for a meeting to discuss the proposed International Bill of Human Rights. Two years later, a similar request was sent to the NAACP's Arthur Spingarn.[18]

The Department of State, and the Truman administration as a whole, also made a concerted effort to publicly address the foreign policy concerns of African-Americans. An Office of Public Affairs (OPA) report from early 1950 looked at the problem of "The flow of information on American Foreign Policy to Negro Americans." One of the main problems was that information from the Department of State was usually directed to the "over-all rather than to a specialized audience." Therefore, there had been little effort to cultivate special relations with the African-American press, organizations, or individuals. In addition, African-American newspapers and journals and groups such as the NAACP were understaffed and underfunded; the OPA suffered from the same problems. Nevertheless, there were certain things the Department of State could do to better reach the African-American community. African-American individuals and organizations should be consulted on a regular basis; "careful consideration" should be given to appointing "qualified talent in the Negro communities" to department advisory boards and U.S. delegations. African-American groups should be targeted for specific speaking engagements, at which "local Negro leaders [would be] invited to sit at the head table"; printed information ("at the sixth to eighth grade reading level") should be made available.[19]

While the OPA report gave a sense of the dawning recognition among some in the Department of State that the African-American voice would have to be taken into account when formulating foreign policy, the document is also valuable for demonstrating why that voice had been discounted in the past. The generally demeaning tone of the report indicates the regard in which African-Americans were held by the department. It was charged, for example, that the African-American press cared nothing for foreign policy issues, unless they touched on "matters of particular and specialized interest to Negroes." Why this was such a terrific problem was not discussed; in any case, the charge was untrue. Even a glance at the most significant African-American newspapers from the late 1940s and early 1950s indicated an interest in a wide range of diplomatic subjects. In discussing department attempts to connect with African-American organizations, such as the NAACP and National Urban League, the report noted that the biggest problem was in "translating materials into a form useful to this constituency where, by and large, the reading skill is substantially less than for other areas of the population." Finally, about midway through the report, there is a sudden digression into the subject of communist penetration of African-American groups in the United States, which, it concluded, was "extensive." The only way to combat this would be to alleviate the domestic problems plaguing the African-American community, which seemed to indicate that this was a subject for which the Department of State was unsuited. The long list of suggestions at the end of the report rang with greater or lesser degrees of paternalism: token appointments of African-Americans; "sixth or eighth grade reading level" materials for the African-American audience; and the special treat of having African-Americans sit at the "head table" when Department of State speakers talked to their groups.[20]

Despite the weaknesses of the OPA's report, its general message was beginning to hit home. American officials were making a greater effort to confront the foreign policy concerns of the African-American audience. Even President Truman made it a point to include it in his speeches. In a talk to the National Emergency Civil Rights Mobilization Conference, he suggested that his civil rights legislation had to be passed "if we are to maintain our leadership in the world. We can't go on not doing the things that we are asking other people to do in the United Nations." In a 1952 address at the graduation exercises at Howard University, he was even more direct in speaking to the issue of race and U.S. foreign policy. After outlining his administration's accomplishments in the field of civil rights, he proceeded to devote a large amount of his speech to international issues. He spoke of America's desire to aid the underdeveloped nations (many of which had been "formerly possessions or colonies"). Point Four would be one of the critical programs, and he made sure to note the program's work in Liberia, Ethiopia, and India. He praised America's diversity, but bemoaned the fact that "much of the trouble in the world today is the result of false ideas of racial superiority. In the past, the conduct of democratic nations has too often been marred by a racial pride that has left its scars on the relations between East and West." It was time to put such thinking aside, to treat "the new nations of Asia and Africa as equals."[21]

While President Truman and the Department of State were, in their ways, reaching out to the African-American audience, some African-Americans were deemed to be beyond the pale; perhaps, even, representative of that "extensive" communist penetration referred to in the 1950 OPA report. For these individuals, the basic approach was to attempt to silence or discredit them with charges of pro-communist sympathies (usually relying on the FBI to spy on, report on, and, on occasion, harass the individual). Paul Robeson and W.E.B. Du Bois, two frequent critics of U.S. foreign policy, were but two of the targets of this campaign of intimidation.[22] Even lesser known figures did not escape the attention of the government. When the singer/dancer Josephine Baker (who often spoke harshly about racial prejudice in the United States) visited Latin America in 1952, the State Department went on alert. Apprised that during her visit to Argentina she had "made strong anti-American addresses on racial discrimination in the United States" and that these were being "welcomed . . . by the Peronistas who had been making much of the discrimination issue in their propaganda against the U.S.," one State Department official suggested that to "counteract" Baker's presence, the United States should send "one or two outstanding negro intellectuals" on a visit to South America. His choices were Ralph Bunche, journalist George Schuyler, or Howard University professor

Rayford Logan. Baseball star Jackie Robinson might also have an impact "where baseball is popular, that is in the Caribbean." A few months later, another department official made a similar suggestion, but with one important difference. Sending "intellectuals" would not reach the proper audience; instead, the United States should concentrate on those groups for whom Baker's rhetoric would have the most appeal—the "negroes and indians in Latin America." These groups were "generally a fairly lowly order in the social and economic sense of things" and were "not particularly articulate." Therefore, sending a labor leader, instead of an intellectual, would make more sense. This would have an additional benefit: "we would be able to send him down *as a labor leader* and not *as a negro*. We don't want to play the negro issue. It will be played for us."[23]

Despite the State Department's reticence to "play the negro issue" in the case of the Josephine Baker affair, it showed little reluctance to do so when it came to propaganda. Throughout the late 1940s and early 1950s, the State Department conducted a sporadic, but increasingly significant, overseas campaign dealing with America's racial problems. A number of different approaches—some direct, some indirect—were tried. The basic theme, however, was consistent: the civil rights issue in the United States was being confronted; progress was being made; and African-Americans were, slowly but surely, being integrated into American society. In addition, the idea that communist propaganda was responsible for the world's "misunderstanding" about America's racial problem continued throughout the early 1950s.

American propaganda dealing with the nation's civil rights problems was part and parcel of a much larger effort, initiated in 1947, christened "The Truth About America"; this, apparently, was the precursor of the much better known "Campaign of Truth" initiated by the Truman administration in 1950.[24] Initially run by the State Department's Office of International Information and Cultural Affairs (OIC), the purpose of the program was, as President Truman put it, to provide "a full and fair picture of American life and of the aims and policies of the United States Government" to the world. The OIC planned to do this by assisting private U.S. groups "seeking to project a better understanding abroad of America," and by supplementing those programs through official efforts where it was judged that it would be "impractical or unprofitable" for private concerns to carry on the task. Exchange programs, movies, radios, publications, and libraries would be used to get the message out to the world about America.[25] In portraying the "truth" about American racial problems, all of those approaches came into play.

Exchange programs worked both ways: bringing visitors to the United States to see the racial problems for themselves and sending African-Americans to various nations to explain the civil rights situation. Writing in the *Foreign Service Journal* in July 1952, Gene Caprio chronicled the experiences of nearly 150 foreign employees of the United States Information and Educational Exchange program (USIE) who had been brought to the United States to get a first-hand view. An Italian employee was optimistic about the plight of African-Americans. While admitting that problems existed, he felt that "it is only a problem of time." After attending an Urban League meeting in Milwaukee, he concluded that "the difference between American democracy and totalitarianism consists in the fact that under the latter the Urban League would have been wiped out." From India, Ambassador Bowles argued that one of the best ways to battle the "Negro question" was to bring African-American speakers to India. He also suggested that the department sponsor a tour by Betsy Graves Reyneau, an artist who had just completed nearly forty paintings of "outstanding Negro Americans." A display of the paintings would serve as a "demonstration that all American Negroes are not trembling under the whiplash of their white oppressors."[26]

In addition to exchanges such as these, the Department of State, the Voice of America (VOA), and the United States Information Service (USIS) were all active in dispensing propaganda dealing with America's civil rights problems. A good idea of the breadth of these efforts was provided in early 1952. In January of that year, Edith Sampson, who was then serving as a U.S. delegate to the United Nations, wrote to Eleanor Roosevelt. She was currently in the middle of a trip through several northern European nations and had been struck by the fact that, "Much of my time is spent answering questions about the Negroes in America." Unfortunately, she concluded, most Europeans suffered from "considerable miseducation" and seemed to believe that *Uncle Tom's Cabin* was an accurate representation of African-Americans' "status today." The communists were busy "spreading misinformation." She called for a "stepped-up, hard-hitting job among the people of the world to offset the damage which has already been done through our enemies." Roosevelt immediately forwarded the letter to Secretary of State Acheson. Acheson replied that he was sympathetic with Sampson's views; "energetic steps" needed to be taken to ensure that the "record is clear." He felt that the "simple truth about the place of the Negro in America is our most effective weapon in meeting this problem." Getting the truth across, he admitted, was a "formidable" task. He assured her that the Campaign of Truth had been "brought to bear on this issue," and that he would forward Roosevelt's and Sampson's letters to the appropriate officers in the department's International Information and Educational Exchange Programs (IE).[27]

From IE, requests went out to several department offices, requesting information on propaganda and education activities dealing with civil rights and African-Americans. The Voice of America replied that "American Negroes receive steady mention in VOA's regular output." Quantifying that statement, it claimed that "at least once every three days Negro achievements and personalities are mentioned in our Americana Roundup." Some typical features had included stories about "Increasing Job Opportunities for Negro Women," the "Negro in International Relations," and one about the Howard University Players, who had just toured Europe. African-American personalities who were featured on VOA broadcasts included Ralph Bunche, Edith Sampson, Gladys Watts (former president of the Illinois Association of Negro Women), author Richard Wright, and singer Marian Anderson. Noting that "the United States is under steady attack by Moscow on the status of the American Negro," the VOA had chosen to indirectly meet those attacks through reports on the "progress of the Negro in different areas of American life." In addition, "statements made by prominent Negroes and Negro organizations on Communism" were usually featured. The responses of Walter White and Congressman Adam Clayton Powell to "various pro-Soviet statements by Paul Robeson" had been used recently. Of course, the VOA continued, it also reported on "tragic instances" of racial bigotry and violence in the United States, though it always tried to put these into their "proper focus . . . by reporting the efforts of law and order to bring the perpetrators of these injustices to book."[28]

The International Press and Publications Division (INP) indicated that it was vigorously attacking the problem of "the damage done among our overseas friends by the torrents of Communist-inspired distortions and lies about the U.S. Negro question." Indirectly, it was taking every opportunity for "introducing the Negro into photographs, publications and news articles as a *normal part* of the whole American society—without drawing attention in text or caption to the Negro." It was also taking a more direct approach, by emphasizing the "achievements of the Negro" or by refuting "Communist distortions of isolated instances of racial conflict, in the United States." One of its recent achievements had been the publication of the article, "The Negro in American Life" in the Russian-language *Amerika*. The success of the piece could be measured by the fact that it had been "attacked by name at least three times in the Soviet press." The INP, it assured the reader, was "constantly on the alert to anticipate Communist moves to exploit the minority question."[29]

A response to IE's query from the public affairs officer for the Near Eastern, South Asian, and African Affairs desk indicated the resources available for these regions where race was often an important concern. The INP had provided "Negro Notes," which summarized "achievements by

Negroes." A "background kit" had also been sent out to the field, containing pictures and articles dealing with African-Americans. A number of films that had been provided to the various field offices dealt "indirectly" with the race problem, by examining "labor unions, farming, and heavy industry," all of which showed "persons of many races and nationalities working together." Features on Ralph Bunche, Edith Sampson, and "Negro artists" were also available. The USIS information centers were stocked with books, newspapers, and journals dealing with African-Americans: Gunnar Myrdal's *An American Dilemma, Ebony, Crisis,* and the *Pittsburgh Courier.* The report especially noted the positive impact of visits by African-Americans. Civil rights activist Mary McLeod Bethune, the Howard University Players, and a number of academicians (usually traveling under the auspices of the Smith-Mundt or Fulbright programs) were cited. Equally important, the report went on, were the visits to the United States by individuals from Southeast Asia, Africa, and elsewhere.[30]

A glance at some of the materials being provided to U.S. posts around the world reveals the general gist of the propaganda approach. For example, the USIS provided materials known as "Air Bulletins" or "USIS Features." These were brief stories designed for "use by newspapers, magazines, or radio stations with or without credit to USIS." In short, they were articles that might be incorporated into propaganda emanating from the specific U.S. post or that might be "planted" in some friendly local media. Specific coverage dealing with African-Americans was sparse. Normally, the stories concerned the activities of an individual African-American; someone who could be pointed to as an example of the tremendous progress of the black race in America. Dr. Jerome Peterson, who was director of the World Health Organization's Division of Public Health Services, was featured in a December 1952 piece entitled, "U.S. Negro Physician Heads International Health Program." More to the point was another article from that same month, this one dealing with Edith Sampson, a U.S. delegate to the United Nations. This was precisely the type of piece the USIS liked to promote. The story recounted Sampson's rise from poverty, how she "worked her way through law school," and had established a practice in Chicago where she served "mostly poor people." The real point of the article, however, was to showcase Sampson's views on minorities—specifically African-Americans—in the United States. She reflected on a recent twenty-nation trip she had just taken. Everywhere she was asked, "Do you, a Negro, like to live in America?" Her response, she noted, "surprised" people: "I think of myself first as an American and second as a Negro. . . . Of course, I like my country." She then went into a long discussion of the progress made by African-Americans: better education; more job opportunities; stronger legal protection of their rights." Unfortunately, "some injustices" still occurred, but by "practicing what we preach," the United States was slowly eliminating the problems. "The Communists," however, "have misled many people about minority groups in the United States." The answer to this problem was clear: "We Negroes of America are more alert to communism and its evils than any other group," Sampson concluded, "Our grandfathers once were slaves, and we know what slavery means. We don't want to be yoked with any people in a communist slave system."[31]

In addition to special reports featuring prominent African-Americans, USIS also turned out other publications for use by American posts worldwide. A report first released in September 1947 (it is probably not a coincidence that its appearance closely follows the State Department's dealings with the PCCR in the preceding months), but later reissued in 1950, was entitled, "Americans of Negro Descent: An Advancing Group." Like the USIS Features, it was provided merely as background or for distribution to the press. It was a fairly straightforward (though not always entirely accurate) retelling of the history of African-Americans from colonial America to the present. This was followed by discussions of specific ways in which African-Americans had advanced in American society. Specific figures such as Ralph Bunche, Dr. Charles S. Johnson (a noted sociologist and member of the U.S. delegation to UNESCO), and George Washington Carver were duly noted. (Interestingly, individuals such as W.E.B. Du Bois, Paul Robeson, and actor Canada Lee, all of whom were targets during the Red Scare, were also mentioned with pride.) The document's basic theme was made in the last paragraph: "the Negro is already an active participant in every phase of American life. . . . In 80 years of freedom from slavery, he has made definite progress toward cultural, social, and economic equality as a citizen of the United States."[32]

The best known of the USIS publications dealing with African-Americans, however, was "The Negro in American Life," which was produced in 1951. This was a much more sophisticated piece than "Americans of Negro Descent" since, unlike that earlier document, "The Negro in American Life" was not intended to serve as mere background material but was to be distributed directly to its intended audiences. Slick, shiny, and full of photographs, this publication was obviously intended for a mass audience. It did, however, follow the same basic format: a somewhat more detailed retelling of the history of African-Americans since their forced arrival in America, followed by a discussion (with graphs and charts) of how much progress African-Americans had made and how that progress had been achieved. The basic theme is a simple one: racial bias in America has "deep historical roots"; it is therefore not altogether surprising that problems still exist.

Nevertheless, the tremendous progress in civil rights for African-Americans was evidence that "the twentieth century, for Negro and white Americans alike, has been one of notable progress." For specific evidence of that progress, the standard cast of characters—Ralph Bunche, Marian Anderson, Louis Armstrong—is once again cited. (Robeson's turn as Othello is mentioned, but Du Bois and Canada Lee are nowhere to be found by 1951.) The last two-thirds of the thirty-three page document is made up of photographs. Some of these are merely portraits of African-American personalities from politics, the arts, and education. Most, however, can be divided into two groups. The first group concentrates on visual displays of African-American progress: medical students at Howard University, brand new public housing developments, factory workers and skilled workers busy at their jobs. The other group of photographs had as its main function the demonstration of how white and black in America were coming together. Here, pictures show white and black children together in classrooms and on the playground; white and black workers shoulder to shoulder at their jobs; black and white government officials and workers; and black and white soldiers and seamen training together. The last photo, showing a black and white family in a housing project, with one of the white women holding a black infant, was captioned: "These neighbors in a housing project, like millions of Americans, are forgetting whatever color prejudice they may have had; their children will have none to forget."[33]

Coming near the end of the Truman presidency, "The Negro in American Life" was an apt symbol for how far the Department of State had come, as well as how far it had to go, in terms of understanding U.S. civil rights problems, both as a domestic and as an international concern. The production of such a stylish publication indicated that the Department of State was coming to the conclusion that indignant denunciations of "communist manipulation" of the race issue were no longer sufficient. The reports of the damage done to America's international reputation from various sources, both official and unofficial, had made it clear that a more affirmative response was needed. In its rather timid way, "The Negro in America" was one of the first examples of this new approach. Yet, despite this important change, the situation remained much the same as during the 1947 Department of State–PCCR imbroglio. While there is no discussion of communist propaganda in 1951's "The Negro in America," it is quite obvious from "Americans of Negro Descent" (re-released just the year before) that there still existed a widespread belief that the international criticisms of America's race problems were manifestations of communist machinations. The general tone of "The Negro in America," therefore, is hardly surprising. While admitting that the United States has a racial problem, the publication consistently downplays its seriousness, while simultaneously publicizing the great strides made in ridding the nation of racial prejudice. By accentuating the "deep historical roots" of America's racism, the report seems to suggest that the mere passage of time will ultimately erode the prejudices built up over the years, resulting in a world in which the present generation's children "will have none to forget."

The differences between the Department of State's views on the issues posed by race and civil rights and those of many African-Americans were significant. For African-Americans, race and civil rights were fundamental problems that the United States, and the world, had to face. They instantly saw numerous connections between their own domestic plight and international issues such as colonialism, nationalism, and apartheid. For the Department of State, race and civil rights were only vaguely comprehended and reluctantly confronted. Those connections, grasped so quickly by many African-Americans, were lost on most Department of State officials, who generally tried to compartmentalize the issue: the demands for civil rights from African-Americans and the racial prejudices they faced were judged to be purely domestic issues, and therefore outside the department's bureaucratic boundaries; the international criticisms about those problems were usually swept away as just more examples of insidious communist propaganda at work.

Perhaps the slowness of the Department of State's appreciation of the scope of the issues of race and civil rights was due, in part at least, to another factor often criticized by African-Americans: the lack of black representation in the department itself. As African-American demands for equal opportunity at home and international criticisms of America's segregated society mounted, the Department of State was forced to confront a more delicate and even more controversial issue: the desegration of America's "lily-white" diplomatic corps.

～ 3 ～

Integrating the "Lily-White Club"

African-Americans in the Department of State, 1945–1952

The Department of State's difficulty in understanding the problems of race and civil rights was no doubt exacerbated by the fact that it had maintained a nearly all-white composition of its diplomatic corps since its inception. By the time of Harry S. Truman's administration, however, a number of factors converged that enabled African-Americans to open the door to career opportunities in diplomacy a bit wider. Both domestic and international issues forced the department to reassess its "lily-white" make-up and begin to break down some unwritten rules that had kept the American diplomatic corps a solidly segregated body.

Prior to 1945, the official role of African-Americans in the Department of State was extremely small and limited.[1] Following the Civil War, the Republican Party, seeking to both reward and secure the black vote, appointed a number of African-Americans to posts in the diplomatic service. Indeed, as Richard Bardolph has noted, "The diplomatic and consular service took more Negro appointees than did any other rank of the federal service."[2] The number of appointees, however, was still minimal. The first African-American appointed to a ministerial position was Ebenezer D. Bassett, who was sent to Haiti in 1869. Two years later, J. Milton Turner was named minister to Liberia. It thereafter became the accepted practice to appoint African-Americans to these two nations, which came to be known as the "Negro posts." Few African-Americans broke the cycle.[3] As a 1978 article in the *Department of State Newsletter* summed up matters, "These posts were small, in tropical countries, and not sought after by most officers. . . . When transfers of black personnel were made, it was usually to another post to which blacks had been previously assigned."[4]

With the passage of the Rogers Act in 1924, however, there was a promise of change. With the act, as Andrew Steigman has explained, appointment to the new Foreign Service of the United States would be by "open, competitive examination with promotion strictly on a merit basis." A better pay scale and living allowances meant that the diplomatic corps was now on a "secure professional basis."[5] It also seemed to promise a more democratic and representative diplomatic corps. And in some ways that promise was kept. As Robert Schulzinger notes in his *The Making of the Diplomatic Mind,* the "social backgrounds of applicants broadened somewhat," with less applicants from private schools and far less from Harvard. There were "two important exceptions to the democratic principles" of the Rogers Act: African-Americans and women.[6]

Joseph Grew, who took over as chairman of the Foreign Service Personnel Board in the same year as the passage of the Rogers Act, made it a point to exclude African-Americans. Though they might pass the written examinations, Grew was clear enough when it came to the oral part of the process: African-Americans would be quietly, but effectively, eliminated. The Executive Committee of the Board of Foreign Service Personnel was equally explicit when it suggested some alternatives for barring blacks and women. It preferred a "frank statement or an Executive Order that, because of the limited availability for service at any and all posts, persons in these groups were not eligible for employment." Failing that, the argument of "limited availability" should then be used as "sufficient grounds for rating applicants so low that they could not possibly obtain a passing mark." Though neither President Calvin Coolidge nor Secretary of State Charles Evans Hughes supported a ban on women and black applicants, the efforts of Grew and others in the department were successful. While African-Americans were still routinely named as U.S. minister to Liberia (Woodrow Wilson having ended the tradition of appointing blacks to Haiti), few others were able to make a career of diplomacy. Three veterans of the pre-Rogers Act Consular Service—William H. Hunt, James G. Carter, and William J. Yerby—were appointed the first African-American Foreign Service Officers (FSOs) when the act took effect in 1924. Hunt and Yerby retired just eight years later; Carter served until 1942. Between 1924 and 1949, only five African-Americans entered the ranks of FSOs; twenty-two others were brought into the Foreign Service as clerks, administrators, or specialists.[7]

Not only were the total numbers of African-Americans admitted to the Foreign Service quite small, but, as Martin Weil has wryly noted, "If a black slipped through the net, he was sent to Liberia until he resigned."[8] A 1949 Department of State report entitled, "Policy of the Department of State with reference to the assignment and transfer of Negro personnel of the Foreign Service," indicated that four of the five African-American FSOs and all twenty-two of the other African-Americans appointed to the Foreign Service since 1924 had as their first assignment Monrovia. (The lone exception was Giles Hubert, who was sent to Haiti.) Once in Liberia, there was little chance of transferring out of the "Negro circuit"—Liberia, Madagascar, the Canary Islands, or the Azores. As the 1949 study showed, the five black FSOs had spent 98 percent of their combined fifty-three years of diplomatic service in those four posts, two of which were considered "hardship posts." This was in striking contrast to their white counterpart FSOs. As an example of the typical career trajectory of African-Americans in the Foreign Service the report cited the example of Rupert A. Lloyd, who had entered the service in 1941, been assigned to Monrovia, and still remained there in 1949. Meanwhile, each of the seventeen other FSOs who had been appointed at about the same time had received from three to seven transfers. The non-FSO black personnel fared even worse: none had been transferred from Monrovia since 1930.[9] It was hardly an encouraging record of employment and opportunity.

The career of Clifton Wharton, Sr., as an FSO from 1925 to 1949 was a microcosm of the dilemma faced by African-Americans seeking a career in the State Department. Wharton graduated from Boston University where he had earned his law degree. In 1924, he was surprised to receive an offer of an appointment to the Department of State as a law clerk. As Homer Calkin of the Department of State's Historical Office learned in a 1978 interview with Wharton, the appointment had "been made on the basis of his background, his name, and his picture. There had been no interview."[10] Indeed, it is not altogether clear that the department knew that Wharton (who, in pictures, appears light-skinned) was black when the appointment was made. In any case, Wharton took the position (which made him the first African-American to hold a classified professional position in the department) and almost immediately after the passage of the Rogers Act took the Foreign Service exam.[11] Wharton passed (only twenty of 144 did so) and was appointed an FSO in 1925. He understood what his fate would be. As Joseph Grew noted in a letter to a colleague after the Foreign Service exams, "Only twenty passed, including one negro who will go at once to

Liberia."[12] The day after his appointment was announced in 1925, he was assigned to Monrovia. There seemed to be a terrible rush to get Wharton to his new post. According to Calkin, he was "not sent to the Foreign Service School where all new appointees were to go for instruction before assignment." The *Baltimore Afro-American* carried an editorial cartoon "showing a man knocking at the door of the 'State Department's Diplomatic School' while someone is throwing a diploma out of the window and saying: 'Here's your diploma, and we have a ship waiting to take you to Liberia!' " Wharton was told that the unseemly haste was "because he was urgently needed in the field."[13]

For the next twenty-four years, Wharton was trapped in the "Negro posts." From 1925 to 1929, he was in Monrovia. After a brief return to Washington in 1929–1930, he formally inaugurated the Canary Islands as a member of the "black circuit" when he began a stay of nearly twelve years. At the end of 1941, it was back to Liberia; six months later, it was off to the third leg of the "black circuit," Madagascar. After nearly three years at that post, it looked as though the cycle might be broken when he received word that he was to be appointed to Oporto, Portugal. His hopes were dashed, however, as he was sent to the fourth and final "Negro post," the Azores. And that is where, after nearly a quarter of a century's service in the Department of State, Wharton found himself in 1948.[14] For Wharton and the other African-American diplomats still in the Department of State, however, things were about to change.

Initially, the position of the Truman administration in regard to African-American diplomats seemed to differ very little from that of its predecessors. Truman continued to appoint a black minister to Liberia. His first appointee replaced Lester Walton, who had served as minister to Liberia for an incredible eleven years, from 1935 to 1946. Walton had, as was usual for presidential appointees, offered his resignation after the 1944 election. It was suggested that he be replaced with an "outstanding Negro" such as Channing Tobias or Claude Barnett. After the death of Roosevelt, Grew wrote to Truman, informing him that "Mr. Walton is a negro and as it has been customary to appoint negro Ministers to Liberia I hope shortly to be able to propose another negro to replace him."[15] Walton's replacement was Raphael O'Hara Lanier, a well-known figure in African-American education who had held posts at Florida A&M College, Houston College for Negroes, and Hampton Institute. Lanier stayed at the post a little less than two years, resigning in the summer of 1948 to take over as president of Texas State University for Negroes.[16] His resignation opened the door for Edward R. Dudley.

Dudley was born in 1911 in South Boston, Virginia. He attended Howard University to obtain a degree in dentistry, but had to drop out because of financial pressures brought on by the Great Depression. From there, he made a rather dramatic career change, going to New York to work as a stage manager with Orson Welles's WPA Federal Theater Project. He also began attending law school, obtaining his degree from St. John's University in 1941. While in New York, he began political work for the Democratic Party, and was rewarded for his efforts with a position as an assistant state's attorney. When the Republicans returned to power in New York, Dudley again changed jobs, landing a position with Thurgood Marshall's group of lawyers with the NAACP. In 1945, he received his first appointment to a federal position, when he was sent to be a legal aide to the governor of the U.S. Virgin Islands. Following another short stint with the NAACP in 1947–1948, Dudley received the news in 1948 that he was Truman's choice to succeed Lanier.[17]

Although Dudley later downplayed his selection by claiming that "I suppose they were looking around for someone to replace whoever was in the Foreign Service in Africa at that time, and they sort of hit on me," this overlooks the domestic and international politics at play in 1948. At home, Dudley's selection must be viewed in the context of the upcoming presidential election. As David Birkhead, one of Truman's advisors, remembered about the 1948 contest, "I personally thought the Negro vote could make the difference because I thought this was going to be a squeaker."[18] Obviously, the appointment of Dudley, a well-known battler for civil rights who was well connected with the NAACP, was part of the Truman administration's efforts to hold onto the black vote in 1948.

Yet, to view Dudley's appointment as merely fulfilling the custom of awarding the Liberian post to an African-American in thanks for black political support would be a mistake. Liberia had become a significant interest for U.S. diplomats. Just four days after the death of Franklin Roosevelt, Secretary of State Edward Stettinius forwarded a *Policy Manual* to Truman. It provided a summary of major U.S. foreign policy objectives and also gave brief nation-by-nation overviews. In respect to Liberia, the report declared, "With the oubreak of the European war the strategic importance of Liberia to the United States was recognized." A military agreement with Liberia had been followed by economic programs that would "strengthen our economic and political ties in the light of our present and future interests in that country." In such a way, Liberia might serve as a kind of showcase: "If we are to be consistent and influential advocates of improvement in colonial administration in the interests of dependent peoples, we must insure as Liberia's 'next friend' that that country shall not compare unfavorably with neighboring colonies." A report from the State-War-Navy

Coordinating Committee two years later echoed many of those same points, emphasizing that the long U.S. relationship with Liberia had made for a special bond between the two nations. That bond was particularly important, given that U.S. investments in Liberia were over $60 million. Much of that amount was accounted for by the Firestone Rubber Company, but Americans were also showing interest in the nation's iron ore deposits, lumber, cacao, and other agricultural products. In addition, during the war the United States had improved and refitted the Roberts Field airport, which was deemed to be of great strategic significance. And in a report prepared at just about the same time that Dudley was being offered the position as U.S. minister, another aspect of the U.S.-Liberian relationship was noted. Claiming that Liberia had been angered at its exclusion from the Marshall Plan, the document pointed out that, "There are 13 million colored citizens of the United States interested in Liberia. They are asking, 'why this discrimination against the only free democracy in all Africa and why all this help for other races.' "[19] By 1948, therefore, Liberia was no longer a diplomatic backwater to which token African-American diplomats could be safely sped and quickly forgotten. Dudley, young (just 37) and vigorous, with acknowledged administrative and leadership skills, fit the bill.

Dudley was convinced that Truman had no chance in the 1948 election and that his tenure in Liberia was likely to be brief. He and his wife believed that "we'll go over and have a vacation and then we'll come back after the elections."[20] As Dudley was shortly to discover, however, his "vacation" in Liberia was about to turn into a stay of over four years. Just a short time after his arrival at his new post, Dudley heard about Truman's miraculous victory. This was followed by the news in early 1949 that the United States was going to raise the U.S. mission in Liberia to embassy level; Dudley would be promoted to ambassador, becoming the first African-American to hold that position. The reasoning behind the U.S. decision once again demonstrated the interplay between international concerns and domestic racial issues. Robert Lovett wrote to Truman in January 1949, laying out the rationale for raising the U.S. legation to embassy status. In terms of strictly foreign policy factors, the document rehashed many of the same arguments made in the earlier reports concerning U.S. interests in Liberia. Lovett also noted the domestic impact of the U.S. action: it "would further demonstrate our deep interest in this republic and would emphasize to the Negro minority in the United States the importance this government attaches to Africa's only independent republic."[21]

Dudley's promotion to ambassador did catch the attention of African-Americans. While most mainstream newspapers such as the *New York Times* carried only a brief notice of Dudley's new role (buried far from the front page), African-American newspapers such as the *Baltimore Afro-American* carried much larger features, usually within their first two or three pages. The *Afro-American* piece was typical: a large picture of Dudley, under the heading, "He's an ambassador now," with an emphasis on the fact that he was "the first colored ambassador" in U.S. history.[22]

At exactly the same time that Dudley was being made a U.S. ambassador, the Department of State was beginning to consider the issue of more African-American appointments and, with Dudley's urging, better opportunities for those blacks already in the Foreign Service. Why the Department of State, which had long operated as a segregated entity, took up these concerns during the period 1948–1952 cannot be precisely documented, owing to the unfortunate loss of some relevant materials.[23] From what remains of the historical record, however, it becomes clear that in addition to the external pressures exerted by African-Americans for more and better employment opportunities in the Department of State, internal pressures were also at work.

President Truman, through the Fair Employment Practices Committee, the PCCR, and the issuance of executive orders in 1948 banning discriminatory hiring practices by federal agencies and ordering the desegregation of the U.S. armed forces, had signaled during his first term a stronger commitment to equal employment opportunities and desegregation than any of his predecessors.[24] While the Department of State was never singled out as a bastion of segregation, Truman's actions during his first few years in office certainly put the department on notice. In January 1946, a copy of a letter sent to all heads of government offices by Truman decrying the fact that during the postwar cutbacks in government employment some "loyal and qualified employees have been refused transfer and reemployment solely because of race and creed," was circulated in the Department of State. Also making the rounds was a copy of the 1944 "Principles and Policies of Departmental Personnel Administration," which clearly stated that, "The Department selects its staff on the basis of merit, without discrimination."[25] When the PCCR requested information on the classified civilian employment of the Department of State in 1947, the failure to meet that goal was glaringly apparent. While the department fared relatively well in the percentage of African-Americans in its total work force (552 out of 5,202, or about 11 percent), the vast majority of those workers were in the lower classifications. Indeed, nearly five hundred were in just three categories, mostly clerical. In the highest category of employment, where there were over 1,300 total employees, African-Americans numbered just four.[26] This was aside from the almost total lack of an African-American presence in the diplomatic corps. This was a particular sore spot since the Department of State, unlike the Department of Commerce or the Department of Agriculture, had a much higher public profile and was America's spokesperson around the world, which trumpeted the nation's commitment to the ideals of equality and fair play.

To achieve more and better opportunities for African-American diplomats would mean, first of all, that the Liberia-Azores-Canary Islands-Madagascar circuit would have to be broken. Henry Villard, who was chief of the Division of African Affairs, approached the subject in a somewhat backhanded manner when he wrote Ralph Bunche in early 1946 about recruiting more African-Americans for the Department of State. Bemoaning the fact that individuals such as William George and Rupert Lloyd were "seemingly condemned to a lifetime of service" in Monrovia "because there is no one to replace them if they should be transferred to another country," Villard asked Bunche to help him find a "suitably qualified Negro." While this was perhaps a step in the right direction, Villard's letter left no doubt that if men like George and Lloyd were to leave Liberia, another African-American would have to fill their spot.[27]

By the following year, the fact that Liberia had become the first and, typically, last stop for African-American Foreign Service personnel was becoming more of an embarassment. In an article entitled, "So You Want To Be a Diplomat," published in the October 1947 issue of *New Republic,* Ralph G. Martin had painted a sarcastic picture of the Foreign Service, which, he claimed, was still dominated by "the pre-Rogers [Act] school of anti-Semitic and Ivy League diplomacy." There were only four blacks among the nearly 1,200 FSOs, and it was common knowledge that "Negroes are limited to Liberia, the Azores, and very few other places." The article made its way to Minister Lanier in Liberia (who knew firsthand that Martin was correct), who immediately wrote the department: "I should be interested to know to what extent, if at all, the statement cited above reflects the Department's policy with regard to Foreign Service Officers of Negro origin." If Lanier had hoped to force the department to face up to the ugly reality, he was disappointed. The reply from the Department was, in short, a bald-faced lie: "assignments are limited only by post needs and individual abilities."[28]

It was obvious, however, that the Martin article (and Lanier's letter) had hit a nerve. In early 1949, a representative of the Department of State made a visit to Liberia to assess the situation. Harold Sims, after consultations with Ambassador Dudley, had prepared the devastating report, "Policy of the Department of State with reference to the assignment and transfer of Negro personnel of the Foreign Service" in May 1949, which contained stark statistical evidence as to the segregated nature of the Department of State and the existence of a "Negro circuit" where African-American FSOs began and ended their careers.[29]

The basic problem, at least from the vantage point of the Department of State, was *where* to send African-Americans outside of Liberia and the other "black posts." It was no coincidence that Assistant Secretary of State for Administration John Peurifoy contacted Director General of the Foreign Service Christian Ravndal at about the same time as Sims's report to ask about the possibility of appointing an African-American ambassador outside of Liberia. Ravndal's reply was not very encouraging. After discussing the matter with several colleagues, he had come to the conclusion that there were only a handful of "appropriate countries" to which an "outstanding Negro" might be sent. "Arab countries" were completely out of the question, since they would regard the appointment of a black ambassador as "just another affront." Latin America also looked bleak. Haiti, Paraguay, Guatemala, El Salvador, or Honduras might be possible, if only the black appointee could "overcome the initial hostility with which he would be met." Ravndal had also considered Ecuador, Bolivia, and the Dominican Republic, but had been informed that "those countries have not evolved enough socially to overcome race prejudice." In the Far East, only French Indochina might be possible. The picture was a bit brighter for Western Europe, though only Switzerland, Norway, and Denmark were "enlightened and generally without the race prejudice found in other places." In Eastern Europe, Romania or Bulgaria. Afghanistan, Ethiopia, and, possibly, Ceylon, rounded out the rather sparse list. As for the list of "outstanding Negroes" who might serve, Ralph Bunche was the only name that Ravndal could come up with.[30]

Ravndal's memorandum was significant on several counts. First and foremost, it posed one of the main arguments consistently raised against the appointment of African-American diplomats outside Liberia: they would not be "welcomed" by the host countries. That, according to Ronald Palmer, an African-American who served as U.S. ambassador to Togo and Malaysia in the 1970s and 1980s, "reflects the prejudice of the people who were making those decisions." Terence Todman, who served as U.S. ambassador to more nations than any other African-American during his long career, was even more outspoken. "I am prepared to say that that business about not being able to send [African-Americans] was purely concocted within the State Department. It was made out of whole cloth. It was a total lie. . . . The problem has been, and is, in the United States of America. . . . So, this was a story concocted by Americans to keep from doing these things. It's damned nonsense." In fact, all of the former African-American ambassadors and FSOs interviewed for this study indicated that they were well received in all parts of the world.[31]

Second, the recommendations of the memorandum set the standard for

African-American appointments for at least the next two decades. From 1949 to 1969, no African-Americans served as chief of mission in a Far Eastern or a Latin American nation. Only one served in the Middle East. One African-American was appointed minister to Romania; one to Norway (and one to another Scandinavian nation, Finland). Luxembourg and Malta rounded out the list of non-African appointments. Through the late 1980s, the pattern changed only slightly, with nearly 80 percent of African-American appointments going to African or Caribbean nations.[32]

Finally, the memorandum was striking for its inability to come up with any name but that of Ralph Bunche as an "outstanding Negro" to serve as a U.S. ambassador. Edward Dudley, already serving in Liberia, was apparently not considered as a possibility for transfer. And Clifton Wharton, who had served in the Department since 1924, was not even mentioned. Nor were William George or Rupert Lloyd, who had served over twenty of their combined twenty-seven years of work in Monrovia. Instead, the Department continued to look to Bunche as a possible answer to its problem. Late in 1949, for example, Philip Jessup of the Department queried Bunche about the possibility of serving as a U.S. ambassador. Bunche's answer was not entirely encouraging. He would not "exclude the possibility" of serving a mission for the Department, "provided it wasn't to Liberia." Aside from Bunche, however, the Department continued to stick to its claim that there was simply a dearth of "outstanding negroes" for possible employment in the Foreign Service. New York Congressman Jacob Javits, writing to the president of Atlanta University, Dr. Rufus Clement, in late 1951, recounted a response from the Department of State to his inquiries about the lack of African-Americans in diplomatic positions. Decrying the 1950 series of articles by Rayford Logan in the *Pittsburgh Courier* concerning this issue, the Department's representative countered that "the proportionately small number of Negroes in the Foreign Service is the result of the very few qualified Negro applicants seeking jobs in the Foreign Service rather than discrimination against Negro applicants by the Department." It was true, the official conceded, that the Department had "received lists of outstanding Negro leaders from Negro organizations." In a bit of tortuous explanation it was argued that, "They are not applicants for positions in the Foreign Service however, but are suggested as possible outstanding candidates for consideration of any position available for which they are found qualified."[33] Why these individuals could *not* be considered applicants for Foreign Service positions was not made clear, but the result of such thinking was perfectly clear: unless an African-American applicant's name happened to be Ralph Bunche, it was going to be difficult to find a Foreign Service position.

Overcoming the biases and prejudices concerning the wider use of African-

Americans as diplomats would be a difficult task. Individuals such as Dudley, Chester Bowles, George McGhee, and others took a variety of approaches to try and undermine the stereotypes and limitations imposed by Ravndal's report and increase both the number of African-Americans employed in the diplomatic service and their opportunities once employed.

From Liberia, Dudley took a number of different tacks in pursuing his efforts to better integrate America's diplomatic corps. In a letter to Deputy Under Secretary Peurifoy in mid-1950, Dudley directly confronted the charge that African-Americans diplomats were not welcome in certain nations. Dudley sharply responded to a memorandum that suggested that the appointment of African-Americans (such as Giles Hubert) to the U.S. embassy in Haiti was a mistake, since neither the Haitian government nor some of the embassy staff wanted them there. He was "at a loss to understand the motives behind" the memo. It seemed to overlook the fact that the outgoing president of Haiti was black, and that "during his tenure, [he] did receive with graciousness and courtesy large numbers of American Negroes of varying color and hue." African-Americans had been "invited to Haiti to participate in the growing economy of that country." The entire report served to "highlight what I believe to be an unfortunate attitude on the part of many persons within the Department today," and Dudley enclosed one of the stories from Logan's series in the *Pittsburgh Courier* as further evidence. As for the memorandum's conclusion that "some members of the (Embassy) Colony are not willing to accept Negroes as social equals," Dudley's blunt response was that if this were true, "I should not be in the State Department today."[34]

Dudley was also extremely active in attempting to break up the "Negro circuit." When the question of his transfer to another post came up, Dudley saw it as a chance to both broaden the opportunities for African-American diplomats and increase the number of African-American ambassadors. It had been proposed in 1949, for instance, that he might be sent to an Iron Curtain country. The possibility of sending an African-American ambassador to one of these nations had been raised in Ravndal's memorandum, the logic being that the appointment would "serve to counteract communist propaganda that Americans are guilty of race discrimination." Dudley was receptive to this suggestion, but indicated that his first preference would be a nation in the Caribbean or in Central America. By 1951, with no movement or word of any transfer, Dudley once again broached the subject. During both the 1949 and 1951 discussions, Dudley emphasized the political and diplomatic advantages that might accrue from his transfer from Liberia. On the one hand, it would "add still greater strength to the Administration, in so far as the Negro vote is concerned," since the appointment of a black to another post would provide "a splendid opportunity to refute the oft repeated charge that the President's appointment of a Negro Ambassador to Liberia is so much 'Window Dressing.'" On the other hand, "in view of the great problems facing our country in winning the Colored peoples of the world to our side, particularly in Asia, now is the time for our government to demonstrate that it does more than assign only one of its negro citizens to another Negro country." Dudley made it clear that, in his opinion, the time had come for the Truman administration to appoint a second African-American chief of mission. He even went so far as to suggest that the United States begin to alternate black and white ambassadors for its post at Liberia, thus providing an answer to communist criticisms of "American pretenses toward the Negro problem by the single appointment of a Negro Ambassador to Liberia."[35]

Dudley's attempts to secure additional ambassadorial or ministerial appointments for African-Americans went for naught, and plans for his transfer never moved beyond the discussion stage. On another level, however, he was extraordinarily successful in securing transfers out of Liberia for African-American members of his embassy staff. Daniel Brantley, in a 1986 article in *The Crisis,* credits Dudley for having begun a "silent revolution," one that eventually succeeded in breaking the pattern whereby African-American FSOs and diplomatic staff were trapped in Monrovia. A perfect example came in 1950 when the Department of State proposed transferring Charles Hanson, a recent FSO who had served about a year in Liberia, to Oporto, Portugal. This was not exactly a groundbreaking assignment. William J. Yerby, one of the original black FSOs, had served there prior to his retirement in 1932. Dudley registered his reservations. While it was "gratifying to know that the Department is implementing its new policy to widen the latitude for Colored officers in the Foreign Service," he wondered whether the department might take a moment to reconsider. Hanson's transfer to Oporto would mean that out of the five black FSOs then serving, three would be in Portugal or Portuguese territory. This seemed a bit strange, Dudley opined, since there was "ample evidence to indicate that there are other posts outside of Portugal and its possessions where Colored FSO's can serve," and he suggested France, Germany, India, and Haiti, among others. Finally, he suggested that the department's new policy might have more success if African-American appointees were sent to "large posts." This, he hastened to add, was simply because the new appointees could be "more easily absorbed both in the large office and in the social pattern of a large city." Dudley's message had its desired effect: Hanson went to Zurich.[36]

In addition to the reassignment of Charles Hanson, several other African-

American FSOs also broke free from Liberia during Dudley's tenure as minister/ambassador. Clifton Wharton was assigned as consul general and first secretary to Lisbon. Rupert Lloyd became second secretary and consul to the U.S. embassy in Paris, and William George took the same position in Copenhagen. Eugene Sawyer was made attaché and public affairs officer in New Dehli. Transfers also went to members of the support staff as two clerks were transferred to the U.S. embassies in London and Rome.[37] Dudley considered breaking the "Negro circuit" one of his greatest accomplishments while in Liberia. In his letter of resignation to President Truman in 1953, he stated that,

> Of one thing in particular I have been most pleased and that has been the degree of cooperation from the Department in advancing its schedule of personnel assignments to all posts without regard to race or religion. Practically all of the gains in this direction by the State Department have been made during the past three years. I am sure you will find that a continuation of this policy both domestically and in foreign affairs can strengthen our country at home as well as give hope and courage to three quarters of the earth's people who expect American leadership based on a democracy that practices what it preaches.[38]

Dudley's actions while in Liberia were critical for the "silent revolution," but he was not alone in his fight. Chester Bowles, from his post as U.S. ambassador to India, was also in the forefront of those pushing for more and better diplomatic assignments for African-Americans. In letters to friends and department officials, Bowles hammered home the point that U.S. racial practices were hurting the nation's image abroad. One solution was the appointment of African-American diplomats and technicians to India. Even before his appointment to India had been finalized, Bowles wrote to Frances Williams, an African-American woman who had been one of his assistants during his years at the Office of Price Administration and had helped him integrate that agency, to seek her help in identifying "some really top Negroes" to take along. A few months later, he complained about the "slow and rocky" progress made on "the racial question in personnel." Although he felt that it would be "unfair of me to say that I had encountered active resistance," he admitted frustration that "somehow the names I suggest do not quite seem to fit the positions that are available." Shortly afterward, Bowles informed Williams that before leaving Washington for his new assignment, "several people told me that it would be a mistake to bring Negroes here because many Indians resented them." It was the same old argument that Dudley and others had heard; like them, Bowles found "there is no evidence whatsoever of any such feeling."[39]

To colleagues in the Department of State, Bowles was even more adamant. In a long and detailed letter to Howland Sargeant in late 1951, Bowles recapped his usual arguments in regard to the damage being done to U.S. prestige in India because of the latter's revulsion at America's racial practices. He had met with little support from anyone in the department; most countered that black appointees were "not liked or respected by most Indians." "I thought this was ridiculous when I was in Washington," Bowles exclaimed, "and I now *know* that it is ridiculous." He had given the department "a list of outstanding, competent negroes. . . . But somehow it was decided that none of them were up to snuff." There had been "one or two symbolical negroes scattered throughout the organization and they are doing a good job, but they are a drop in the bucket." Even as his tour of duty in India came to an end, Bowles continued the attack. In a letter to the director general of the Foreign Service, Bowles explained that he "would like very much to have top notch Negro Foreign Service Officers assigned here." His rationale was twofold: Indians seemed to "open up much more freely to an American Negro than they will to others," and such appointments would "help us to combat to a certain extent the feeling in India about the Negro problem in the U.S." Writing to his soon-to-be successor, George V. Allen, in early 1953, Bowles listed what he considered to be some of the problems to be faced by the new ambassador. He had "tried in every way I know to get qualified negroes assigned to our posts in India." Allen should disregard rumors that African-American appointees would be resented: "The Negroes we have had have done us a world of good."[40] Ultimately, however, Bowles left India frustrated in his efforts. Despite the fact that individuals such as Giles Hubert were transferred to posts in India, such appointments were, as the ambassador concluded, "a drop in the bucket."

George McGhee, who served as assistant secretary of state for Near Eastern, South Asian, and African affairs from 1949 through 1951, also played a key role in pushing for desegregation of the U.S. diplomatic corps. He consistently made the point that Africans, in particular, took a dim view of the state of race relations in America and that this was hurting U.S. objectives in the area. As one way to help that situation, he argued for the appointment of more African-Americans to posts in Africa.[41] McGhee also developed a close relationship with Edward Dudley. In a letter to the ambassador in early 1950, McGhee noted that Deputy Under Secretary Peurifoy had sent him a memorandum concerning African-American appointments. "I was gratified to know," McGhee stated, "that the other divisions of the Department feel as we do regarding the important problem of Negro assignments in the Foreign Service, and I am sure that you share my feelings in this regard."[42] McGhee's work did not go unnoticed in the black press. In a 1951 article in the *Afro-American,* the assistant secretary was cited as one of "a small group in the State Department" who had "been urging the integration of colored persons into various embassy and legation staffs."[43] In mid-1951, another of that "small group in the State Department," Harold Sims, who had visited Dudley in Liberia and worked with the ambassador to try and break the "Negro circuit," wrote to Dudley summarizing the progress that had been made so far. He noted the transfers of individuals such as Wharton, Hanson, Lloyd, and others out of Liberia since 1949 and remarked that "it is heartening to know that this great democracy of ours does practice some of the things it preaches." His concern now, however, was "what can be done to insure a continuation of this policy." Regretfully, "not all FSO's and Departmental Officers view this matter in the same light as others." Sims suggested that "valuable benefits would result if an organization like the NAACP or a group of prominent Negro leaders could in some way make known to the Department or preferably to President Truman their pleasure over the Department's action in widening the Foreign Service field for Negro personnel." Such "proper and gentle pressure from the outside" could also result in a transfer for Dudley, perhaps to Southeast Asia.[44]

Sims's call for "outside pressure" to keep the ball rolling in terms of more African-American appointments to the Department of State was a good one, but, unbeknownst to Sims, had already been put into practice. On February 28, 1951, a body called the Committee of Negro Leaders had a face-to-face conference with President Truman. Among the dozen members of the committee were A. Philip Randolph (who served as chair), Walter White, Channing Tobias (director of the Phelp-Stokes Foundation), Mary McLeod Bethune, Lester Granger, Charles S. Johnson, and Benjamin Mays (president of Morehouse College). The purpose of the group was to assure Truman of their support in "the fight to stop the spread of communism and to maintain and improve our democratic way of life." To that end, the group argued, "it would increase our national unity, weaken communist propaganda, strengthen our cause among the colored peoples of Asia, Africa, the Isles of the Sea, the West Indies, the United States and freedom-loving peoples everywhere" if Truman would make "the fullest use of the services of the Negro citizens in this hour of national emergency." The committee then made six recommendations: abolish segregation in Washington, D.C.; appoint African-Americans to the "policy-making level of our government"; integrate "all new agencies" that had been set up to cope with the world crisis; initiate an Executive Order "guaranteeing the maximum use of all manpower in all production efforts" regardless of race; ensure complete desegregation of the U.S. Army; and, appoint African-Americans "more widely in the foreign and diplomatic service of our country."[45]

It was a clever tactical move by the committee. As historians Brenda Gayle Plummer and Gerald Horne have noted, the civil rights movement had had a hard time coping with the exigencies of the new Cold War. The criticisms of U.S. policies, both domestic and foreign, had brought down the fire of conservative forces on the heads of many African-Americans.[46] This document attempted to subvert those criticisms by making it appear that the desire for civil rights and equal opportunity was simply part of a larger plan to help combat the spread of communism. And it seemed, at first, that the approach might be working. Elmer Henderson, who was director of the American Council on Human Rights and one of the twelve members of the committee, wrote the day after the meeting that President Truman had responded by saying "it was difficult to awaken the country to the peril it was in at this time. . . . He seemed to appreciate the fact that this group had come to him in a spirit of helpfulness and cooperation."[47]

Even more promising was the fact that Secretary of State Dean Acheson had agreed to meet with a subcommittee of African-American leaders to discuss ways to implement the demand for more black diplomatic appointments. The meeting was scheduled for mid-April. Shortly before it was to take place, Randolph contacted Rayford Logan to ask for his assistance and participation in the meeting. Randolph noted Logan's series of articles that had appeared in the *Pittsburgh Courier* in mid-1950, and asked him to serve as a "technical consultant" and to prepare a memorandum that might be given to Secretary Acheson at the meeting. Logan agreed, and was part of the six-person subcommittee that met with Acheson on April 13, 1951.[48]

The statement presented to Secretary Acheson at the meeting was perhaps a bit more combative than Randolph and some of the other African-American leaders might have desired. It picked right up from where Logan had left off in his 1950 articles, charging that, "The State Department suffers from the unenviable reputation of practicing discrimination in employment against Negroes both at home and abroad." The Foreign Service was particularly bad: here, blacks were basically "restricted to custodial and clerical positions" and "with few exceptions they are assigned to only 'colored' countries." He brushed aside department arguments that there were few "competent" African-Americans to hold the jobs and that few of those handful actually applied. The first argument was "manifestly not in accord with the facts"; as to the second, a number of blacks had applied, but "to no avail." The statement went on to blister the Foreign Service for locating its School of Foreign Service on a campus "that until very recently has not admitted Negroes to any of its classes." All of this obviously weakened the nation's foreign policy. Logan then went on to list six demands: that a "complete review" of Department of State hiring practices take place; that an African-American be appointed as an assistant secretary of state; that African-Americans "be employed in professional and policy making positions in the Department and the Foreign Service"; that African-Americans have membership on advisory and consultative committees; that African-Americans be used in "representative capacities" at the UN; and that the department "facilitate admission, without distinction based on race, to schools that prepare a large number of men and women who hold responsible positions in the Foreign Service."[49]

According to a summary of the meeting prepared by one of Acheson's assistants, the secretary's attitude was pleasant, if noncommittal. After brushing off the sixth demand as not being "directly related to his responsibilities," Acheson then went on to address the other issues. He first "outlined his own personal attitude on this general subject, which was well known to the group," and then advised it to meet with Director of the Office of Personnel Haywood P. Martin. As for appointing an African-American as an assistant secretary, he informed Logan and the others that an offer had been made to Ralph Bunche, who had refused. Nevertheless, Acheson wanted it made perfectly clear that Bunche had not been tapped for the position simply because he was black. Theodore Brown (representing Randolph) informed Acheson that "many Negroes felt that Dr. Bunche was offered the appointment because of the effect such an appointment might have had at that time." At this point, Acheson "amplified the situation concerning Dr. Bunche more fully and to the apparent satisfaction of the group." Logan and other members of the group assured the secretary that he had their full support, although Brown concluded that there was "a longstanding resentment by Negroes of the State Department's discriminatory personnel policy—as he put it."[50]

Logan remembered things a bit differently in his diary. Acheson had indeed begun in a conciliatory fashion, encouraging the group to meet with Director Martin. The discussion about Bunche, according to Logan, was somewhat tense. Acheson had begun with this disclaimer: that Bunche had been chosen because of his qualifications, not his color. At this point, Director of the Washington Bureau of the NAACP Clarence Mitchell interrupted, stating that he "hoped the secretary would not feel that the list of competent Negroes had been exhausted when Bunche was offered [the] position; that most Negroes did believe that Ralph had been appointed because he was a Negro." Acheson grew annoyed and denied the accusation. Theodore Brown reiterated that most African-Americans felt Bunche had been selected because he was black. It hardly appeared, therefore, that the secretary had explained the situation to the "apparent satisfaction of the group." His frustration evident, Acheson then announced that "he was not going to try to run the schools of Foreign Service." Somewhat taken aback, another member of the group reassured the secretary that they simply wanted to help during a "critical period" when the nation needed to "utilize all its resources"; unfortunately, the "State Department had not done so in the past." Logan hoped that Acheson would use his power to "stop the State Department from being the most vulnerable Department in the Government as far as discrimination against Negroes is concerned." Acheson merely promised to investigate the matter.[51]

Following up on Acheson's suggestion, the group scheduled a meeting for April 19 with Director Martin to discuss personnel matters. Three members of the group—Elmer Henderson, Clarence Mitchell, and Theodore Brown—met with Martin and came to agreement on several points. First, Martin would appoint a special assistant to deal with the relevant personnel problems. Second, the director would "welcome recommendations" from the group concerning qualified African-Americans for diplomatic service and for participation in the Department's internship program. In a letter to Martin the day after the meeting, Randolph assured him that the Committee of Negro Leaders was "ever ready to cooperate in assuring equality of opportunity in all categories in employment in the Department of State."[52]

After meeting with Martin in April, members of the committee continued to meet regularly with the director, and with his successor, E.N. Montague.[53] At least one member of the committee, however, was less sure of Martin's commitment to integrating the Department of State. Channing Tobias commented on a letter from Martin in May 1951. "Quite frankly," he began, "I did not like Mr. Martin's letter." For one thing, he believed that Martin should be made aware that use of a lower-case "n" in "Negro" was unacceptable. More important, he expressed surprise at Martin's claim that he did not believe that the Department of State was guilty of racial discrimination in its hiring. Such a statement "indicates that he does not know a great deal about the policies of the Department, or is resorting to the usual procedures of government officials who do not want to face the issues involved." Tobias indicated that he had no interest in appointing a committee to work with Martin. Instead, he suggested that "different national organizations" should encourage highly qualified persons to apply for "top level positions on merit. It would then be our job to see that well qualified persons were not shunted aside in spite of their qualifications."[54]

Whatever Martin's personal feelings about the situation, it was clear that little if anything was accomplished during the next few months. A report to the NAACP's Board of Directors in June indicated that "several wellqualifed individuals" had inquired at the department for interviews. Not much had come of this: "Although these people have not yet been employed, it appears that their applications are being considered favorably." One African-American applicant *had* been hired, and it was thought that "the sudden notice to report is due to Mr. Acheson's pledge of a general effort to assure all people of employment on the basis of merit." In July, the Division of Departmental Personnel sent a form letter to Walter White asking for help in "developing a reservoir of top-flight manpower" for positions in State.[55]

It was not a very auspicious start, and by March 1952 Randolph felt compelled to remind Acheson of the meeting that had taken place nearly a year earlier. Randolph first recapped that meeting and the six demands made by the committee. He indicated that a number of meetings had taken place with Martin and Montague. Indeed, Montague had promised to finally appoint an African-American to help with personnel matters. As politely as possible, Randolph stated that the importance of such an appointment was due to the fact that it would "aid in encouraging young Negro students to prepare themselves for service to their country in the State Department with the assurance that upon being duly qualified the expense and years of preparation will not be in vain." Once again, Randolph assured Acheson that the committee's demand for equal opportunities for African-Americans was due to the desire to serve the nation during a time of "international crisis." Randolph's gentle prodding had at least one effect: a few months later, John A. Davis, a professor of political science at Lincoln University and a well-known figure in the study of discrimination in employment, was hired by the Department of State as a "Consultant to the Director of Personnel."[56]

Randolph, in a form letter to other members of the Committee of Negro Leaders, was optimistic about the appointment of Davis and expressed the hope that "a new day may be approaching for all qualified Negroes who might desire to serve their country in the facilities of the Department of State." He promised that further information would be passed along "at such time as some concrete information is available." "Concrete information," however, was hard to come by. The committee had been waiting for a progress report from the Department of State for some time, but by November 1952, as Clarence Mitchell indicated after a talk with the new Deputy Secretary of State for Administration, Carlisle Humelsine, there was still only the promise of such a report.[57]

It was only after the Truman administration had left office, in late March 1953, that the long-awaited progress report saw the light of day. Clarence Mitchell's frustration was evident in his letter to Walter White: "Finally, we have the State Department Report on personnel." He was not completely satisfied, and suggested that "a conference with Secretary Dulles is indicated." The report, entitled, "Progress Report on the Employment of Colored Persons in the Department of State," had arrived at Mitchell's office with a cover letter from Montague; the report itself, however, was prepared by John A. Davis. It began with a brief summary of Department policy on fair employment, claiming that "the utilization of non-whites has been well received in all parts of the world by the people of the free nations as an evidence of American belief in democracy." There then followed a detailed report on the State Department and Foreign Service positions held by African-Americans. The numbers were necessarily incomplete. Since the Department of State did not "request information on the racial identity of its employees," many African-Americans in the "lower positions" in the Department would be impossible to identify. It *was* possible, however, to note those in "professional" positions and in the Foreign Service, "for their number is small."

The report began with "Departmental Lower-Grade Positions." While the various "clerks, typists and secretaries" could not all be identified, it was possible to list Foreign Service Staff (FSS) workers at the FSS-12 and FSS-13 levels. In all, eighteen employees were listed as working at overseas posts; nine of these were in Monrovia, two each were in Paris and Athens, with one each in Bonn, Rome, London, New Dehli, and Tel Aviv. From there, the report then detailed African-Americans in the "professional and upper-grade positions" in the Department in Washington. Ten African-Americans held positions ranging from Chief of Northern and Western European Branch, Division of Research for Europe, Office of Intelligence Research to various assistants and specialists, mostly in the Office of Intelligence Research, the International Information Administration, and the Division of Foreign Service Personnel. Two other African-Americans worked as Voice of America writers in New York. In the prestigious Foreign Service, there were only five FSOs: Wharton, Hubert, Hanson, George, and Lloyd. Thirty-six other African-Americans served overseas as FSS-11s or above and in the Foreign Service Reserve (FSR). Fifteen of these served in Monrovia, the Azores, and the Canary Islands, while the rest were spread among fourteen different nations in all parts of the world.

The overall evaluation was that there had been "considerable progress" in hiring African-Americans. Nevertheless, it needed to be "admitted that there is much to be done before it can be said that the Department of State has hired non-whites fully and fairly and has utilized them to the best effect in various parts of the world." There were but fifty-five African-Americans among the 8,321 Foreign Service personnel serving overseas. The numbers were equally dismal when looking at the number of African-Americans at the GS-7 level and above in the department in Washington: only fifteen of 6,700 total employees. Even worse, due to budget cuts, the employment outlook was not very good.[58]

It was little wonder that Mitchell wanted to have a conference with Secretary of State John Foster Dulles, for, in truth, there was very little in the report that could be classified as encouraging. True, there had been some increase in numbers. In his 1950 articles, Logan had noted that there were only thirty-three African-Americans in the Foreign Service; that number had now increased to fifty-five. According to the report, however, eight of those were in the Technical Cooperation Administration, where the outlook for long-term employment was far from good; how many others were with USIS was not specified. More noticeable was the fact that there were only five African-American FSOs in 1953, and only two had been appointed during the Truman administration: Giles Hubert in 1947 and Charles Hanson in 1948. This hardly boded well for a long-range black presence in the Foreign Service. Hubert would retire in 1953 and one of the other black FSOs, William George, would retire just three years later. A handful of African-Americans held professional positions in the Department of State, but besides the abortive attempt to lure Bunche into the department as an assistant secretary of state none were in high-level jobs. There had never been any further movement either to transfer Dudley to another post or name another African-American ambassador.

Taken as a whole, they were indeed meager results. That there had been some slight progress during the Truman years could not be denied. Dudley's elevation to ambassador was significant, for it broke a very important barrier and set the stage for further appointments. Although there had been only two African-Americans appointed as FSOs during the Truman presidency, six other African-Americans had been appointed as FSSs or to professional positions in the department; all would later become FSOs, and three—David Bolen, Samuel Adams, and Terence Todman—would go on to become U.S. ambassadors.[59] The "Negro circuit" had been broken. In 1949, Monrovia had been the beginning and the end as far as most African-Americans in the Foreign Service were concerned. By 1953, African-Americans served in Asia, the Middle East, Latin America, Europe, as well as other areas in Africa.

Much, however, remained to be done: twenty-four of the fifty-five individuals cited in the 1953 progress report served in Liberia, the Azores, or the Canary Islands. Outside pressures from organizations such as the NAACP, groups such as the Committee of Negro Leaders, and individuals such as Rayford Logan, combined with the efforts of Dudley, McGhee, Sims, and others within the Department of State, had, to some degree at

least, forced a reevaluation of the department's hiring and placement practices. The question in 1953, however, was whether there would be a commitment to *real* and *sustained* progress in the coming years in the face of
budget cuts, a new Republican administration that seemed to have a cloudy
vision on civil rights, and the knowledge that efforts to desegregate the
department and Foreign Service were not universally accepted by some
members of what was still, to a large degree, a "pretty good club" with a
nearly all-white complexion.

4

The Domination of Whites Must Go

African-Americans, Diplomacy, and Race, 1953–1961

In the May 1960 issue of *The Crisis* an editorial entitled "Rising Tide of Color" appeared. It took its title from the immensely popular 1921 book by Theodore Lothrop Stoddard, *The Rising Tide of Color Against White World Supremacy,* a racist creed warning about the coming battle between white civilization and the forces of barbarism emanating from the hordes of people of color. The editorial agreed that a battle was brewing, between "the unfree peoples of the world, who are predominantly colored" and were "tired of being vassals of empire, helots, hirelings, and often pariahs in their own countries," and the forces of "exploitation and degradation." The revolt against "race prejudice and discrimination" was taking place on many fronts: at North Carolina lunch counters; in the African empires of the Portuguese, British, French, and Belgians; and in the apartheid system of South Africa. As the editorial concluded:

> What is the meaning of these events in the present world context? The world has become small; what happens in one corner affects the welfare and the destiny of people everywhere. A riot in the Congo, an election in Nigeria, and a "sit-in" in North Carolina affect the future of mankind. American Negroes take courage and hope from an independent Ghana and Guinea;

revolts in the Congo stiffen the resolve of Africans in South Africa. Everywhere the colored peoples are resolved that the arrogance and the domination
of the whites must go. The tale is the same wherever you turn. What the
colored world wants and what white men of good-will want is real better-
ment, a world in which all men can walk with human dignity and freedom.[1]

The editorial suggested that by 1960 many African-Americans believed
that their goal of educating their white counterparts as to the significance of
race as both a domestic *and* international problem was far from being
achieved. The struggle to do so, which involved criticism of colonialism and
a U.S. foreign policy that seemed to support it, warnings about the deleteri-
ous effect that America's racial problems was having on the nation's world
prestige and effectiveness, and a persistent striving for more African-American representation in the Department of State and Foreign Service, had continued throughout the presidency of Dwight D. Eisenhower and, obviously,
would have to be continued on into the next presidential administration.

It would be misleading, however, to assume that the African-American
criticisms continued without change from the early 1950s through the end
of the Eisenhower years. As a number of scholars have argued, the bur-
geoning Cold War mentality in the United States changed the tenor and
focus of the African-American stance on international issues. James Roark
claims that by late 1947, "most American Negro leaders abruptly altered
their public statements about world affairs." Groups such as the NAACP
and the black press muted their criticisms concerning colonialism and
pulled back from any denunciation of U.S. diplomacy that might be perceived as "radical." Instead, their emphasis turned to domestic civil rights
issues. In the area of foreign policy, most African-American leaders fell in
line with the anti-communist crusade. African-Americans found that, "In
order to protect the civil rights movement from a disastrous Red smear"
they were "constrained to affirm their Americanism and to prove that their
crusade was not Kremlin-inspired."[2]

Recent monographs by Gerald Horne, Penny Von Eschen, and Thomas
Borstelmann tend to support that conclusion. Horne, focusing on the clash
between Du Bois and the rest of the leadership of the NAACP concerning
foreign policy issues, describes the association's change from "militant
anti-imperialism to virulent anticommunism" as "a torturous path." Von
Eschen's work describes the break between the "leftist" position on the
issue of colonialism advocated by organizations such as the Council on
African Affairs (CAA) and the "liberal" position embodied by the NAACP
during the late 1940s. Walter White personified the stance of the NAACP,
which "continued to link foreign and domestic policies but adopted a strat-

egy that embraced American foreign policy while pushing for domestic rights." Borstelmann concludes that the Truman administration's "simulta-neous moves in 1947 to contain communism and to discourage domestic racial discrimination" resulted in the "effective separation of the issue of civil rights in the United States from racial and colonial problems abroad." Organizations such as the NAACP "chose to stay close to the Truman administration by taking anti-communist stands."[3]

Brenda Gayle Plummer, who has given us the most detailed analysis of African-Americans and U.S. foreign policy from the 1930s through the 1950s, is more cautious in her evaluation. While she acknowledges that the Cold War did drive a wedge between African-American concerns about U.S. diplomacy and their domestic agenda, she also notes that "civil rights had always been and remained a greater priority for Afro-Americans than foreign policy." The NAACP and other organizations certainly did not want the domestic civil rights movement to be crushed in the machinations of the Red Scare. Therefore, in place of harsh criticisms of U.S. foreign policy came "tempered, upbeat responses" to America's Cold War policies.[4]

It is certainly true that as the Cold War heated up, more mainstream African-American organizations—most notably the NAACP—distanced themselves from the radicalism of groups such as the CAA. Du Bois's break with the NAACP and Walter White's very public denunciations of Paul Robeson were but two examples of this new stance. There is also no denying that the NAACP spent less and less of its time considering matters relating to foreign affairs. Finally, no one who looks at black periodicals and newspapers for the 1950s can doubt that, in general, the tenor of Afri-can-American criticisms of U.S. foreign policy had changed: there was less stridency and more instances of raising the communist specter when analyz-ing Africa and Asia.

Another look at the evidence, however, reveals that along with these changes there was also a great deal of consistency in the African-American analysis of U.S. diplomacy during the Eisenhower period. Blacks were still keenly interested in the foreign scene. Colonialism was still denounced and the growing independence movements in Africa and Asia attracted a great deal of notice and enthusiasm in the black press. And criticisms of U.S. policies, while often less harsh than in the past, were still leveled. More important, the emphasis on the issue of race as an international problem for the United States was constantly reinforced. It was stressed over and over again that America's race problem—which climaxed with the Little Rock incident in 1957—was hurting the United States overseas. Reminders that the United States lived in a world that was made up largely of people of color were reiterated. And the demand for more African-Americans in the

Department of State and Foreign Service grew even louder.

African-Americans continued to evidence interest in a variety of foreign policy issues during the Eisenhower years. Colonialism, for instance, remained a focus. In January 1955, *The Crisis* published a compilation of resolutions passed by the NAACP during the last few years. The effort to distance the group from any perceived radical critiques of U.S. policy was apparent: "we dissociate ourselves from any critique based solely upon the contentions of declared Soviet protagonists." Nevertheless, the stance on colonialism was clear. The organization declared its "support of the legitimate aspirations of colonial peoples for independence or self-government" (1950); called on the United States policy in Southeast Asia to "give support only to genuine freedom movements which aim to set the people free from domination by America, West European countries or Russia" (1950); expressed regret over the decision by America's UN delegation to refuse to support a resolution demanding attention to Tunisian demands for independence (1952); and denounced imperialism as "unjust and a threat to world peace" and urged France to end its domination in Indochina and Africa (1953). Various articles during the 1950s criticized French colonialism in Indochina and the Portuguese empire in Africa.[5]

Criticisms against European colonialism also came from other sources. A. Philip Randolph, writing to President Eisenhower in June 1953, implored the president to alert the colonial metropoles to "the danger of Africa, blazing with the fires of nationalism, to world peace and democracy." Randolph took the Europeans to task for their "ruthless colonialism," and heartily condemned the "Fascist Malanism in South Africa." He asked that Eisenhower not be "deceived by the cry of Communism as a cause of the violent unrest and uprising, revolt and revolution of the black man against the white man in Kenya and South Africa." A long history of colonial and racist oppression was the real culprit. P.L. Prattis, executive editor of the *Pittsburgh Courier,* wrote in early 1953 that the world was confronted with two revolutions. One involved the rebuilding of Europe. The other—"the big one"—involved "1600 million human beings, mostly colored," in Asia and Africa. "These are the peoples who have suffered from a colonial or near-colonial status. These peoples constitute two-thirds of the world's population, but enjoy only one-sixth of the world's income." The United States, Prattis argued, should stop focusing on "stopping Communism" and instead turn its attention to programs designed to "cure the maladies from which the world is suffering."[6]

The United States continued to come under attack for its own brand of "colonialism" in Panama and elsewhere. The biased policies of Canal Zone officials were criticized throughout the 1950s. Writing to John Foster Dulles in 1954, Roy Wilkins called on the United States to "end color discrimination in the Panama Canal Zone." A 1953 article in *The Crisis* noted that for many Panamanians, "North American occupation of Isthmian territory has come to symbolize discrimination, exploitation, and domination." A 1960 editorial zeroed in on the real cause of the problem: "at the bottom of these complaints, all legitimate, is Panamanian resentment of our old friend, Jim Crow."[7]

American officials also found themselves criticized for supporting the colonial powers. Claude Barnett, director of the Associated Negro Press, informed Assistant Secretary of State George V. Allen in May 1956 that African-Americans were keeping a close watch on events in the colonial world:

> Interest in African affairs among Negroes in America is increasing rapidly. They have not been unaware of the position taken by our United States representatives in supporting measures before the United Nations which favored the position of the colonial powers rather than the welfare of their black subjects. Frequently the position taken seemed to clash with the traditional principles of our nation when the aspirations of subject people toward freedom and independence are considered. Negroes in America are beginning to question the governmental links our country has forged with South Africa, with Belgian Congo and East African areas including, it is understood, even Portuguese East Africa. Just what is the position of our State Department upon the problems of the colonial areas?[8]

Others were more specific in their criticisms. In an article in *The Crisis* published shortly before the French defeat at Dien Bien Phu, correspondent William Worthy, Jr., warned his readers of "Our Disgrace in Indo-China." For years, he charged, the United States had supported French colonialism in its brutal and futile war against Vietnamese nationalism. Now, with the French effort at a standstill, Secretary Dulles was hinting that perhaps the United States would have to become involved directly in the conflict. He called on the American people to fight against this "counter-revolutionary direction of America's policies among the darker people" of the world. Horace Cayton, writing in the *Pittsburgh Courier* in early 1960, argued that America's history of supporting the colonial powers was an impediment to the nation's diplomacy in Africa. The United States would have to realize that the new African nations "represent the future; the colonial governments represent the past."[9]

However, it was the new nations in Africa that drew the most attention during the 1950s. The independence of Ghana in 1957 was of particular interest. Horace Cayton wrote a long piece for the *Pittsburgh Courier* in February 1957, in which he declared that, "Independence for this small black nation will be the hole in the dike for the vast continent of Africa," since this would "speed up the time table" for the independence of all African nations. Writing later in 1957, George Padmore expressed a note of concern. In an article published in *The Crisis*, he decried the "campaign of vilification, misrepresentation and slander" against the new government of Ghana being carried out by British newspapers. The goal of this campaign seemed clear: by bringing the government of Ghana into "ridicule," these newspapers and their supporters hoped to influence "British colonial policy against the granting of independence to Nigeria and other territories predominantly inhabited by Africans." These efforts to tarnish the new government, and particularly its prime minister, Kwame Nkrumah, had little effect on African-American observers, who quickly latched on to Nkrumah as a symbol of African independence and black pride. A photo essay in the August 1958 *Ebony* celebrated Nkrumah's visit to the United States. Observing that the prime minister had once scrubbed pots while going to college in America and had been "refused a drink of water in a bus station because he had been born black," Nkrumah now returned in triumph as the "symbol of the dark man's entry into world affairs" and the "voice of the new Africa."[10]

This interest in events in Africa and Asia was also much in evidence during the Asian-African Conference held in Bandung in 1955. Roy Wilkins, executive secretary of the NAACP, sent along the organization's greetings and admiration for "this effort of the darker peoples to merge as an independent world force in the struggle for order, dignity and peace among nations." A Department of State report noted the large number of African-American journalists in attendance, including such well known figures as Carl Rowan from the *Minneapolis Tribune,* Mary Cartwright of the *Chicago Sun Times,* Louis Lautier from *Ebony,* and novelist Richard Wright.[11]

The apartheid system of South Africa also attracted a great deal of interest from African-Americans.[12] Numerous pieces in *The Crisis* testified to the anger and horror felt by American blacks. Matters came to a head in March 1960 when the Sharpeville massacre took place, in which South African security forces opened fire on a crowd of black protesters, killing over 100 people. Roy Wilkins wrote to Secretary of State Christian Herter to express his indignation at this "shockingly brutal slaughter." The United States "cannot remain inactive in the face of mass murder," and he reminded Herter that the American government had protested similar repressions in North Korea, the People's Republic of China, and Hungary. Nor could the United States claim absolute innocence; Wilkins hinted that the weapons used to murder the protesters might have been provided "with funds made available to the Union of South Africa by the United States under its international aid program." Wilkins demanded that the United

States sever relations with a nation that had shown itself to be "outside the pale of Western democratic society."[13]

Beyond these specific criticisms of international problems in general, and U.S. foreign policy in particular, African-Americans also continued to demonstrate their concern over the fact that U.S. policymakers did not seem to understand the importance of the race issue in the new global arena. According to an editorial in the *Pittsburgh Courier* in 1957, the outburst of nationalism in Africa and Asia reflected the desire of the inhabitants of those continents "to control one's own destiny . . . to be considered as equals." Yet, the United States did not grasp these simple truths. This was displayed at the domestic level by its "lack of comprehension of the American Negro's mentality. The American Negro is mad. . . . In this he is no different from the Indian of India, the African of Ghana, of Nigeria, or Kenya, the Indonesian who is willing to strangle his economy to get rid of the Dutch." The East-West struggle paled in comparison to "the more immediate goals (sic) of throwing off the yoke of white supremacy."[14]

In place of understanding, however, U.S. officials more often displayed ignorance and arrogance. The ignorance was sometimes evident in intemperate outbursts, such as the one by Representative Wayne Hays of Ohio in 1958 after his tour of Asia and Africa: "We can't turn these countries over to these half-baked half-educated natives." An editorial in the *Chicago Defender* cited the statement as "typical of the kind of blundering boorishness exhibited by too many Americans abroad who should rightly be labeled Our Ill Will Ambassadors." More often, however, it was displayed in more benign, but just as frustrating ways. In two articles in the *Pittsburgh Courier* in early 1958, P.L. Prattis and George Schuyler commented on a recent visit, organized by the State Department, by the editor of an East Pakistani newspaper. Prattis noted that the editor's itinerary took her first to the South. When she traveled north, she was invited to stay at the home of a black attorney in Buffalo. This put the editor on the spot since her visit to the South had convinced her that "Negroes were to be avoided." Eventually, however, she made the visit and learned some facts about African-American life in the United States that were "quite different" from what she had heard in the South. The experience left her "amazed by the deception." This kind of deception, Prattis claimed, could only hurt the United States. "If our State Department were half as smart as it thinks it is, it would work to see that some of these foreign visitors see and visit with some American Negroes. . . . The lies Americans tell are wearing out on them." Schuyler had a more personal take on the visit. He also thought it "incredible" that the editor's first exposure to American life was through a visit to the South. He was offended, however, that no time had been made in her tight schedule

for a visit with "intelligent, articulate Negroes" such as himself. "It is probably not," he opined, "that the State Department particularly wants to keep
these visitors away from talking to Negroes, but simply that it does not
occur to them that these visitors *should* talk to some Negroes." Or, perhaps,
the State Department simply feared exposing visitors to the "seamy side of
U.S. 'democracy' and what Negroes have been and still are up against in
making the grade in this land which lectures the world about freedom."[15]

American arrogance, which was complemented by its ignorance, was
also plainly evident to African-American observers. An editorial in the
Pittsburgh Courier in early 1958 commented on the "surprise" in the Department of State occasioned by the plan of Egypt and Syria to form a
united power. The editorialist expressed no surprise, however, since "State
Department thinking is always getting a jolt when other so-called backward
peoples in Asia, Africa or the Middle East show independence, skill, or
political maturity." The action by Egypt and Syria was obviously a reaction
to the "ramshackle Baghdad Pact," which had been an obvious response to
Soviet "pressure" on the area. What was needed was real economic assistance for the region, but "What have the State Department boys offered . . .
to the industry-hungry darker peoples of the Middle East, Asia and Africa?"
In addition, the United States needed to export "the ideas of the Declaration
of Independence" (which were also needed "right here"). "But," the editorial concluded, "will Mr. Dulles stop treating the dark peoples like inferiors
needing his unwanted protection?" For the aging civil rights warrior W.E.B.
Du Bois, the ultimate demonstration of America's arrogance concerning the
international ramifications of the race issue was to be found in the UN,
where, as he explained in a letter to the Human Rights Commission in 1957,
"white Americans who know nothing and care less about Negroes have
been selected to tell the United Nations about the 'Negro Problem,' while
not a single black man has been given opportunity to speak." Would it not
be "too much to ask that the United Nations itself invite some Negro to
address them on this problem which is not local nor merely internal but
affects the majority of the peoples of the earth?"[16]

Perceiving that officials in Washington had little understanding of or
concern for the issue of race as an international problem, African-Americans combined their criticisms of U.S. actions with renewed warnings about
the harmful effects such disinterest would breed. Black newspapers and
journals were constantly reporting on foreign perceptions and criticisms of
white America's racial attitudes. Sociologist John E. Owen, after spending
over a year and a half in Finland, wrote of his experience in *The Crisis*. He
had discovered during this stay that "race was the one topic above all others
about which young Finnish students wanted to learn." As a whole, the Finns

could not "understand the attitude of many American white people" concerning race. The larger problem for America was clear: "As long as a man cannot be served in a restaurant or be offered accommodation at a hotel because of his skin color, we must not expect the rest of the world to be enthusiastic about 'the American way.'" Otto Leichter, an Austrian who had recently become a naturalized American citizen, reflected some of the same concerns in an article he also published in *The Crisis*. Though he believed that Europeans held grossly mistaken opinions concerning the situation of African-Americans, he admitted that there was "immense interest in the Negro problem" in Europe and that most Europeans believed the worst about the race problem in America.[17]

More often, African-American newspapers and journals let the foreign observers speak for themselves. J.A. Rogers of the *Pittsburgh Courier* wrote in early 1958 about a group of foreign students brought to the United States by the *New York Herald-Tribune* to get a firsthand look at the race problem. Their attitudes before arriving were harshly critical of the United States. One student from Thailand stated that the "Little Rock incident made me hate the American people." Another, from Iran, indicated that she believed there were "secret organizations that wear masks and go out to kill colored people." A young man from the Sudan warned that he was "deeply concerned at the way the Communists keep on insisting on this weakness of yours to strengthen their position all over the world." Their stay in America had convinced many that "matters weren't as bad as they had heard at home," but Rogers concluded that many more around the world might agree with a statement from an Indian newspaper: "A white man is always a nuisance to the rest of the human race."[18] Speaking before a group in Virginia, the Ceylonese ambassador declared that discriminatory behavior against minorities "cast dark doubts in the minds of other people as to your sincerity and the reality of what you say you are." America's "greatest wealth lies in your belief that all men are created equal. . . . When you fail . . . you let down yourselves and millions of other people who look to you to uphold this ideal."[19]

Some African-Americans traveled abroad to find out for themselves what the world thought about America's race problem. At least two, Carl Rowan, then a journalist from Minneapolis, and Saunders Redding, a professor at Hampton Institute, published books recounting their experiences. Both had been approached by the U.S. government to undertake speaking engagements; Redding spent his time in India, while Rowan traveled throughout South and Southeast Asia. Redding's book, entitled *An American in India* and published in 1954, detailed his three-month visit to India in 1952. In large part, the book deals with what Redding saw as the main

problem facing India: communism. Much of the book deals with his encoun-
ters with "communist agitators" who attempted to heckle him during his
speeches; in nearly every case, Redding is able to put them in their place
with a few well chosen words. However, the descriptions of communist
activity and growing strength in India are drenched in drama and worries for
the future. The book also directly confronted the issue of race. Upon his
arrival in Bombay, he was met by one of the few African-American FSOs
outside of the usual "Negro circuit." With some hesitation, the FSO warned
Redding to be prepared for questions on the race issue: "it's a bigger issue in
the thinking of the rest of the world than Americans have let themselves
believe." Later, when a mob formed on one of the streets of Bombay, Redding turned to one of his Indian companions and asked whether there would
be trouble. The indignant response was that, "These are not the Negro communities in your American South protesting their many inequalities. There
are no armed police to shoot them down." Redding, "shriveled with humiliation and embarrassment," could only blurt out a reflexive " 'But . . .' " "I
might have said, 'The right of Negroes to protest has never been abridged by
guns. Why,' I might have said, 'even in Mississippi and Texas—' Lies! . . . It
is much easier to tell an unpleasant truth than to take one." Yet, everywhere
he went in India, he was faced with unpleasant questions about civil rights in
America. "It seemed impossible for these Indians to conceive of a dark-
skinned American as being other than the enemy of white. . . . I was asked
more than once whether the Negro community of America would join with
the colored peoples of the world in a war against the white man." Redding
was puzzled by the lack of any American effort to deal with these issues.
"Was this because . . . America was somehow afraid to concede the importance of the race question? Was it fear, or shame, or blindness, or—shriveling
thought!—the inculcated habit of not considering 'colored' folks?"
Redding's personal defenses of American progress in the field of civil rights
were met with disbelief and skepticism.[20]

Rowan's book, published in 1956 under the title *The Pitiful and the
Proud,* reported on his travels throughout much of Asia, ending up with his
attendance at the Bandung Conference. His first stop in India had been at
the behest of the Department of State, which wanted Rowan to spend three
months there lecturing under the auspices of the International Educational
Exchange Program. Another month in India, and the rest of his time spent
in South and Southeast Asia, would be as a reporter for the *Minneapolis
Tribune.* Like Redding, Rowan spent much of the book describing the dangerous growth of communism in the countries he visited and detailing his
run-ins with communist agitators and left-leaning journalists. Also like
Redding, Rowan discovered that race was a significant issue wherever he

went in Asia, particularly in India. As he concluded, "this concern with color had become close to an obsession and I was convinced that for many years to come race would be an important factor in India's foreign policy." Rowan's response was twofold. First, he was convinced that Communist propaganda was the main problem: when he felt he was making progress in creating goodwill among the Indian population, this was the time for the "Communists to open a new attack by hitting me where I was supposed to be weak—on the race question. The wily Reds realized that in the Indian's deepest emotional kit lies a long-unsatisfied desire not only for individual status but for the right to believe that his country is great." As for the Indian newspapers who carried stories decrying America's racial problems, Rowan had "the impression that they were unwitting pawns in this campaign." Second, Rowan was simply exasperated by the lack of understanding by the Indians and other Asians with whom he came in contact. "With many such people, I was banging my head against a stone wall" in trying to paint an objective picture of the "startling strides toward first-class citizenship" being made by African-Americans. For Rowan, the race problem in America was largely the result of the work of a small, but vocal minority of bigots; instances of discrimination and bias, then, were isolated incidents, not truly representative of the American nation as a whole. The answer to the Asian criticisms was relatively simple: "I had been convinced that our propaganda experts must dig deeper into this thing *race* to see how it is a factor in the struggle for Asia today."[21]

While African-American observers may have disagreed on why race had become such an issue in places such as India, they all agreed that America's domestic racial problems were hurting the nation overseas. As he had during the Truman years, Walter White of the NAACP kept pushing this point right up to his death in 1955. In early 1954, he wrote to the editor of the *New York Times Magazine,* complimenting a recent article by Chester Bowles on the international implications of race prejudice in the United States. White noted that "I have attempted to point out on the basis of personal experience in Asia, Africa and Latin America that the stream of news of mistreatment of dark-skinned people in the United States is doing us harm." Obviously attempting to link the issue to recent notions put forward by President Eisenhower (which would find their ultimate expression in his "domino effect" speech in April 1954), White argued that there was a "connection between our racial practices in the United States and the source of many of the indispensable ingredients of our industrial production." If America's racial prejudices helped in pushing the people of Asia and Africa "into the orbit of the Soviet Union, the Western world would lose much, if not most, of its uranium, cobalt, tungsten, tin, rubber and other essential raw materials." Writing to Secretary Dulles a few weeks later, White was more direct: "Race discrimination threatens our national security. We can no longer afford to let the most backward sections of our population endanger our country by persisting in discriminating practices. We must meet the challenge of our neighbors, not only because discrimination is immoral, but also because it is dangerous."[22]

The most dramatic example of the damage that could be done to America's international prestige by episodes of racial prejudice and violence in the United States was the Little Rock school desegregation incident of 1957. Writing in the *Pittsburgh Courier* just months after the ugly scenes in Arkansas, Horace Cayton suggested that Little Rock, like the recent launching of Sputnik, was an international debacle for the United States: "What the Little Rock affair did was show the world that our high-sounding pronouncements on morals, on democracy and the brotherhood of man, did not mean much when it came to internal problems. It demonstrated to the two-thirds (some say three-fourths) of the world that is not white that democracy in the United States is more of a hope than a reality."[23]

During the next two years, African-American newspapers, journals, and organizations constantly reemphasized the international damage done by Little Rock. A story in the *Baltimore Afro-American* in May 1958 reported on the upcoming meeting of the International Labor Organization, which would be attended by Secretary of Labor James P. Mitchell. Expecting strong Communist denunciations of U.S. race relations, and the Little Rock incident in particular, Mitchell was prepared to fire back with a "strong counter-offensive." This would involve, for example, telling the world that "colored Americans are paid better than workers are paid in the Soviet Union." The writer of the article seemed decidedly unimpressed: "Meanwhile, as the Labor Secretary prepares to explain away the Little Rock situation, the legal battle for first class citizenship continues." Horace Cayton, in an editorial of the same month, was equally skeptical about any claims that the furor over Little Rock was the work of Communist propaganda. "The damage done to our prestige abroad—among the majority of the world's people who are non-white—by this incident of violence and brutality was and is incalculable. And none of this was Russian inspired; none originated in Pravda. It was all our own doing."[24] As another African-American commentator noted, the world had indeed been watching the events at Little Rock with keen interest. As reported in an October 1958 editorial in the *Norfolk Journal and Guide*, the impact of Little Rock in the Middle East had been dramatic. As a U.S. diplomat in the region had commented, prior to Little Rock, Israel had been "the enemy." Now, after the events in Arkansas, America was "the enemy," all because of that state's governor, "Orval

Faubus and those other apostles of pure lily-whiteness who stand with him." Since Little Rock, "The race issue has been emphasized on almost every state-owned broadcasting station in the Middle East."[25]

Civil rights leaders implored President Eisenhower to understand the international reverberations of Little Rock. In a statement signed by A. Philip Randolph, Lester Granger, Martin Luther King, and Roy Wilkins, the point was clearly made: "It is no secret that the foreign relations program of our nation has been hampered and damaged by the discriminatory treatment accorded citizens within the United States, solely on the basis on their race and color. In our world-wide struggle to strengthen the free world against the spread of totalitarianism, we are sabotaged by the totalitarian practices forced upon millions of our Negro citizens." A resolution presented at a meeting of the NAACP's Board of Directors shortly before the start of the 1958 school year reiterated that point: "One of the factors in the cold war in the Far East, in the Middle East, in emerging Africa and along the borders of the Iron Curtain is the demonstrated failure of America to guarantee democratic rights within its own borders. The Little Rock situation, because it epitomizes so sharply the negation of democracy, is the dramatic symbol to the world of America's delinquency."[26]

In the aftermath of Little Rock, African-American leaders and journalists kept up the attack, reminding their readers that the damage done to U.S. foreign policy by racism was immeasurable. In October 1957, just a few months after the Little Rock incident began to explode, William P. Robinson of Central State College published an article in the *Negro History Bulletin*. Reviewing the world situation, the impact of racial incidents in America on international public opinion, and the machinations of Communist propagandists in making use of such incidents, Robinson concluded that, "We must be free not because we claim freedom but because we practice it; our freedom must be clear and unequivacal (sic) no matter what the color of the skin may be. In this struggle for the minds and hearts of men," he declared, "we can successfully plead the cause of freedom and equality for others only if we resolve our own racial problem, and do it now."[27]

In July 1960, Alice A. Dunnigan published a piece in the *Pittsburgh Courier* summing up matters. She reported on her meeting with several Nigerian government representatives who had been visiting Washington. The interview began rather lightheartedly, with the Nigerians snickering about how little Americans knew about Africa, while Africans knew all "about Arkansas and Faubus." Soon, however, the talk turned to the issue of discrimination in America. Just before speaking with Dunnigan, they had had a meeting with a select group of African-American employees of the Civil Service Commission. As Dunnigan reported, "The Africans listened interestingly and patiently, but let it be known afterwards that they were not fooled by this 'rosy picture.' " As the Africans put it, "We realize that we will never see a true picture of America's discrimination. Everywhere we go, word has gone on before announcing our visit." Finally, one of the Nigerians stated that he had already formed some definite opinions about America but refused to verbalize them. Dunnigan finished what he had started: "He would say no more, but in his eyes was that modest glare which seemed to be shyly saying, 'You'd better tidy up, America, your "phony" is showing.'"[28]

One corrective to the unsavory reputation America was acquiring around the world, according to many African-Americans, was the appointment of more blacks to diplomatic positions. The election of Republican Dwight D. Eisenhower as president in 1952, which ended twenty years of Democratic control of the White House, did nothing to decrease the activities of African-American civil rights leaders, politicians, and journalists geared toward increasing the integration of blacks into the nation's diplomatic service. They continued their meetings with Department of State officials and kept up their two-pronged line of attack developed during the Truman years: criticizing the department for its lack of African-American employees, while giving praise and publicity for the handful of black diplomatic appointments that were made. Not surprisingly, Rayford Logan was one of the first to press the attack. Even before Eisenhower and Dulles took office, Logan published a "4-Point Program For New Secretary of State" in the *Pittsburgh Courier*. These points included appointing a full-time personnel consultant to bring "competent Negro men and women" to the attention of the Department of State; naming African-Americans to "non-colored countries"; sending African-American diplomats to African nations, "other than Liberia"; and appointing "competent Negroes. Use other departments to pay off political obligations."[29]

In the first months of the Eisenhower presidency, however, African-Americans expressed disappointment and pessimism about the new administration's inactivity in this regard. In early 1953, Claude Barnett wrote to John W. Davis, who was serving as the director of the U.S. Technical Cooperation Mission in Liberia, to express his concern. As Barnett understood matters, the Truman administration had been "dickering with the idea" of taking Ambassador Edward Dudley out of Liberia and putting him in a "non-African country as a part of a program of integration. The change in administration probably scotched all this." Barnett concluded that politics was to blame: "The new administration has had no posts to give to Negroes due to the great demands on the part of white applicants for sundry recognition so it may be they will sacrifice efficiency to expediency."[30]

The NAACP, attempting to maintain the very slight momentum toward integration of the diplomatic corps that had begun during the last years of the Truman presidency, saw its early optimism fade into dejection in the first months of the Eisenhower administration. Clarence Mitchell, who directed the NAACP's Washington, D.C., office, set up a meeting with Department of State officials in April 1953 to see what could be expected from the new president and secretary of state. On April 30, Mitchell met with four department professionals and personnel consultant John A. Davis. In a memo to Walter White, he expressed his satisfaction with the talks. Edwin Montague, director of the Office of Personnel, had assured Mitchell about his commitment to further integration: "as long as he was there this project will be continued." A memorandum by Scott McLeod, one of the Department officials at the meeting, also indicated that the discussions had gone smoothly. Mitchell, he stated, had "commended the Department on the progress made on employment of non-whites over the past two years." There had been broad agreement that the "employment of non-Caucasians in the Foreign Service of the United States was of real importance to the effectuation of our Foreign Policy, especially in non-white countries and in Iron Curtain countries." McLeod's stance was unequivocal: "I concur in the conclusions of the group," and suggested that they be sent on to Secretary Dulles.[31]

Not all of the news had been good, however. In a report to the NAACP Board of Directors, Mitchell noted that the meeting with the Department officials had come on "the same day that the House Appropriations Committee heavily cut State Department's funds." McLeod had informed Mitchell as to what this would mean: the Department would suffer "a reduction in force of approximately 25%, and that in all probability both the Technical Cooperation Administration and the International Information Administration would leave the Department." Matters quickly went from bad to worse. The NAACP's Board of Directors heard in May that there was "great confusion in the Department of State because of budget cuts." Of the four officials Mitchell had met with on April 30, only one remained "firmly placed"; another had resigned, one had been dropped due to budget cuts (consultant John A. Davis), and another "may leave any day." "However," the report gloomily concluded, "we are trying to pick up the pieces."[32]

From there, things continued to go downhill. About a month after his meeting with the department officials, Mitchell wrote to McLeod expressing his dismay at what had happened since that time. Most particularly, he was upset that John A. Davis had been "dropped from the payroll." "We are trying very hard to act in good faith in this situation, but, frankly, the long delays we have encountered in getting approval of qualified persons and the latest adverse action on Dr. Davis causes me to doubt that some of the people in the Department are fully cooperative with the principle of fair employment." Those doubts were expressed more directly in a report to the NAACP's Board of Directors: "The NAACP's program to increase the employment of qualified colored persons in the Department of State has been thrown into severe jeopardy by two factors." One were the budget cuts mentioned earlier; the other was that "some political individuals and Department officials who are opposed to integration of colored people have combined forces in halting a program under the direction of Dr. John A. Davis." In mid-June, Mitchell informed the NAACP's Youth Secretary, Herbert L. Wright, that the "State Dept. has curtailed its integration program in its current economy drive. 2,500 graded and experienced members of State Dept. units are being laid off. Possibility of employment with agency not good at this time."[33]

With this rocky beginning as a background, it was not surprising to find African-American politicians, civil rights leaders, and media attacking the Eisenhower administration's record on black hiring for the Department of State and pleading for more action in this area. One of the most consistent critics was New York Congressman Adam Clayton Powell, Jr. Just months after the new president took office, Powell reminded Eisenhower of his campaign promises to take direct action in the field of civil rights. Powell suggested that, as an act of good faith, "the discrimination in the Department of State which now allows only fifty Negroes in Foreign Service out of six thousand employed, shall be discountinued and opportunities extended to all people." About a year later, Powell's tone had changed. Writing to an official in the Department of State's Personnel Bureau, Powell indicated that he had conducted a personal survey of Department employees, which revealed that, "Out of 8,231 persons employed abroad in the Foreign Service, only 55 are Negroes. Out of the 6,700 departmental employees, GS-7 and above who are in Washington, D.C., only 15 are Negroes with other grade classifications." With a good deal of sarcasm, the congressman stated that "it is little short of amazing that I could do this since you, as one of the top echelon of the Department of State was unable to . . . in view of this ridiculous and tragic disparity, what is the Department of State going to do concerning remedying this situation?"[34]

In a meeting with President Eisenhower in mid-1955, Powell reported on his attendance at the Bandung Conference. One way of counteracting some of the anti-Americanism that issued forth from the conference was "to have Negroes placed in embassy service in those countries where there is large non-White population." Powell kept up his attack during Eisenhower's second term. In a speech in April 1958, the congressman called the State Department "the weakest spot in our democratic offensive." He charged that a "great mistake" of the Department of State was its "steadfast refusal ... to employ colored Americans in embassy positions." An article in *Jet* also carried Powell's speech, in which the congressman declared, "The full impact of the American way of life in all its vast and progressively advancing fields is not being sold to the people of Asia and Africa. It is not being sold because there is a road block at the highest peak, and the road block is in the Dept. of State."[35]

Representative Charles C. Diggs also criticized the Department of State's hiring patterns. Following a congressional study mission to Africa in late 1960, an obviously angry Diggs argued that the "skillful use of non-whites as foreign service officers and in diplomatic posts may swing the sympathy of independent African nations in our direction." However, "propaganda that 'American Negroes are second-class citizens' was being used by some State Department personnel as an excuse to not send more non-whites to Africa." "Their excuse," Diggs claimed, "is that it would be an insult to an African nation to send second-class citizens to represent the United States there." His own discussions with African leaders had revealed that "in every case where non-whites were utilized by the State Department, they accomplished a superior job of communications."[36]

Some of the leading figures in the civil rights movement also lambasted the Department of State for its underutilization of African-Americans. Lester Granger of the National Urban League wrote to one of Eisenhower's aides, Maxwell Rabb, in September 1953 to register his complaints. He began by noting that during the past two or three years, the Department had begun using blacks in the USIS in "strategic areas," mostly in India. Due to budget cuts, however, this positive trend was endangered, since "the last hired" would naturally be the "first fired." He noted a case in point: Herbert Tate, who had been working as a cultural affairs attaché in India, had been terminated, even though the current U.S. ambassador had recently commented on the need for "a qualified, devoted and skillful Negro in that particular post." This was particularly troubling, since there were "not more than a half-dozen Negroes in such posts in our whole foreign service." Why should these people, with "irreplaceable experience," be sacrificed simply because of a lack of seniority? Furthermore, Granger argued, seniority obviously was not the only principle at work. Another individual holding a foreign service reserve position in India, who was white, was allowed to hold onto his job, even though he demonstrated "almost complete ignorance on the subject of racial conditions in the United States" and tended to "shy away from the subject whenever it was brought up." This was a perfect, but tragic, example of "a hard-and-fast bureaucratic procedure which still does not seem to have been adjusted to meet the very touchy racial aspects of our foreign service problems."[37]

A. Philip Randolph, who was scheduled to meet with Eisenhower in June 1958, requested that Martin Luther King, Roy Wilkins, and Granger—who would also be at the meeting—raise criticisms against "the continued flagrant discriminatory practices by the State Department and U.S. Foreign Service." Department officials consistently demonstrated their "desire to greatly limit and in many areas exclude, qualified Negroes from State Department positions here at home and the Foreign Service abroad." President Eisenhower should be asked to immediately "appoint and integrate Negro citizens to the various Presidential appointive positions in the Foreign Service."[38]

The NAACP, which had turned its attention to other matters following the rebuff it received from the Eisenhower administration in 1953, revisited the issue of more African-American appointments to diplomatic service in late 1960. A memorandum to Roy Wilkins from James Farmer and E.J. Odom in December 1960 expressed the NAACP's continuing frustration with the situation in State. As they reported, "Hardly any African leader with whom we have talked has failed to express disappointment that our State Department uses so few Negroes in diplomatic posts on that continent." These talks put the lie to the Eisenhower administration's contention that "African nations do not want Negroes in diplomatic posts in their countries." Farmer and Odom called for a "full-fledged campaign to persuade the Department of State, under the new administration, to make adequate use of qualified Negroes in every diplomatic capacity."

The U.S. government had been content to use African-American "show people and teams of entertainers on tours," but this raised "the danger of exporting the stereotype of Negroes as merely entertainers." Based on their experiences in Africa and Latin America, Farmer and Odom believed that "Negro Americans are generally in a better position than white Americans to develop and maintain rapport with the peoples therein."[39]

Journalistic criticism of the Eisenhower administration's record on African-American appointments to the Department of State was a constant, but it grew decidedly stronger during Eisenhower's second term. This may have been due to the growing black dissatisfaction with the president's undistinguished record on civil rights during his first four years in office; or perhaps the Little Rock episode simply reawakened the criticisms. Whatever the reason, the attacks in newspapers and magazines began to take on a much more cynical and combative tone after 1956. A long piece by Ethel Payne in the *Chicago Defender* in May 1957 was typical. Payne launched a bitter attack against the "iron-fisted dictators in the State Department" who showed every indication that they would continue their policy of "keeping Negroes out of the foreign service." She criticized the fact that the new Bureau of African Affairs had not named any African-Americans to high positions; nor had any blacks apparently even been considered for the ambassadorship to Ghana.[40]

Louis Lautier, writing in the *Baltimore Afro-American,* took the Department of State to task for its use of African-American "tokens" at state dinners or in groups greeting visiting heads of state, particularly those from Africa. With the Soviet Union making tremendous headway in the underdeveloped world, Lautier stated, "it would appear that the United States would have some colored Americans in responsible positions in the State Department" to work with the heads of state from those regions. Like Payne, he bemoaned the fact that no blacks were being considered for the position of assistant secretary of state for African affairs. An African-American in such a position would be America's "Exhibit No. 1 of how colored persons are treated in this country." In July of 1959, Lautier continued his criticisms. After congratulating the Eisenhower administration on its choice of African-American educator John Howard Morrow as U.S. ambassador to Guinea, Lautier then went on to ask why more blacks were not being used for diplomatic work. In many areas of the world, Lautier argued, black U.S. diplomats would have an advantage: they would "mingle with the people and win friends for the United States, while the white American would hold himself aloof and stay within official and diplomatic circles."[41]

Jet often carried brief, but slashing attacks on the "lily-white" make-up of the Department of State. In November 1958, it reported that UN officials were having difficulty in getting African-Americans to support an event featuring black opera singer Marian Anderson. The reason was that many in the African-American community had come to feel that Anderson "allows herself to be used to cover up the fact that the State Dept. pursues a lily-white racial policy." Fewer than five of the top jobs in the Department were held by blacks—"and none of them in the African Bureau." Months later, *Jet* reported that, "Here's more on the State Dept. color bias: not a Negro is employed in the Department's African Bureau, and in the U.S. mission to Nigeria—the large African country which gets its independence next year—the same thing." This had provoked a Nigerian official to ask "why the U.S. was using a lily-white policy in his country."[42]

An editorial that appeared in the *New York Age* in late 1959 took a somewhat different approach. Instead of arguing that more African-American diplomats be sent to Africa, the editorial protested that blacks be given opportunities in other areas, particularly Europe. It was futile to argue that African-Americans were being given equal job opportunities, since "everybody who has an ounce of sense knows that the State Department's lily-white hiring policy from Consul General down to errand boy has prevented Negroes from acquiring diplomatic experience." All that was being asked was that "not all the Negro ambassadors and Negro State Department employees (bless their few souls) be sent to Africa and all the white ambassadors and white State Department employees be sent to Europe."[43]

Occasionally, however, the Department of State garnered praise. The *Baltimore Afro-American* noted with approval Congressman Powell's declaration that the Eisenhower administration was "Ready to Appoint Tan Diplomats." This announcement came on the heels of Powell's 1955 meeting with the president following the former's trip to the Bandung Conference. Powell had urged Eisenhower to send more African-American diplomats to the Far East. According to the congressman, "President Eisenhower indicated that action would be taken on this immediately." A short time later, a story in the *New York Amsterdam News* reported that the Department of State seemed to be following up on the matter. The substance of the action was that the Department would make a greater effort to recruit from black colleges. And as a feature in the *Baltimore Afro-American* in early 1956 argued, there were good opportunities for African-Americans in the diplomatic service. Focusing on a recent report by Dr. Francis Hammond, a former psychology professor working as the "minority affairs advisor" for United States Information Agency (USIA), the story argued that the old rumors about African-Americans not being welcomed in certain countries had been proven false. What that meant was that "with the U.S. government now fully aware that colored representatives will be greeted with open arms in these potentially explosive places, it seems certain—as well as sensible—that the foreign service will be sending out more colored diplomats than ever before."[44]

Although this anticipated explosion of opportunities for African-American diplomats never materialized, the achievements of the handful of blacks in the Department of State, USIA, and the UN never failed to attract intense interest in the black press. Sometimes this meant examining a particular foreign post, as when William Worthy reported on the work of African-American diplomats in India in mid-1955. "Today," he noted, "one sees brown faces in nearly every embassy, Point Four mission and U.S. Information Service office."[45]

More often, however, stories focused on individual African-American diplomats. Journalist Marguerite Cartwright wrote a number of articles on African-Americans who served on the U.S. delegation to the UN. One, published in the *Pittsburgh Courier,* featured Charles H. Mahoney, who was the first black permanent U.S. delegate (all others had been alternate delegates). Her portrayal of the life-long Republican, head of his own $5 million insurance company, was not complimentary: "Speculation on what to expect of future development is difficult with a man quite so cold, cautious and uncommunicative as Charles H. Mahoney." An *Ebony* photo feature on U.S. Ambassador to Liberia Richard L. Jones took a much more favorable slant. A successful businessman, and only the fifth black to rise to the rank of brigadier general in the U.S. Army Reserves, Jones had first gone to Liberia in 1954 to head the Foreign Operations Administration program there. In 1955, when Ambassador Jesse D. Locker (who had succeeded Edward R. Dudley) died, Jones had been selected to take the vacant position. He had also served in the UN, and, the article stated, "was rumored 'in line' for a high-level Middle East Ambassadorship or U.S. Undersecretary of State role."[46]

The *Baltimore Afro-American* reported on the work of O. Rudolph Aggrey as an information officer at the U.S. embassy in Paris. The appointment of Frank Snowden, who was head of the Department of Classics at Howard University, as cultural attaché to Rome was front-page news in 1954. *Ebony* ran an article on Dr. Francis Hammond in 1958, featuring his work as a USIA representative in Morocco. And a lengthy article in the *Baltimore Afro-American* in 1959 publicized the appointment of John H. Morrow as the first U.S. ambassador to the new nation of Guinea.[47]

Without a doubt, however, the individual who received the most press coverage (besides Ralph Bunche, who continued his highly publicized work for the UN) was Clifton Wharton. By the time Eisenhower came to office, Wharton had served nearly three decades in the Foreign Service but, as noted in the previous chapter, had only recently broken free from the "Negro circuit." His appointment as consul general to Marseilles in 1953 was highlighted both in a front-page story in the *Baltimore Afro-American* and in the lead story in *Jet*. As the latter article noted, the job was "the most important and highest in rank ever assigned to a Negro career diplomat in a major country."[48]

Wharton's promotion to U.S. minister to Romania in 1958 sparked a tremendous amount of coverage in the black press. The *New York Amsterdam News* carried the announcement of the appointment on the front page and also ran an editorial congratulating Eisenhower for playing "an ace in the race" by appointing Wharton to an Iron Curtain country. As the editorial opined, "the Negro is a trump card which our government has stubbornly refused to make appropriate use of in the propaganda war with Russia." Naming Wharton as minister to Romania would be "a confusing answer to Red propaganda. We hope the President will give us more of the same." The nomination also made the front page of the *Baltimore Afro-American*. This was followed by a story a few weeks later that declared, "The United States is credited with scoring a major decision over the Communist regime here by the recent appointment of Clifton Wharton." The selection of Wharton as U.S. minister "sharply counteracts Communist exploitation of the American race issue" and had already "quieted down Communist drumbeating on the American racial issue." *Jet* and the *Norfolk Journal and Guide* also noted Wharton's nomination. An editorial in the *Pittsburgh Courier* stated that Wharton's selection "broke a long-standing American diplomatic pattern," which had limited African-American diplomats to service in a handful of nations.[49]

In a variety of ways, African-Americans during the Eisenhower years had tried to convince their white counterparts that race was a significant international issue—that a "rising tide of color" had to be confronted by the makers of U.S. foreign policy. Continued attacks on colonialism, increasingly harsh denunciations of apartheid in South Africa, and excitement with the growing independence movements in Africa were just a few of the foreign policy issues commanding the attention of black Americans. Their perceptions of the importance of the racial issue in the international arena compelled them to continue with their pleas to U.S. officials to recognize that American racial attitudes and problems were having devastating effects on the nation's prestige and influence abroad, particularly in the underdeveloped areas of the world. A corollary of all this was the continuing insistence on more black representation in the Department of State and Foreign Service. Because it was morally justified, because it would be a damaging blow to communist propaganda about America's race problem, and because African-Americans might better relate to peoples of color in the nations of Africa and the Far East, black civil rights leaders, politicians, and journalists kept up steady pressure for an increased black presence in the U.S. diplomatic service. If the tone and temper of the African-American criticisms and suggestions differed somewhat from the Truman years, there was no denying that throughout the 1950s American blacks continued to believe that "the domination of whites must go," both at home and abroad.

~ 5 ~

Token Gestures

The Eisenhower Administration, Race, and Diplomacy, 1953–1961

Despite the steady stream of criticism and suggestions from African-Americans concerning the issue of race and U.S. foreign policy, the Eisenhower administration demonstrated only lukewarm interest in the matter. In terms of responding both to the damage done to American prestige abroad by the nation's civil rights problems and to arguments for the desirability of appointing more blacks to diplomatic positions, the new administration offered only token gestures. It was only after the terrific international repercussions of the Little Rock incident that Eisenhower and his assistants took more forceful action.

This lack of initiative was not surprising. Neither Eisenhower nor Secretary of State John Foster Dulles could be characterized as trailblazers in the area of race relations. The president's attitudes toward domestic race problems have been well documented, with most scholars arguing that his reactions to the growing civil rights crisis were slow and inefficient at best. Robert Burk concludes that the president demonstrated a great deal of sympathy for Southern whites during the desegregation crises of the 1950s.[1] He demonstrated the same outlook when race became a foreign policy issue. This is perhaps best illustrated by his response to the 1960 effort in the UN to pass a resolution condemning apartheid in South Africa. In a telephone conversation with Secretary of State Christian Herter (who had replaced the ailing Dulles in 1959), Eisenhower explained his reluctance to criticize South Africa: "He said that while we, the United States, were trying to better condition [sic], he could not escape the feeling that we are not entirely in a different position ourselves. He said the South Africans have a right to say they want to make progress any way they want to do it." Besides, he declared, "if we vote for a tough resolution, we may find ourselves red-faced—in other words concerning our own Negro problem."[2] And there was the crux of the problem for Eisenhower: to take more direct action on the race issue overseas, he would first have to deal more actively and effectively with the "Negro problem" at home. That did not happen.

Secretary Dulles essentially dismissed the issue of race out of hand. Despite some lip-service public statements about race and America's foreign policy, Dulles shared Eisenhower's ambivalence on civil rights and believed that the issue was not really a matter for his department. His feelings came through very clearly in his correspondence with Robert Houston, an acquaintance who lived in South Carolina. In February 1956, Houston wrote to complain about the "constant agitation" by the NAACP, which was resulting in "bitter disunity" in the nation—"something all the cleverest Communist propaganda and infiltration ever devised couldn't do before the NAACP started stirring up hatred in the South." The secretary's response was telling: "The segregation issue is fortunately not a foreign policy issue." However, he was glad to have Houston's views, "which I am disposed to share insofar as relates to gradualism." Over a year later, Houston was still complaining, this time focusing on the school desegregation issue, which he seemed to consider a "staggering danger to national security." Dulles assured him that most "Northerners feel a great deal of sympathy for those in the South of both races who face the problem of integration." There was "no reason for any part of our country to feel a sense of superiority over any other part." What was needed was patience: "these matters can and will be worked out gradually."[3]

In confronting race on the international scene, he showed the same caution. U.S. Representative to the UN Henry Cabot Lodge wrote to Dulles about a potential problem in South Africa: the U.S. embassy and consulates were not inviting "colored persons" to the Fourth of July parties. This might result in some "extremely damaging publicity." Dulles's response was measured: "invitations should not be issued on a basis of caste, color or creed." Nevertheless, "As regards the applicability of this principle to specific posts abroad, I believe our people should apply it to the extent the traffic will bear. The equally American characteristic of good common horse sense should also apply." Little wonder that Representative Adam Clayton Powell implored President Eisenhower to replace Dulles in late 1955. A new secretary of state, he declared, would need to "realize that the day of the domination of the world by the white man and by Western civilization is finished, and that this is a day in which there must be complete equality on an international basis of all peoples whether they are black, brown, yellow or white."[4]

Of equal importance to the personal proclivities of the president and his secretary of state was the fact that the Eisenhower administration did not feel domestic political pressure in the same way the Truman administration had. Simply put, the black vote mattered less to Eisenhower and the Republicans; African-American criticisms and demands, therefore, had less impact. A study prepared after the 1952 elections stated that the vast majority of black voters had gone for Adlai Stevenson. The result was that, "The Negro leaders know the President and the Republican Party owe them nothing politically." And, as even the few African-Americans to support Eisenhower admitted, nothing was exactly what most blacks believed they got from the Republican administration. E. Frederic Morrow, who had been appointed as a special advisor in the Eisenhower White House, wrote in mid-1957, "I can state categorically that the rank and file of Negroes in the country feel that the president has deserted them in their current fight to achieve first-class citizenship via Civil Rights legislation, etc." Morrow suggested a meeting between the president and Martin Luther King, A. Philip Randolph, and Roy Wilkins. Yet even after the meeting took place a few weeks later in June 1958, the results, at least from the African-Americans' perspective, were disappointing. *Jet* reported that at least one of the black representatives felt that Eisenhower "just doesn't have the grasp of the (race) problem. It's far removed from him, probably because his racial aides are second- and third-string men in the White House order and don't get to him often enough." Each of them (including Lester Granger, who had also attended) believed that the president "was considerably less informed on race relations than were his predecessors, Truman and Roosevelt," and "seemed unaware of 'specifics' of segregation and discrimination problems."[5] Personally disinterested in (and uninformed about) the civil rights issue, and with no special interest in pleasing the black electorate, Eisenhower was an unlikely candidate to take forceful and innovative measures to deal with the international side of the issue. Nor would his Department of State take the lead, since his secretary of state did not consider civil rights issues to be foreign policy problems.

The lack of insight into the problem of race was demonstrated most vividly by the propaganda campaign on civil rights carried out by the Department of State and USIS during the early Eisenhower period. Campaign is probably too strong a word, since there was never any considerable or sustained effort made in this regard.[6] The USIS work was largely confined to issuing news briefs and feature stories highlighting the progress of African-Americans. Musician Louis Armstrong, for example, was the focus of a 1953 release, which emphasized his rise from a broken family to a star jazz musician. Black athletes were also prominently featured in stories dealing with "The American Negro in Baseball," and in profiles, such as those on boxers Henry Armstrong and Jersey Joe Walcott.[7]

The appointment of J. Ernest Wilkins as Assistant Secretary of Labor was a typical feature story. A note to the public affairs officers at the various U.S. missions around the world urged them to use it to stress "the principle of equal rights and opportunities for all citizens, regardless of race or color"; Wilkins's appointment "highlights progress of American Negro." Another instance of this general approach came in a photo feature dealing with "Fair Employment Legislation in the United States." The overall theme of the pictures was the "U.S. progress in eliminating racial and religious discrimination, with particular reference to the American Negro." Each picture accompanying the story featured at least one African-American.[8]

USIS features used the *Brown* school desegregation case as yet another example of the steady progress toward civil rights. As a story from June 1954 explained, the *Brown* decision was "not a sudden reversal of former United States policy," since most states already had desegregated schools. "In reality," the article went on, "as all students of U.S. history know, the Supreme Court's decision is only the logical culmination of a long series of steps." Even before the Court's announcement, "the southern States have been doing a great deal to improve their public school facilities for Negro students." The story went on to note that Southern schools had always lagged behind the rest of the nation, so the poor state of black schools in that region was not unusual. The piece hurried to point out that African-Americans were gaining in employment, wages, and home ownership: "No other group of people in any part of the world has made comparable progress during that period [since 1940]." Thus, the Supreme Court ruling was "an official action expressing the will of the great majority of the American people."[9]

Beyond the stories disseminated by USIS, there were other minor attempts to convince the world of America's racial tolerance. One was explained by Henry Cabot Lodge in early 1956. He believed that one of the main problems faced by the United States in dealing with the "Afro-Asian governments" was the "insufferable superiority" of "some tactless Americans" who traveled abroad. This attitude raised the "suspicion that Americans, like European colonial powers, are willing to work with the 'natives', but are not willing to play with them and treat them as social equals." Cabot suggested, in a rather awkward turn of phrase, that "high-ranking American officials who are temperamentally so inclined, and who have the necessary physical stamina (preferably with their wives)," take some goodwill trips overseas "to do a certain amount of sociable drinking, dining, dancing, and laughing." In dealing with the "natives," the "main point would be simply to be agreeable and to make them feel that *we* think *they* are attractive." As an example, Lodge recounted his recent trip to Khartoum. After the formal dinner, Lodge and his wife had been asked to accompany the foreign minister to a local nightclub. There, the foreign minister "who was coal black" danced with Mrs. Lodge. Word had spread around town that "the Americans are not stuffy." Eisenhower responded that the idea "seems to make good sense to me," and asked Dulles to consider the matter. The secretary was less enthusiastic, believing that "on a selective basis" the notion had "merit."[10]

C.D. Jackson, the administration's point man for psychological warfare, pushed for an interesting approach in early 1955: having John Foster Dulles speak at a meeting of the United Negro College Fund (UNCF). Jackson had been involved with the UNCF for years. As Jackson discovered, the UNCF could also be an effective tool for promulgating the message that the civil rights problem in the United States was being dealt with. In November 1952, Jackson had chaired a symposium put together by the UNCF, entitled "Color in Democracy." Featured speakers included Carl Rowan, Robert Weaver (director of the John Hay Whitney Foundation), Albert Dent (president of Dillard University), and UN delegate Edith Sampson, all of whom trumpeted the great strides made in civil rights in America during the last few years.[11]

Two years later, Lindsley F. Kimball, National Chairman of the UNCF, wrote to Jackson concerning plans for the upcoming fund meeting. Kimball suggested that "perhaps Ralph Bunche might arrange some sort of a shindig over at the United Nations. A reception by [Dag] Hammarskjold and the attendance of both Negro and white Americans on an equal footing might do no harm as an international demonstration." This obviously got Jackson thinking about the propaganda angle, and he was soon writing to Dulles to ask if the secretary would speak at the March 1955 convocation: "I know how you feel about America's racial problems and the right and the wrong ways to go about solving them." There was also "a tie-in between America's diplomatic work with the non-white nations of the world and the higher education of American Negroes, and the ammunition that our Negro problem has furnished the Soviets." Finally, there was "real political value in top level Administration identification with these people."[12]

The idea that U.S. propaganda on the race issue merely needed to clear up some misunderstandings and indicate the progress made on the civil rights front was solidified by the widespread belief that most of the misunderstandings were the result of communist lies. A 1953 report prepared by Captain John Silvera for the Psychological Warfare School at Fort Bragg noted the rising tide of expectations among peoples of color around the world: "Soviet propagandists have capitalized on this unrest, stirring up hatreds and creating new ones." The United States was the "principal victim" of this propaganda. "America's treatment of its Negro minority has been an Achilles heel, and needlessly so." All that was needed, Silvera argued, was "proper use of the Negro in propaganda themes." The goal was to make the world see that, "The story of the Negro is indeed the saga of America. It is a 'rags-to-riches' idyll which could literally inspire millions of people in other parts of the world." Africa was the real battleground, where "Russian and Communist propaganda reaches . . . through various channels," branding "Americans as capitalists and imperialists." This, then, was the job for America: "The native African of all peoples should know the truth about the Negro development in the United States. To him it would serve as both inspiration and bulwark against the enemies of Democracy, whoever they may be."[13]

Others reached many of the same conclusions. The Office of African Affairs prepared a report in 1956 entitled, "Africa: Problems of United States Policy." One of the factors was the "anti-white and anti-Western sentiment" in Africa; there was little doubt, however, that it might be "intensified as it is stimulated by other external pressures," one of which was Communism. Vice President Richard Nixon, after his visit to Africa in early 1957, claimed that, "As a result of skillful propaganda primarily inspired by the enemies of freedom, a consistently distorted picture of the treatment of minority races in the United States is being effectively presented in the countries I visited." Any example of mistreatment or bias was "blown up in such a manner as to create a completely false impression of the attitude and practices of the great majority of the American people." Necessarily, then, the United States needed to "do a far more effective job than we are presently doing in telling the true story of the real progress that is being made." In a report to the National Security Council, Nixon elaborated, arguing that there had been a tendency to "underestimate the seriousness of the Communist threat in Africa." The Communists were particularly effective because they could "clothe themselves in Islamic, racist, anti-racist, or nationalist clothing."[14]

These unsophisticated and tentative efforts by the Eisenhower administration seem positively groundbreaking when compared with its policies in regards to increasing the number of blacks in the Department of State and Foreign Service. Here, a policy of tokenism was glaringly apparent, as the administration was satisfied with a few well publicized appointments.

The numbers for African-American diplomatic appointments speak for themselves. A study of key African-American appointments to the Department of State prepared by the Department's Office of Equal Employment Opportunity in 1969 indicated that little progress was made in increasing the number of blacks in the Foreign Service. The report shows that seven African-Americans were appointed FSOs during Eisenhower's years as president. Four of those—Terence Todman, David Bolen, James A. Parker, and William Boswell—had joined the Department of State during the Truman presidency: Todman as a regular civil service hire, and the other three as FSSs. Only three African-Americans who received appointments as FSOs during the Eisenhower administration, therefore, were "new" appointments: Archie Lang (1956), Ronald D. Palmer (1957), and James E. Baker (1960). Harold D. Snell was appointed as FSR in 1958. In addition, two veteran black FSOs retired or were fired during Eisenhower's term of office. William George, who had served in the Department since 1931, retired in 1956. Giles Hubert, who had been appointed to the Foreign Service in 1947, suddenly found himself terminated in late 1953. In a letter to Atlanta University President Rufus Clement in which he sought employment for the coming school year, Hubert wrote that, "The knowledge of my separation from the Foreign Service has come as a sudden shock with very little forewarning." He had been told only that his firing was the "result of necessary reduction in the staff of the Foreign Service"; he had "not been in the Service long enough to pile up service points in competition with career officers in the same grade who have been in the Service many more years than I."[15]

The administration's record in terms of ambassadorial appointments for African-Americans during its first term was equally unimpressive. Eisenhower continued the trend of appointing an African-American as U.S. ambassador to Liberia. The first appointee, Jesse D. Locker, was an Ohio lawyer and politician who was endorsed by Senator Robert Taft. Locker arrived in Liberia in late 1953 and died at his post in April 1955.[16] His replacement was Richard L. Jones, a Chicago businessman and brigadier general in the U.S. Army Reserve who served until 1959.[17] Despite constant rumors in some of the black newspapers and magazines, there were never any serious efforts to appoint an African-American ambassador to any other nation during Eisenhower's first years in office.

In fact, there were never any serious efforts to progress beyond the first tentative steps taken during the Truman presidency. This is not to say that voices from within the Department of State and the Eisenhower administration did not continue to raise the issue. John A. Davis, who had been hired by the Department as a personnel consultant in 1952, argued that, "A special effort will be needed on the part of Recruitment to develop non-Caucasians as a source of Departmental personnel since for many years everything in our society and in the Department has tended to discourage the preparation of such people for Foreign Service employment." Davis soon found his own employment terminated.[18]

Approximately a year and a half later, Davis's place was taken by John Roxborough, an African-American lawyer. Roxborough immediately prepared a memorandum entitled, "Rationale for the Full and Fair Utilization of Non-Whites in the Foreign Service of the United States." There was first, he argued, a "moral rationale": the equal employment of African-Americans was simply the right and Christian thing to do. A "legal rationale" also existed, since various acts and executive orders mandated equal employment opportunity. There was also a "manpower rationale": if the Foreign Service was to grow in size, it would need the "untapped reservoir of non-whites." Finally, and most importantly, there was a "foreign relations rationale." All around the world people were speaking out against racial discrimination. In such an environment, African-American diplomats were increasingly necessary. Quoting from a recent article by the writer Alan Paton, the report concluded, "But it is he [the African-American] more than any other American in this century who has helped America to know what her Constitution is, and that it is fit for all mankind. Perhaps now he can help America to tell the world." Despite his early enthusiasm, Roxborough had no better luck than Davis. As journalist Ethel Payne explained in a 1957 article in the *Chicago Defender,* the new personnel consultant "went to work in quite deadly earnest" upon being hired in 1955. During his first two years, however, he saw Secretary Dulles only once, and that was when he was sworn into office. In addition, he "soon found himself up against a stone battlement of cold subtle resistance" from Department of State oldtimers. He had prepared a lengthy report, but, "Nothing has been heard from his report. Certainly no action has been taken on its recommendations, and it is further doubted that Secretary Dulles has ever seen it." In frustration, Roxborough had gone back to his law practice.[19]

It is pertinent to note that these concerns over the lack of African-American representation in the Department of State and Foreign Service were raised almost exclusively by black insiders, and that their concerns were almost entirely ignored. It points to the lack of any comparable complaints being raised by their white counterparts. So many of the people who had been pushing for more black appointments during the Truman years were gone. John Peurifoy had died at his post in Thailand in 1955. George McGhee had gone on to serve as U.S. ambassador to Turkey, had left that position in 1953, and did not hold a policy-making position in the Department until 1961 and the return of the Democrats. Chester Bowles had been replaced as U.S. ambassador to India and, though he continued to push for civil rights issues, would not be involved with the Department of State again until the Kennedy years. Even Dean Rusk, who had hesitantly brought the issue of civil rights and U.S. foreign policy to the attention of

Secretary of State Marshall, had left the Department for private life and, like Bowles, would not return to the diplomatic fold until the 1960s. In addition, there is little evidence that either Jesse Locker or Richard Jones fought for desegregation in the Department of State with the vigor of Edward Dudley. The progress begun during the Truman years, which had been agonizingly slow to begin with, nearly ceased altogether.

The old excuse that many foreign nations just did not want African-Americans diplomats was trotted out as one justification for the low numbers of blacks in the Foreign Service. John A. Davis came face to face with this argument in mid-1953. Except for the "African colonies" of our European allies, there were "very few areas where non-Caucasians may not be used." Nearly everywhere else, "Negroes either are readily acceptable or the matter can be worked out." Obviously, Davis's argument fell on deaf ears, since his successor, John Roxborough, was still grappling with the issue three years later. Roxborough quickly came to the same conclusions as Davis: "The favorable experience of recent years in the fuller overseas assignment of non-white Foreign Service personnel strongly indicates that such personnel can be assigned to practically every country with which our Nation maintains diplomatic relations."[20]

The debate over naming a new U.S. ambassador to Haiti in 1953 indicated, the reasoning of Davis and Roxborough notwithstanding, how powerful the argument could be. In early 1953, Mrs. Robert L. Vann, a well-known African-American Pittsburgh publisher, was being considered for U.S. ambassador to Liberia. According to a memorandum prepared in March, Mrs. Vann had asked whether she might be assigned to Haiti. The problem with Haiti, however, was that "the Haitians do not consider themselves negro but French and resent any feeling that we are dropping nego [sic] ambassadors on them for political reasons."[21] In the end, Jesse Locker went to Liberia and Roy Tasco Davis, a Maryland politician who served in the Department of State during the Republican era, 1921–1933, went to Haiti. The African-American press was dismayed and skeptical. An editorial in the *Chicago Defender* argued that, "The President missed a golden opportunity to demonstrate the type of democracy we try to practice in this country and to develope [sic] closer ties with the colored nations of the world when he failed to name Negroes either to Haiti or Ethiopia." An article in the *New York Amsterdam News* focused on the reason given by the Eisenhower administration for the Davis appointment. According to a statement released by the White House, the decision was made based on Haiti's announcement that it "preferred not to have a colored representative." The reporter was not buying the argument, since the "Haitian Consulate in New York . . . denied that a Negro was unacceptable sometime ago when Mrs. Robert L. Vann . . . was being mentioned for the post."[22]

Another example is provided by John Reinhardt, an African-American who joined the USIS in 1956. Assigned first to India, Reinhardt discovered the plans had been changed: "I learned many years later that USIA personnel then in India objected to the sending of a black there, on grounds that Indians would not gladly receive persons from a segregated minority, and the Agency accommodated their wishes." Instead, he went to the Philippines, since "it was probably reasoned that Filipinos, as kinds of wards of the United States, would accept blacks, while others may not." In Reinhardt's opinion, "this assumed objection was a product of prejudicial thinking on the part of American whites in the diplomatic service." He could not "remember a single 'problem' in any way traceable to race, creed, color or religion."[23]

Another reason for the low number of African-Americans in the diplomatic service was alluded to by Secretary Dulles in a phone conversation with Republican National Committee Chairman Leonard Hall in May 1953. There was, according to Dulles, a "problem of getting colored people cleared by the FBI." The fact was, he continued, "that there was practically no negro, even Ralph Bunche, who could come through an FBI check lily white, because all of their organizations had been infiltrated at one time or another." He then proceeded to pass the buck, claiming that the problem was with Eisenhower and Sherman Adams: "they have been very particular about getting lily white clearances on everybody, but it is impossible to do this with negroes." A short time later, Dulles received a memorandum concerning Walter White's recent complaint that "loyalty boards were asking white persons if they or their co-workers invited colored people to their homes, the implication being that such association connoted disloyalty." In response, it was suggested that Dulles inform the NAACP leader that "no one in Security feels that association of white employees with colored people is any indication of disloyalty or poor security."[24] The argument was a bit disingenuous. After all, if no African-American could get a "lily white clearance" and if all African-American organizations had been "infiltrated at one time or another," then the "association of white employees with colored people" could very easily be construed as "disloyalty or poor security," and color did indeed become a factor. And Dulles's arguments were equally suspect. In 1953 and 1956, the FBI had prepared detailed reports on "The Communist Party and the Negro." Both reports had been sent directly to the White House, and both came to the same basic conclusion: Communist influence among African-Americans had been entirely negligible, despite an "almost overwhelming effort" by the Communists. While some organizations, such as the National Negro Congress, had been infiltrated by Communists, efforts to penetrate more mainstream and prestigious groups such as the National Urban League and the NAACP "have met with failure." The 1956 report noted that while overall Communist Party membership had declined since 1953, "the Party has experienced an increasingly greater decline, percentage wise, in its Negro membership."[25] It seems unlikely that Dulles could have been completely unaware of such reports. If the secretary truly believed his arguments about African-American candidates for Department of State positions being less than "lily white" (which was a telling choice of words), then he did so in the face of official evidence directly contradicting his position.

For the handful of African-Americans who made it through such obstacles, life in the Department of State and Foreign Service was full of evidence of the slight progress that had been made during the Truman years as well as of how far the push for integration had to go. Ronald D. Palmer came out of the intellectual ferment of Howard University of the early 1950s, where he came into contact with people such as Rayford Logan, Merze Tate, Frank Snowden, and Mercer Cook. Drawn to work in the Department of State because it "advertised itself as a merit service," Palmer passed the Foreign Service examination in 1955 and joined the Service in 1957. "It was," he observed, "a very much Ivy League, East Coast, upper class kind of outfit. . . . There were people who had had no professional contact with blacks before." Yet, Palmer saw signs of encouragement, since most of the people "in the Foreign Service, the State Department, were really first class people and first class people don't have these problems. They may have a problem with lack of familiarity. . . . But if they're really good, it's a moot question."[26]

Terence Todman, who had been with the Department since 1952, but only joined the Foreign Service in 1957, recalled his frustration with the dining facilities available for individuals such as himself who were attending the Foreign Service Institute in Virginia. There was only a small coffee shop at the FSI; "at lunchtime, all of the white officers went across the street to a regular Virginia restaurant and had their meals." Barred from the segregated restaurant, Todman complained but got little satisfaction. The officials running the FSI "regretted that they were in Virginia, and the laws of Virginia didn't allow blacks and whites to eat together." Todman was incensed and fired back that either the FSI had to adjust its class schedule to allow him to go into Washington to eat or find an establishment "where all State Department people could eat." Still, the Department showed little understanding: "They said, people had gone there before I had and no one else had complained, they had just managed to get by on it, they had taken it. I said, that's fine, they took it, but I'm not going to, and so we need to work something out." The result, "after a lot of unhappiness on the part of many people, was that the State Department leased a half of the restaurant and a partition was put up," between the segregated private side and the integrated State Department–leased side. "I was considered a troublemaker, and that was all right."[27]

While the progress toward desegregating the Department of State and Foreign Service ground almost to a halt, there was one area in which the Republican president surpassed his Democratic predecessor. Whereas Truman had appointed but three African-Americans as alternate U.S. representatives to the UN, Eisenhower selected eight. In addition, one of those, Carmel Carrington Marr, had been named legal advisor to the U.S. mission to the UN; another, Charles Mahoney, had been made the first African-American permanent representative; and Genoa Washington had been named a member of the U.S. delegation to the General Assembly in 1957.[28] The discussions preceding some of these appointments, however, reveal that the selection process reeked of tokenism. In July 1953, for instance, Sherman Adams telephoned Dulles to discuss delegates for the UN mission. Dulles pointed out the main problem: "what we really are stuck on is a negro." Adams suggested Mrs. Vann, but Dulles responded that "that was not the way to do [it], the delegates were for emminent [sic] people and it would be wrong to put her on it." Undeterred, Adams mentioned a letter from Walter White suggesting a number of African-American candidates, including Ralph Bunche. Dulles fell back on the security argument, claiming that "all of them have such doubtful records from the FBI standpoint—and few have attained a position of prominence usually associated with the Delegates." Adams gave it another try a few hours later. In particular, he wanted "the Secretary to think about J. Ernest Wilkins, National Trustee, Presbyterian Church, Chicago, negro." Adams indicated that he wanted to have "a negro as a full delegate for political reasons, the boss has been critized [sic] for not having appointed a negro to a high office." Dulles again raised the security issue, arguing that there was not time to get a clearance for Wilkins; Adams indicated he would have the FBI rush it through. Dulles declared that "he is not prejudiced because he is a negro but in general we have kept those positions for people of high standing." Adams would not be put off, however, concluding that, "If we find a good one for the UN let's take him. The Secretary said all right."[29]

A few days later, however, Dulles and Adams were going over the same ground. Dulles informed Adams of his top five choices, one of which was former secretary of state and now Governor James Byrnes, a well-known opponent of integration. Adams immediately asked if the secretary was "afraid that Gov. Byrnes would object to a negro?" On the defensive, Dulles replied that he "had not thought of that," but noted that his own objection would be if an African-American candidate "goes to the top of the list, not because of the right to do so as an individual but because he is a negro." He added that "hereafter, unless a negro had the top spot each year, the cry would be raised that they were being discriminated against. He did not want the UN Del. to become like the NY State slate where a Protestant, a Catholic, a Jew and an Italian were on everything." Adams and Dulles mulled all of this over for a time, and then came to the conclusion that a choice would be made between Wilkins and another African-American Chicagoan, Archibald Carey. Afterward, Dulles phoned Illinois Senator Edward Dirksen to see which candidate was preferable. Dirksen had no personal preference but did note that Carey had been pestering him about the appointment. Two days later, Adams, fearing that Carey would get the appointment instead of Wilkins, complained to Dulles. Carey, Adams claimed, was a "demagogue, and very hard to handle." Dulles, obviously impatient to get the matter over with, replied that "the National Committee and Dirksen favored Carey and we had a pretty good name check on him, and nothing on Wilkins."[30] Carey got the appointment.

A year later, Adams was pushing for an African-American to be named as a permanent delegate. The list of names he sent over to Dulles included Charles Mahoney, an African-American from Michigan who was an executive with a large insurance company. Dulles indicated a bit of surprise, stating that he "had not heard of" Mahoney. He was, Adams explained, someone the "Comm. [Republican National Committee] recommended." Dulles was skeptical about having "someone with no stature as a full delegate," arguing that it was "hard to get alternates who have to serve under such delegates." They went over some other names (Ralph Bunche, again), but Dulles finally gave in on Mahoney, saying he would not "quarrel with it." After all, both men agreed, Mahoney's selection would provide "a boost" for the Republican senator from Michigan.[31] Mahoney got the nod.

The lack of action on and interest in the international implications of the race issue blew up in the Eisenhower administration's face with the Little Rock crisis in the Fall of 1957. As Eisenhower and his aides quickly discovered, Little Rock was a world issue as well, one for which they were completely unprepared to deal. One of the first warnings of what was to come came in a letter from the American Veterans Committee (AVC) to President Eisenhower in early September 1957, just as the crisis in Little Rock was heating up. The AVC (which included "Honorary Members" Ralph J. Bunche and Eleanor Roosevelt, as well as African-American Congressman Charles C. Diggs Jr., on its Advisory Counsel) warned Eisenhower that, "The international reaction to what is happening in Arkansas will be devastating." America's friends around the world "must be completely disillusioned when they hear of federally supported troops being used as they are in Arkansas." The fact that the UN would soon be taking up the matter of Russia's brutal suppression of the Hungarian revolt made it doubly important to do something about the situation in Little Rock: "It would be tragic if at the time the UN meets, the world was reading of the continued suppression of civil rights in Arkansas by federally supported militia."[32] The AVC's words were prophetic. The Eisenhower White House was soon aware that the Soviets were playing the Little Rock incident for all its propaganda value and were mocking the hypocrisy of the United States for condemning the Hungarian situation while "the cries of hundreds of Negro children, ill-treated by the whites, rise from the Southern states."[33]

Matters steadily got worse. The Soviets were giving "increasing attention to integration incidents in the Southern states." They continued to counter American denunciations of their actions in Hungary by arguing that "white-faced but black-souled gentlemen commit their dark deeds in Arkansas, Alabama, and other Southern states, and then these thugs put on white gloves and mount the rostrum in the UN General Assembly, and hold forth about freedom and democracy." Some French newspapers were also lambasting the United States, sarcastically noting that "the US has in the past sought to give France 'lessons and advice on how to treat men of color.' " Even the Swiss media had expressed "sober dismay" at the "incalculable harm done to the occidental position throughout the non-European world." USIA was "attempting to minimize the damage by summarizing anti-integration events on a factual basis." Nevertheless, it concluded that "photos were particularly damaging to U.S. prestige. Agency officials are apprehensive that this week's violence in Little Rock will have serious adverse public reaction abroad."[34]

In Washington, Eisenhower got the bad news from political friend and foe. Congressman Adam Clayton Powell telegraphed Eisenhower and informed the president that, "I have just returned from Europe where American prestige is at its lowest ebb. It is imperative that we do all we can to restore worldwide good will and confidence." Henry Cabot Lodge praised Eisenhower's handling of the crisis but was blunt in evaluating its international impact: "Here at the United Nations I can see clearly the harm that the riots in Little Rock are doing to our foreign relations. More than two-thirds of the world is non-white and the reactions of the representatives of these people is easy to see. I suspect that we lost several votes on the Chinese communist item because of Little Rock." Even Dulles, who had shown little if any interest in the race issue, declared in a telephone conversation with Attorney General Herb Brownell that "this situation is ruining our foreign policy. The effect of this in Asia and Africa will be worse for us than Hungary was for the Russians." Brownell indicated that Eisenhower was "very alert to this aspect."[35]

Over the next few months, the Eisenhower administration tried to sift through the mountain of reports from overseas concerning the Little Rock crisis and evaluate the information. A report from the Foreign Broadcast Information Service in late September 1957 took media reaction from around the globe and divided it into geograpical and political (communist and non-communist) groupings. Not surprisingly, the "Sino-Soviet Bloc" had given a tremendous amount of coverage to the Little Rock incident, all of which had been uniformly negative. Coverage in Western Europe had been more favorable, but noted that "communist exploitation of the unfortunate events would inevitably make it more difficult for the free world to win the allegiance of uncommitted nations." British and West German radio and newspapers had generally applauded Eisenhower's handling of the situation, but many criticized the president for the delay in taking firm action. The French media was a bit harsher, noting that "the biggest democracy in the world has not been able to solve any better than anybody else the problem of the peaceful coexistence of two communities." One French newspaper charged that "Lincoln, Roosevelt, or Truman would never have tolerated" the "racial excesses in Little Rock." In the Far East, the Japanese "viewed the events as an unfortunate blow to American prestige," while in Indonesia there was a good deal of comment to the effect that "it would be difficult to undo the damage that had been done to the American image in Asia."[36]

A report prepared just a few days later by USIA's Office of Research and Intelligence (OIR) was even more negative. "In points so distant as Leopoldville, Seoul, and Quito, U.S. internal affairs had been exposed to a scrutiny and interest comparable to that given the respective Soviet and British-French attacks upon Hungary and Suez last fall." Articles and editorials from newspapers in the Far East, Europe, Latin America, and the Middle East had driven home the same point again and again: the Little Rock crisis had severely damaged America's standing in the world community, particularly among people of color. "In general," the report concluded, "the Free World press has heavily reported the racial incidents, deplored their occurrence, and appeared genuinely to lament the loss in American stature." Since this "pointed and varied publicity" already existed, the Soviets "have felt no compulsion to develop a world-wide campaign to lacerate further the prestige of the U.S."[37]

Perhaps the most damaging of the post–Little Rock reports was that prepared by USIA's OIR in late October that analyzed the results of public opinion surveys done in thirteen large cities around the world. Not surprisingly, given the intense media coverage of the events in Little Rock, the study found that the "incidents had captured the attention of the very large majority of the population in most of the cities surveyed." This was contrasted with the fact that those same populations knew little or nothing about recent civil rights legislation in America. Almost without exception "general opinion of the treatment of Negroes in the U.S. is . . . in most cities overwhelmingly adverse." In addition, there was the very widespread feeling that "Negro-white relations have been worsening rather than improving over the past few years." The one positive point that came through was that a majority (though sometimes a slim majority) of the people polled believed that the U.S. government was doing a good job in trying to remedy the problem. The net result of all of this was that a sizable majority of individuals in each city indicated that America's racial problems had resulted in a lowering of the nation's world standing: "these losses are of such a magnitude as to outweigh the effects of any recent factors which have contributed to increases in U.S. standing." Attempting to end on a good note, the report noted that, even with the recent problems "it should not be assumed that as a consequence present U.S. prestige . . . is in any sense in ruins." The "adverse effects [of Little Rock], while substantial, have been less than sweeping and have been partially offset by gains in U.S. prestige." Although this directly contradicted the previous statement that the impact had been of such "magnitude" that it "outweighed" any recent gains in the U.S. standing in the world, it was obviously felt that something positive needed to be said.[38]

Finally, in January 1958, OIR attempted to put all the data together and draw some overall conclusions. Efforts were made at putting as positive a face on matters as possible—with mixed results. The report began that "the Little Rock happenings have apparently had no major effect in worsening opinion of the treatment of Negroes in the U.S." The bad news was that this might be due "to the fact that America's standing in the area of race relations was already in a very depressed state prior to the Arkansas desegregation incidents, and hence not readily susceptible to further decrease." What did seem to be apparent, however, was that Little Rock had had "considerable effect in confirming and solidifying already held unfavorable attitudes." Overall, world opinion of the United States was good. (In this case, the "world opinion" was limited to polling done in Europe.) More importantly, there seemed to be a large number of foreigners who believed that civil rights progress was being made in America. Before celebrating this finding, however, the report reminded its readers that "not less than a plurality in France and sizable proportions of those with opinions in Italy and West Germany apparently believe that even in the perspective of a decade the Negro's lot in the U.S. has not improved, or has deteriorated." Such results, the study concluded, "underscore the value of making every effort to place recent racial developments in a broader perspective in the projection of America abroad."[39]

The Eisenhower administration was obviously taken aback by the international criticisms provoked by the events in Little Rock. At least initially, however, there was little indication that the worldwide backlash would make for any substantive changes in the propaganda approach taken by U.S. government agencies and individual officials. From the UN, Ambassador Lodge insisted that the way to "counteract the harm of Little Rock" was to "make a sustained effort to extend hospitality to distinguished colored people." This rule should apply not only to U.S. diplomats overseas or to the UN, "where I entertain non-whites regularly," but also to "'white' countries" where "distinguished colored people who may be visiting should be given hospitality." The American consul general in Dakar, French West Africa, also proposed more "personal contacts" with people of color as a response to Little Rock. He noted, however, that an even more effective plan "would be the sending to Black Africa of American negro athletes and athletic teams (such as the Globe Trotters, and Althea Gibson). . . . The Africans at this stage are insatiably interested in sports of all kinds. . . . Good negro jazz musicians or jazz orchestras would also make a very favorable impact."[40]

The official Department of State response was also a rehashing of an old position: portray the events at Little Rock as isolated instances of misguided behavior, and accentuate the positive gains in civil rights made during the last decade. In a memorandum sent to U.S. missions around the world, it was indicated that the first order of business was to put Little Rock in "perspective." The unpleasantness in Little Rock had been "widely misunderstood and misinterpreted." The proper interpretation was that the disturbances "arise from the force and strength of the American people's insistence upon complete equality." The United States was already making "progress toward integration," which had "already been achieved in most parts of the country; it will inevitably spread throughout our entire nation." There followed the usual list of numbers concerning African-Americans enrolled in colleges, their average wages once in the work force, and the strides toward equal employment they had made. The conclusion seemed obvious: "The attention given to the rare misdeeds of an occasional small minority highlight the respect with which the overwhelming majority of the American people regard their laws." And, of course, it needed to be pointed out by U.S. officials that "[t]he problems we are experiencing are not unique to the US." Incidents such as those in Little Rock were the natural result of American society's attempts to "maintain and expand the freedom and equality of the individual. They are not to be confused with those tragic disturbances that arise through the efforts of certain other nations to repress human liberty." That last sentence was an obvious attempt to regain the moral high ground on the Hungarian issue, but just in case it was not completely clear, the memo concluded, "In the Little Rock incident national authority has been invoked to maintain equal rights of a minority. In the Soviet Union national authority has been repeatedly invoked to suppress the rights of minorities." In a follow-up message to U.S. missions in Africa, the Department admitted that "remedial action will be a long range operation and that the damage that has been done the United States by sensational newspaper accounts and photographs cannot be repaired overnight." Through proper efforts, however, "not only can the harmful effects of the Little Rock story be overcome but also the people of Africa be made aware of the real progress being made in the United States in racial matters, a progress that is both rapid and steady despite occasional outbursts of violence such as have received so much publicity recently."[41]

These were the usual responses to international criticisms of U.S. racial problems, but questions were being raised as to their effectiveness in the wake of the Little Rock fiasco. An editorial from a Philippine newspaper went right to the crux of the matter. It downplayed the value of USIA's practice of including "paragraphs in its releases" highlighting "the careers and achievements of outstanding Negroes," and concluded: "These paragraphs are clearly intended to give lie to the accusation that race prejudice prevails in the U.S., but the official glorification of a Marian Anderson or a Richard Wright hardly proves anything. Men and women of whatever race or color who have attained excellence in their chosen fields cannot be ignored even in so arid a region as the American South. What must be shown is what is being done to save the millions of colored Jacks and Janes from the score or so of Governor Faubuses." An Indonesian newspaper put the matter succinctly. Despite the protestations from the United States about its progress in civil rights, all it took was one Little Rock and "all patient good will garnered by American Foreign Service, ICA and USIS dissipated in a matter of minutes."[42]

John Reinhardt, who was serving in the Philippines when the Little Rock incident occurred, came to many of the same conclusions. In nations such as the Philippines, "the United States was widely viewed as a racist society." American efforts to counter this belief "were not very persuasive." Despite the fact that USIS "had extensive programs about successful American blacks, . . . stories about Marian Anderson and Ralph Bunche never caught up with Little Rock." There was "practically no way to overcome the worst racial incidents at home. . . . [T]he Agency had far more success in being forthright . . . than in trying to show progress despite bloodshed."[43]

Such criticisms had an effect, if only for a short time, on the American government. While it continued giving many of the pat responses to the chorus of international critics it also took one very well publicized stab at "being forthright" about the nation's race problem. The attempt was made in the bright spotlight of the first post–World War II world's fair held in

Brussels in 1958 and resulted in the ill-fated "Unfinished Business" exhibit on the grounds of the U.S. pavilion.[44]

From its beginnings, the 1958 World's Fair was viewed by U.S. officials as "a major opportunity to advance important U.S. objectives." With the events at Little Rock casting long and destructive shadows over U.S. international relations, it is hardly surprising to learn that one of those objectives was to confront the race issue in a new and direct manner. As one report noted, "maybe the way to 'handle' Little Rock is not to ignore it and distract the world with gadgets and applicances. Maybe the best way is to try to show the miserable events at Little Rock in the long context of the Negro's rise from slavery and his spectacular recent progress."[45]

To that end, the Department of State sought some fresh insights and turned to what came to be known as the Cambridge Study Group. Made up primarily of faculty from MIT (including Walt W. Rostow), the group developed the idea for the "Unfinished Business" exhibit. The fundamental premise of the exhibit was that American problem areas had to be faced, in particular the problem of segregation. Certainly, the group concluded, "positive progress should be shown, but the problem should be faced squarely. . . . Our ideals should be shown at work in the dirtiest part of the job of American life." These rough ideas were forwarded to C.D. Jackson at *Time,* who had served as Eisenhower's special assistant on psychological warfare. He liked what he saw and devised a plan whereby the staff at *Fortune* magazine (a sister publication to *Time*), using Department of State funds, would design an exhibit displaying three of America's pressing national problems: urban renewal, natural resource depletion, and segregation.[46]

The uncertainty as to just how well this new approach might fly was indicated by the setting of "The Unfinished Business." Instead of being housed in the main U.S. pavilion, it was set off by itself on the grounds of the U.S. exhibit. It was a rather strange looking affair, with three separate rooms linked together by a sort of catwalk. In each of the three rooms there was an area devoted to each of the three problem areas. The first room introduced the visitor to the scope of the problem; the second provided evidence of the progress being made in solving the problem; and the third room indicated the desired outcome. For segregation, this meant that room number one contained a collage of newspaper headlines detailing many of the recent racial disturbances in the United States. The second room contained photographs and charts indicating the progress African-Americans had made in terms of schooling, employment, and voting rights. Finally, in the third room (which had as its theme "Hope for the Future"), visitors were confronted with a huge picture of black and white children playing ring-around-the-rosy. The caption of the photograph indicated that, "American communities, like American individuals, like to emulate and surpass one another. By this process, democracy's unfinished business, already partially mastered, will get done on a national scale. To be followed, no doubt, in other (and perhaps nobler) challenges. The goal that draws us together is not utopia, but larger freedom with more justice. Democracy is our method. Slowly but surely, it works."[47]

The exhibit was certainly more along the lines of what John Reinhardt had called for: a "forthright" statement that America did indeed have a serious race problem, but that it was working to try and solve it. What its impact would have been on the hundreds of thousands of visitors to the U.S. pavilion (most of them the same Europeans who had expressed such glum opinions about America's civil rights situation in polls taken just months earlier) can only be guessed at, since only a handful ever got to see it. Even before the fair opened, a vocal group of Southern congressmen, together with some sympathetic Department of State officials, were tearing away at "The Unfinished Business"; eventually, they succeeded in shutting it down.

The four loudest Southern voices came from Senators Olin Johnson and Strom Thurmond and Representative L. Mendel Rivers, all from South Carolina, and Senator Herman Talmadge from Georgia. All bitterly expressed their anger and disappointment that the United States would subsidize an exhibit that, as Senator Talmadge claimed, would "apologize for racial segregation in the United States"; Rivers called it "unimaginable stupidity." They made it very clear that should the Department of State persist in efforts to open the exhibit the cry from the South would be loud.[48]

These complaints sent Department of State officials scrambling. Their reviews concluded that perhaps the Southern congressmen had valid arguments. The newspaper headlines in the first room were "far too specific"; pictures in the second room, particularly one that showed two teenagers—a black male and a white female—dancing, would have to go; the large picture of the children playing in the last room would have to be recaptioned so as to indicate that the photograph "does *not* represent any national objective defined by law, but freedom of choice to play as one wishes." Undersecretary Christian Herter, who had never shown any great enthusiasm for the project, now went on the attack, arguing that the exhibit should simply be shut down because of its "failure to tell [a] balanced story."[49]

Supporters of the "Unfinished Business" exhibit, such as Howard Cullman, who was U.S. Commissioner General for the American effort at the fair, managed to get a brief reprieve by arguing that the display was popular with European visitors. The exhibit was shut down after only a few weeks of operation to undergo revisions. The changes made, which were largely cosmetic, failed to placate the growing chorus of congressional critics, who were now joined by Styles Bridges of New Hampshire, Prince Preston from Georgia, and William Ayres from Ohio. All argued that the exhibit was an open invitation for communist propaganda. Besides, as Preston noted, there were other problems, such as "crime and the influx of Puerto Ricans," which might be shown in place of the section on segregation. President Eisenhower had heard enough. In a meeting with his advisors, he exclaimed that the United States needed to "put our best foot forward at an exhibit such as this"; he also indicated reluctance to engage in "finger pointing" at the South for its "racial problems." All of this signaled the end for the "Unfinished Business" exhibit, at least in its original form. At Eisenhower's "suggestion" the exhibit was again closed, and then reopened with a focus on a single problem—public health.[50] The "forthright" approach to America's race problem had lasted for approximately three months.

One of the many ironies of the "Unfinished Business" debacle was that the European audience seemed receptive to the approach. The only poll of visitors to the exhibit, which was done by a Belgian firm hired by USIA, indicated that while they were rather evenly split on the issue of whether progress was being made in America concerning civil rights, nearly half of those expressing an opinion stated that the exhibit had helped raise their opinion of the United States (with most of the others indicating that it had made no difference in their opinion).[51] Apparently, it was easier to try and sell the story of America's civil rights progress abroad than it was to live it at home.

Just as Little Rock had spurred the United States to attempt (albeit halfheartedly) a new approach to its international propaganda on segregation and civil rights, it also served as the catalyst for rethinking the issue of African-Americans as diplomats. The very obvious tokenism in the selection of blacks as chiefs of U.S. overseas missions, for example, did not disappear, but it did take some interesting new forms. The selection of Clifton Wharton as minister to Romania was the most obvious example of this new thinking. After thirty distinguished years in the Foreign Service, no one could deny that Wharton had earned the right to serve as a chief of mission. Yet, somehow, when openings came up they were always filled by someone else. In 1958, however, Wharton finally received his just reward when he was appointed as minister to Romania. Though his good friend in the Department, Deputy Undersecretary of State Loy Henderson, assured him that his race played no role in his selection, this assertion must be viewed with some skepticism. Coming hard on the heels of the Little Rock fiasco, the appointment does appear to be more an answer to communist propaganda than a well-deserved reward for services rendered. And ever since Ravndal's 1949 memorandum about "outstanding Negroes" and "appropriate countries," the idea had circulated among U.S. officials that appointing an African-American to an Iron Curtain country would pay big propaganda dividends. Certainly that is the slant the *U.S. News and World Report* took on the appointment, informing its readers that, "Communist-run Rumania is in for a surprise upon the arrival of Clifton R. Wharton." The Eastern-bloc nation, the story continued, "has been sharply critical of the U.S. for 'suppressing' Negroes. And Mr. Wharton is a Negro."[52]

Another hint that Wharton's assignment was more for international consumption than to demonstrate to the domestic audience a new and more enlightened employment policy on the part of the Department of State is found in the newspaper coverage of the event. While African-American newspapers gave it front-page play, coverage in other media sources was muted. The *New York Times* carried the story of Wharton's swearing in on page five. This was no doubt due to the Department's rather secretive approach to the ceremony. As the *Times* story indicated, Wharton had to go through *two* ceremonies due to a "mix-up." For the first ceremony, there was only one reporter present, and he had "stumbled onto the initial ceremony when, his curiosity aroused, he followed a large group . . . into the State Department's diplomatic reception room." Wharton's friend Henderson was present, but not Secretary Dulles. Very quickly, however, another ceremony was announced by the Department's news division, which indicated that it had not known about the first swearing-in "in time to invite the press and photographers." For this "re-run," Secretary Dulles was suddenly available to pose for photographs with his new minister to Romania. The resulting picture shows an unsmiling and completely disinterested Dulles staring off somewhere past Wharton's face.[53]

The second big change in the appointment of African-Americans as chiefs of mission occurred in 1959, when Professor John H. Morrow (who was chair of the Department of Modern Foreign Languages at North Carolina College) was named U.S. ambassador to the newly independent nation of Guinea. Loy Henderson, once again acting as facilitator, indicated that the Eisenhower administration was "impressed by your knowledge of African affairs and French politics, your friendly relations with many Africans, your academic record, and your fluency in French." There was more at play, however, than these qualifications. Henderson had made it clear in a memorandum written a few weeks before his meeting with Morrow that naming an ambassador to Guinea "should be linked with the appointment of a new Ambassador for Liberia." The "Liberians have been restless because the United States has been uniformly represented at Monrovia by a negro Ambassador," and this suggested that "the United States is treating Liberia on a racial basis." The solution to both problems was clear: "appoint a negro as Ambassador to Guinea . . . and simultaneously to replace Ambassador [Richard] Jones, who has now been in Liberia as Ambassador and head of the ICA Mission for more than five years, with a career Foreign Service Officer." Morrow was a possibility for Guinea, and his brother, E. Frederic, a special assistant to the president, had indicated that he "might be available." Henderson suggested Elbert G. Mathews, a white FSO with nearly twenty-five years experience, as the new ambassador to Liberia.[54] Henderson's suggestions were put into effect: Morrow took the position in Guinea, and Mathews replaced Jones in Liberia.[55]

The basic idea behind all of this, of course, was not new. Edward Dudley and others during the Truman years suggested that one way to break the perception that Liberia was the "Negro post" would be to appoint a white as ambassador. Those calls, however, had been coupled with some other notions: that other (and *more*) posts would open up for African-Americans; that those other posts would be outside of Africa; and that FSOs, not political appointees, would fill those positions. None of this follow-up occurred. The Morrow and Mathews appointments meant that there was still just one African-American serving as a U.S. ambassador; the new African-American ambassador was assigned to Africa; and Morrow, despite his excellent record, was not a professional diplomat. The end result was a zero-sum game: a new African-American appointee meant the loss of another.

Considering the views of new Secretary of State Christian Herter, it was not surprising that, even with the impact of Little Rock, Department of State employment patterns were unlikely to change very much. In a letter to the editor of *The Saturday Evening Post,* Herter admitted that "we have a given asset here which the Russians do not have, namely, Negroes." Yet, "our experience in a number of instances has been an unhappy one in that the Negro States of Africa have often felt that we were downgrading them if we sent Negroes as ambassadors or diplomatic representatives." He quickly noted that "Negro athletes, of whom there are many in this country . . . can, however, be of great value to us in USIA material showing how successful they have been, not only in this country but at the Olympics."[56]

Despite the unexpected jolt provided by the Little Rock incident, by 1960 the Eisenhower administration seemed to be back to square one concerning race and foreign policy. On the propaganda front, the "Unfinished Business" exhibit had been a complete failure. As Herter's letter indicated, America was left with promoting the success of "Negro athletes" as its answer to international criticisms and communist attacks. On the question of promoting a larger African-American presence in the Department of State and Foreign Service, there had been some reshuffling, but, as John Reinhardt concluded, "The State Department . . . altered its essential personnel policies in no way to cope with the problem; only lip service was paid."[57] There had been but a handful of African-American FSOs and one African-American ambassador when Eisenhower took power; nothing had really changed by the time he left office eight years later.

How little impact alternative viewpoints had on the Eisenhower administration is exemplified by the response to a 1958 study made by Matthew Marks, who was with the Office of International Finance in the Treasury Department. Marks's basic position was that the nation's "race difficulties . . . are weakening U.S. national security." America's race problem was of enormous interest to the "three quarters of a billion colored peoples" around the world. The Soviets were successfully "capitalizing on U.S. race incidents"; "Little Rock has, by now, become an international symbol of white race intolerance in the U.S." Marks was convinced that the United States was doing almost nothing to counteract this situation, beyond some propaganda that sought to present "a more balanced view of the race situation in the U.S." He called for a "broad gauge attack." Besides increased propaganda, which might focus on racial problems in the Soviet Union, the country should consider "the possibility of better enlisting the services of the more than two hundred thousand colored Americans with four or more years of college training." In 1959, Marks sent the paper to Karl Harr, a special assistant to Eisenhower for security matters; this finally ended up in the hands of Kenneth Landon of the Operations Coordinating Board who responded in February 1960. His skepticism was overwhelming. While he agreed that using more African-Americans as diplomats was a good idea, he did not agree with Marks that "the cleaning up of domestic race segregation as quickly as possible and the reassertion of our revolutionary traditions . . . are the most important steps to erase existing international tensions." The former would "require the achievement of the Sermon on the Mount or Nirvana, and the second would require the loosening of our political ties with our most important European allies." According to Landon, the "practical solution would be to improve our own propaganda in order to dissociate international relations from personal morality." In conclusion, he stated, "we should never mislead ourselves into thinking that our success in international relations will stand or fall on our moral practices and principles."[58] He need not have been worried that the Eisenhower administration would fall prey to such radical ideas; "lip service" and token gestures were the preferred responses to both domestic and international critics of America's race problem.

∼ 6 ∼

New Frontiers in Race Relations

African-Americans and
U.S. Foreign Policy, 1961–1969

In June 1961, Carl Rowan gave a talk to the Catholic Interracial Council of Washington, D.C. entitled "New Frontiers in Race Relations." He decried the violence being directed toward the Freedom Riders—black and white civil rights activists riding into the South to fight for desegregation. One of the overlooked consequences of the racist attacks was the harm such incidents did to the nation's foreign policy. Rowan cited recent remarks by new Secretary of State Dean Rusk to the effect that, "The efforts of the United States Government in international affairs to build the kind of world we want to live in—with peace, prosperity, and justice for all—cannot be divorced from our ability to achieve those same purposes for all the people of our own country." He also used a long passage from his 1956 book dealing with his trip to Asia, *The Pitiful and the Proud,* which described the ways in which Communism was preying on the "anti-racism" feelings of peoples in the underdeveloped world. Too many American people, Rowan claimed, "persist in entertaining the notion that we can have our cake and eat it, too. They think they can smile at a Nigerian and scowl at an Alabaman and their split personality will go unnoticed." Despite the enormity of the nation's racial problems, he remained optimistic. The strength of the United States was in the "freedom to express our conviction as to what is and what is not wrong in our society"; the Freedom Riders were a perfect example. There were "millions of people in the world who understand and envy this kind of freedom."[1]

By the time Rowan gave this speech, he had been appointed deputy assistant secretary of state for public affairs by the incoming Kennedy administration. He would later go on to serve as director of the USIA and as U.S. ambassador to Finland. Yet, Rowan's optimism concerning the ability of the United States to face the race problem both at home and abroad should not be dismissed as just another example of official rhetoric. Many other African-Americans shared (albeit somewhat more cautiously) the belief that, with the coming to power of the new Democratic president, the country might finally be able to come to grips with race. The very fact that Rowan had been appointed to a high position within the Department of State was cause for hope. Perhaps John F. Kennedy (and, after his assassination, Lyndon B. Johnson) was prepared to allow blacks more of a voice— and a presence—in the nation's diplomatic service. With more hope for success than ever before, African-Americans during the Kennedy-Johnson years continued their efforts to convince U.S. officials of the significance of race in international affairs; to direct the attention of those officials to issues in Africa and Asia; to press home the point that racism in America was an international disgrace; and to push for the appointment of more blacks to the Department of State and Foreign Service.

As the pages of *The Crisis* attest, African-Americans during the 1960s maintained a strong interest in foreign affairs. Typical stories include a 1961 article dealing with racial discrimination in Castro's Cuba; a reprint of a 1964 letter from Archbishop Denis E. Hurley from South Africa criticizing racial bigotry in America and South Africa; an item on the efforts in New Zealand to keep its sports teams from playing against South African teams; and a report from Denmark about the alternately enlightened and naive racial views of the Danish people. Other features examined the ethnocentric way in which geography was taught, in which the focus was on European "discovery" and "civilization," and how African-Americans had been discriminated against at the world's fairs held in the United States.[2]

Two international issues highlighted African-American concerns about race and U.S. foreign policy. One was the Vietnam War. Martin Luther King Jr., became one of the most vociferous critics of U.S. policy in Vietnam, and he often made explicit reference to the links between American racism and the war. David Garrow, in his biography of King, explains that, "King also spoke of how the [civil rights] movement could not ignore violence and racism when they appeared in the international arena. 'Violence is as wrong in Hanoi as it is in Harlem,' stated the civil rights leader.

People had 'to see that there is a mutual problem involved. Racism and militarism are very closely tied together,' especially in what was 'basically a war of colonialism.'"[3] And the experiences of thousands of African-American servicemen who, as James E. Westheider has noted in his study, were "fighting on two fronts"—against racism at home and against the enemy in Vietnam—also heightened awareness of the interrelations between race and American foreign policy.[4]

Africa also remained a primary focus of African-American interest. As Martin Staniland argues, black intellectuals and writers were "wholeheartedly enthusiastic about decolonization in Africa. Their response to the emergence of independent African states was marked by a warm, almost intimate, pride in the achievements of people whose goals and sufferings many African-Americans felt they had shared." Such enthusiasm permeated black popular culture, as the study of Swahili, the wearing of African clothing, and the popularity of the "Afro" hairstyle attested. Interest was also documented in the books produced by African-American scholars during the late 1950s and 1960s. A 1958 volume entitled *Africa from the Point of View of American Negro Scholars,* edited by John A. Davis, contained articles by nearly every leading black intellectual of the day. In 1966 Davis co-edited a study entitled *Southern Africa in Transition,* which brought together articles by leading U.S. and African scholars. Both of these volumes were issued under the auspices of the American Society of African Culture (AMSAC), an organization devoted to the study of African history and culture, which had been formed following the Bandung Conference.[5]

As in previous years, the apartheid system in South Africa was soundly condemned. *The Crisis* reprinted recommendations that had been passed at a conference on the South African Crisis and American Action held in March 1965. The strongly worded statement read, "We believe that racism, whether in Alabama, New York, or South Africa is an abomination in the eyes of God and men, an offense to human decency, and a gross violation of the emerging common law of mankind." The case in South Africa, however, was different, since it was "the only country in the world officially dedicated to a policy of racism. . . . This policy is maintained by a totalitarian system strongly reminiscent of Hitlerism."[6]

In particular, however, the independence of nation after nation in Africa, begun with Ghana in 1957, began to capture the imagination of many American blacks. As Dennis Hickey and Kenneth C. Wylie explained in their 1993 book on U.S. perceptions of Africa, "The independence of Ghana in 1957 was a turning point for many African-Americans in their relationship with the mother continent. This event, which was dramatically underscored by the march to freedom of a majority of the African colonies over the next five years, was a tangible source of inspiration for black activists involved in the American civil rights struggle: it demonstrated that victory was, indeed, a real possibility, that the 'promised land' was within reach."[7]

As the British and French African empires began to dissolve in the 1960s, African-Americans focused their criticisms on the remaining colonial holdings in Africa, especially Portugal's empire. George Houser of the American Committee on Africa, writing to other African-American activists prior to a 1962 meeting with President Kennedy, urged that Portuguese colonialism be strongly condemned. It should be made clear in the discussions with Kennedy that "the American Negro people are firmly opposed to Portuguese policy in Africa." An editorial from the April 1961 issue of *The Crisis* stated that, "Little Portugal has managed for years to deceive the general public about the real nature of her colonial system." While the "Lusitanian racism" of the Portuguese rulers was "relatively more refined" than South Africa's apartheid system, "the fruits of Portuguese colonialism in Africa are human degradation and slavery" for the native population. The next year, *The Crisis* reported on the outbreak of violence between Angolese rebels and Portuguese military forces. Portugal's use of a "modified form of slavery" to dragoon Angolese natives into work forces made its claims that it was serving a "civilizing mission" in Angola "a gigantic fraud."[8]

More and more, however, African-Americans were turning their attention to the newly independent nations of Africa. African-American Congressman Charles Diggs, after a two-week tour of Africa, suggested in early 1961 that, "The United States must learn to consider the problem of the new African nations from the African's concept not those of the European colonists." He continued, "We in this country must become aware of the fact that independence is coming to Africa and the Africans are going to run the show." And, as John A. Davis argued in a 1969 article in the *Journal of International Affairs,* American blacks were demanding more of a role in U.S. policy toward those new nations. Davis concluded that, "If the United States is to develop a true community of interests with an important segment of black African nations . . . then it must develop economic, cultural and political enterprises to bind mutual goals. In such an undertaking the American Negro must play a significant role, or become a source of embarrassment both to the United States and to those African nations sharing the common mission."[9] One dramatic example of putting that concept into practice was the African-American participation in the Peace Corps program. Of the approximately 1,000 African-Americans who served in the Corps from 1961 to 1971, six- to seven-hundred went to Africa.[10]

One of the forces pushing African-Americans to demand a more "significant role" was the fact that they so concretely grasped the similarities between the black Africans' struggle for rights and equality and their own at home. Anticipating a Democratic victory in the 1960 election, African-American journalist Ethel L. Payne wrote to Louis Martin, who headed the Democratic National Committee's Civil Rights Division. She proposed that the Capital Press Club set up a number of public forums dealing with the situation in Africa. Her reasoning was clear: "While Civil Rights is the burning domestic issue, world peace looms more and more in the minds of people, including Negro-Americans as the No. 1 issue. The events in Africa and particularly, the Congo crisis are making colored Americans more aware of international relations and the reciprocal effect upon their own struggle for full citizenship. Therefore, the Civil Rights problem and world peace are inextricably linked together."[11]

The point seemed so obvious that even white journalists, such as James Reston, picked up on it. In one of Reston's pieces, reprinted in the *Pittsburgh Courier* in early 1961, the reporter noted that "we are beginning to see a confluence of the world struggle for freedom in Black Africa and the struggle for equal rights in the Negro communities of America." Reston concluded that this was "an event of momentous importance, and officials here [in Washington] are just beginning to realize that even their foreign policy will be affected if the causes of these Negro frustrations are not dealt with more effectively." African-American writer Langston Hughes was more poetic in describing the interrelationship between the civil rights movement in America and the fight for freedom and respect in Africa during a speech in Ghana in 1962. In undertaking cultural exchanges with Africa, "America is seeking a bolstering of her *own* basic dreams, and finding here in Africa a new strengthening of the old concept of freedom in your liberated lands." Continuing with the theme, Hughes declared that, "Black Africa today is sending rejuvenating currents of liberty over all the earth reaching even as far as Little Rock, Birmingham and Jackson, Mississippi."[12]

Roy Wilkins of the NAACP, in a 1966 letter to Frank Ferrari of the African-American Institute discussing Rhodesia, came directly to the point: no one should overlook the "psychological inspiration and lift which any project aimed at improving the Rhodesian situation will give to the civil rights movement here in America." African-Americans had been fighting against many of the same "obstacles" confronting the black Rhodesians in dealing with the Ian Smith regime. "Any effort in Rhodesia to bring the same kind of advances to black Rhodesians will have a tremendously bolstering effect upon the morale and, more importantly, on the democratic convictions of American Negroes." Wilkins concluded, "It is important . . . to demonstrate that freedom is attainable and that participation in government can be won."[13]

African-Americans also saw another link between domestic and international issues: racial discrimination in the United States hurt the nation over-seas, particularly in areas such as Africa. Roy Wilkins attempted to explain the situation to Secretary of State Rusk in early 1961. Disturbed about reports that Rusk planned to speak before a segregated audience in Atlanta, Wilkins argued that, "We cannot imagine a more disastrous blow to the image of the United States which your Secretaryship is seeking to project in the present world situation than an address ... to a professional society meeting within the United States in which the participants are separated in seating according to race." Nearly a year later in an article in *Current History,* Rayford Logan examined the Kennedy administration's policies on race both at home and abroad and, while giving credit to the new president for initiatives in several regards, found the record disturbing: at home, no new civil rights act, no new laws concerning discrimination in housing, embarrassing treatment of African representatives in Washington, D.C., and Maryland; and abroad, a tepid policy toward European colonialism in Africa and a refusal to censure South Africa in the United Nations. Logan warned his readers that, "Since many African and American Negroes, in particular, link United States policy toward Africa with the treatment of Negroes in the United States, they keep a watchful eye on the Kennedy administration's civil rights record."[14]

On occasion, the criticisms came from Africans themselves. An August 1962 story from the *Norfolk Journal and Guide* reported on a speech by Achkar Maros, a counselor with the Guinea mission to the UN. In his opinion, "The racial situation in America hurts the U.S. position throughout the world more than anything else." When queried as to what Africans in general thought about America's race problem, he replied, "They pay more attention to the racial problems of the U.S. in Africa than you do here." Those views were substantiated by Reverend James H. Robinson, who directed a program called Crossroads Africa, a volunteer organization dedicated to improving living conditions in Africa. After a two-month tour of thirteen African nations in 1965, Robinson was convinced that, "Two things hurt us most in Africa; one is race relations in the United States and the other is that we haven't been able to take a forthright stand on Apartheid in South Africa." The race problem, in particular, "raises a big question in the minds of Africans, about the United States."[15]

The organization that perhaps best brought together the various strands of African-American thinking concerning U.S. foreign policy during the 1960s was the American Negro Leadership Conference on Africa (ANLCA), which was formed in 1962. The list of members and sponsoring organizations was truly impressive. James Farmer of the Congress of Racial Equality, Dorothy Height of the National Council of Negro Women, Martin

Luther King Jr., of the Southern Christian Leadership Conference, A. Philip Randolph of the Brotherhood of Sleeping Car Porters, Roy Wilkins of the NAACP, and Whitney Young of the National Urban League were the primary movers. Numerous black fraternities and sororities, the American Committee on Africa, AMSAC, Operation Crossroads Africa, the Phelps-Stokes Fund, the Student Non-Violent Coordinating Committee, and various labor unions sponsored the group's activities. Theodore Brown, who worked with Randolph, was primarily responsible for organizing the ANLCA conferences.[16] The purpose of the organization was clearly laid out in an announcement for the first conference, to be held in November 1962 at the Arden House Campus of Columbia University: "We believe the 19 million American Negro citizens must assume a greater responsibility for the formation of United States policy in sub-Sahara Africa. Negroes are of necessity deeply concerned with developments in Africa because of the moral issues involved and because the struggle here at home to achieve in our time equality without respect to race or color is made easier to the extent that equality and freedom are achieved everywhere."[17]

The organization's realization of the links between the domestic civil rights struggle and U.S. relations with Africa was made even more strenuously in Roy Wilkins's opening address to the conference. He began by stressing the hard road ahead for his listeners: "We American Negroes know something about the difficulties of getting our nation to move on political, economic and social inequalities and injustices where race and color are involved." Recounting the hardships faced by African-Americans, he drew a comparison to those faced by black Africans, stating that, "Yes, American Negroes have a wealth of experience on this issue. . . . We have no doubt that the same kind of system that works to our disadvantage in areas of the United States (and with special effect in the Deep South) works also to humiliate and to hamper our brothers in Africa." He was even more explicit in using the example of South Africa: "South Africa, like Mississippi, justifies her course unashamedly upon the inglorious and debasing theory of white supremacy." And finally, Wilkins noted that the African struggle for freedom and equality had positive side effects for African-Americans, particularly emphasizing that "the very physical presence of their representatives in the United Nations and in their Washington embassies have given the crusade a push toward its goal." Given this situation, and drawing attention to the fact that "28 new African nations have emerged in the past ten years," Wilkins argued that this new situation demanded "something more than deploring resolutions coupled with business as usual."[18]

The series of resolutions passed at the conference gave concrete form to Wilkins's ideas. The "Preamble" began: "The struggle for freedom and equality is world wide." Noting that "we have a serious civil rights problem which exhausts much of our energy," the preamble went on to conclude that "we cannot separate this struggle at home from that abroad." The conference, therefore, was evidence of the African-American intention to "launch a more aggressive determination to make our influence felt on the policies of our government." Among the specific resolutions adopted were ones condemning U.S. policy toward South Africa and urging the United States to take more forceful actions in dealing with problems in South West Africa, Angola and Mozambique, the Congo, the Central African Federation, and Kenya. All of these reflected the conference members' resolve to "rededicate and reaffirm our ethnic bond with and historic concern for the peoples of Africa and our complete solidarity with their aspirations for freedom, human rights and independence." As Whitney Young summed up in a statement in the *New York Times,* the "decision to link the integration struggle in the United States with the fate of the sub-Saharan African states would represent a 'new phase in the civil rights struggle.' "[19]

The conference was followed by a meeting between ANLCA leaders and President Kennedy. As Theodore Brown explained in a post-meeting summary, this was "the first White House conference by American Negro leaders on U.S. foreign policy." At the meeting, the leaders implored Kennedy to increase economic and technical assistance to Africa; urged him to put more pressure on Portugal concerning that nation's African colonies; and reminded him that, "It is not enough to embrace the principle of racial equality; that principle must also be implemented at home and abroad," and asked him to initiate economic sanctions against South Africa.[20]

In 1964, a follow-up conference was held. While noting some progress in a number of areas, the participants were, "[m]indful of the unfinished political and economic problems remaining in Africa and aware of the need for an effective United States policy in regard to those problems." One of these, Dr. Adelaide Cromwell Hill from Boston University, summarized where things now stood: "Is it now really possible for Africans or persons of African descent to 'call the plays?' . . . After a somewhat tenuous or tangential involvement in Africa . . . the accepted (one is tempted to say respected) Negro leadership as a group has now definitely concerned itself with Africa. This leadership sees Africa and the progress and problems of that continent as germanely related to the position of Negroes in this country."[21]

Yet, as the resolutions adopted at the conference indicated, recognition of the connections between the race problem in the United States and the struggle for independence and equality in Africa did not necessarily translate into suggestions acceptable to the U.S. government. The preamble to the resolutions basically reiterated the points made in 1962. The resolutions again urged the United States to "increasingly emphasize or direct its attention to the underlying social and economic causes of political crises" in Africa. The U.S. policy toward South Africa needed to be more "dynamic," and the conference once more called for economic sanctions. More aid to Africa was urged, and one resolution chided the United States for playing a "secondary role in her relations with the 'independent' countries of Africa, leaving the primary responsibility for aid to the European 'metropolitan' powers." Unlike in 1962, there would be no meeting with the new president, Lyndon Johnson. In any event, the 1964 conference was the last significant action of the ANLCA. In just a short time, internal divisions and reports that CIA money had funded some of the group's activities crippled the group and, aside from another conference a few years later, it ceased to function as a forum for getting the African-American message about foreign policy across to U.S. foreign policy makers.[22]

The optimism that African-American leaders had in 1961–1962 concerning their ability to influence U.S. foreign policy makers as to the necessity of coming to terms with the issues of race and civil rights as international factors was also reflected in their efforts to place more blacks in the Department of State and Foreign Service. Ten years after publishing Rayford Logan's articles that had excoriated the Department of State and Foreign Service for their hiring practices, the *Pittsburgh Courier* carried another series, written by managing editor Harold L. Keith, entitled, "Where Do Negroes Fit in State Department Hiring Practices?" The five pieces, which appeared during November and December of 1960, were far different in tone. Replacing Logan's criticism and sarcasm were optimistic appraisals of the roles available for African-Americans in the U.S. diplomatic service. As Keith summed up after meeting with Department of State officials, "a new day has arrived opportunity-wise for the Negro in the foreign service." For qualified applicants, "The State Department stands ready to welcome him or her with open arms."[23]

Perhaps Keith was simply being politic. John F. Kennedy had just been elected, promising his African-American constituency more attention to civil rights matters; olive branches in place of brickbats in discussing the Department of State's minority hiring policy must have seemed the more prudent approach to securing more foreign policy jobs for blacks. Yet, Keith's focus on the future was telling. More than a decade after internal and external criticisms had forced the Department of State to reevaluate its hiring policies, ten years after Logan's biting commentaries, and over nine years after the meetings held between department officials and African-American representatives such as Logan, White, and Randolph, very little had changed in terms of the numbers of and the opportunities for African-

Americans in the field of U.S. diplomacy. By 1960 much of the initiative (which had hardly been overwhelming) in regard to the desegregation of the nation's diplomatic corps created during the second Truman administration had evaporated. A "new day," if it were to come, would depend on the actions of the new administration.

It was clear that many African-Americans expected the Kennedy (and, later, Johnson) administration to make a tremendous impact in the area of black employment in the Department of State and Foreign Service. Just a few weeks after Kennedy's election in 1960, the *Baltimore Afro-American* expressed itself as very pleased with the incoming president's choices for top foreign policy posts. Citing his selection of Dean Rusk as secretary of state, Chester Bowles as undersecretary, G. Mennen Williams as assistant secretary for African affairs, and Adlai Stevenson as ambassador to the UN, the newspaper claimed that "this new foreign policy team speaks with one voice on the urgency of utilizing more diplomatic appointees of color in a world in which the influence of Asian and African nations is on the ascendancy." Bowles had complained about the situation for years and Rusk had "long deplored this neglect." The editorial excitedly concluded that, "Truly new and expanding frontiers in the diplomatic service hitherto closed are soon to be opened for hundreds of our alert and imaginative young people ready to be of service."[24]

Other stories in the black press echoed this new optimism. The *Pittsburgh Courier* noted that Assistant Secretary Williams wanted "qualified Negroes" for diplomatic service, and promised not to isolate them in African posts. In an article entitled, "A new day in foreign policy—JFK may name 3 as diplomats," the *Afro-American* revealed that Ralph Bunche was being considered for ambassador to Italy; Benjamin Mays, president of Morehouse College, was being mulled over for Israel; and Clifton Wharton might get the nod for Denmark. These appointments signified that the new administration sought to "remove the historical cry that they are 'second-class' citizens sent to 'second-class' countries."[25]

Hopes soared even higher when in August 1961 the Department of State announced a Conference on Equal Employment Opportunity and invited an impressive list of leading African-American educators, civil rights leaders, publishers, businessmen, and reformers. After a day of reports and discussion, the participants came up with a list of nine recommendations, including the appointment of African-Americans to " 'high level policy positions' in the Department," the lateral transfer into the Foreign Service of African-Americans from other agencies such as USIA, and the appointment of more blacks to "middle and high level posts by making Foreign Service Reserve appointments." They also urged that African-Americans become more involved in the process, as recruiters from the Foreign Service, examiners for the Foreign Service oral examinations, and educators preparing their students for careers in diplomacy.[26]

The response to the conference in the black press was very positive. Benjamin Mays (though no ambassadorial appointment had appeared) editorialized in the *Pittsburgh Courier,* stating, "For years I have said in this column and from the American platform that more Negroes should be in Foreign Service, more Negroes should be sent to represent this country on every continent, especially Europe, Asia and Africa." According to Mays, the long wait was over: "Thank goodness that we have an Administration in Washington that senses this point thoroughly." A story in *Jet* informed readers that one result of the August meeting was that, "Faced with doing business with a world already two-thirds colored, the U.S. is conducting an unusual, nationwide talent hunt for Negro representatives to send around the world." And a story in the *Afro-American* began by declaring, "The immediate appointment of a person of color to a top position in the State Department would do more than anything else to dramatize to young people job opportunities now available in the foreign service." A more direct response was an article in *Ebony* a year after the conference, which highlighted State Department efforts to find "talented Negroes for foreign service," and followed this with a picture essay made up of shots of nearly twenty African-Americans currently employed by State or the Foreign Service.[27]

Pursuing what they perceived to be the new opportunities offered by Kennedy and Johnson, African-Americans pushed with renewed vigor the idea that black diplomats could bring important and, indeed, unique benefits to the United States. Just two months before Kennedy's election, the title of a long story in the *Norfolk Journal and Guide* said it all: "Russia Can't Match USA's Ace In the Hole: 18 Million Negroes." The basic theme of the piece was that, "There is a strong blood tie between America and Africa which beats anything Russia has to offer"; that bond "could well be the turning point to win Africa on the side of the West." That idea was also at the heart of a March 1961 letter from John W. Davis, an African-American veteran of U.S. technical assistance programs overseas, in which he argued, "One of America's greatest assets in the battle for the minds of Africans and Asians and, indeed, Europeans is the American of African descent." Especially in terms of dealing with Africa, it was clear that "the African wants a truly representative American team. A representative team from the point of view of the African is neither exclusively white nor Negro."[28]

Benjamin Mays, in another editorial in the *Pittsburgh Courier,* emphasized the propaganda value of black appointments. Arguing that Ralph Bunche and others could be appointed to posts on any continent, he concluded that, "Such appointments would go a long way to offset Communist propaganda." Roger Wilkins, an African-American employee in the Agency for International Development, in a letter to Special Assistant to the President Ralph Dungan in 1962, concurred with Mays's idea that African-American diplomats should be spread across the globe and not automatically sent to Africa: "Appointment of Negroes to important foreign affairs posts in which the concerns are not Africa will demonstrate to Africans, Asians and Americans that American Negroes are deemed able and useful citizens by their government." However, Congressman Charles Diggs, responding to the resignation of G. Mennen Williams as assistant secretary of state for African Affairs in 1966, argued that African-Americans still had a special role to play in relations with Africa. Suggesting several blacks for the vacant post, Diggs argued that, "all other things being equal, an American Negro could offer an extra dimension of considerable utility, somewhat analogous to the advantages of having John Grounski as our ambassador to Poland."[29]

Once again, ANLCA was in the forefront, pushing for more African-American appointments to diplomatic positions. In its 1962 resolutions, the organization argued that "we find that Negro citizens are still excluded from top level jobs in the area of policy making." It then reiterated most of the same points raised at the 1961 equal employment conference. At the postconference meeting with President Kennedy, leaders of the group presented the president with a memorandum that noted, "Our Nation has a huge reservoir of potential good will in our relations with African Nations which has scarcely been tapped. We urge, therefore, more extensive use of qualified Negro Americans in foreign service and policy-making positions in the State Department." Theodore Brown reported that at the meeting, Kennedy had expressed his "particular interest" in this issue. In January 1963, Brown cited Carl Rowan's appointment as ambassador to Finland as evidence of ANLCA's influence on the president.[30]

The interest of the African-American community in the appointment of blacks to, and promotion of blacks within, the foreign policy making bureaucracy of the United States was evident by the amount of newspaper and magazine coverage dedicated to the subject. Nearly each appointment or promotion was cited by the black media as another example of a barrier breached or a new precedent set. The attention given to the career of journalist Carl Rowan provides a good example of this. When Rowan was selected to be deputy assistant secretary of state for public affairs by the incoming Kennedy administration, *Jet* magazine proudly noted that this would make him "the highest-ranking Negro in the U.S. State Dept." Two years later, when he was named as ambassador to Finland, the *Afro-American* reported that Rowan saw his appointment "as a challenge to help blaze a trail in the foreign service for other colored citizens." He was quoted as saying that "'doors might be opened to more colored students' in the foreign service if he and others of his race demonstrate that colored citizens can serve America's interest abroad with as much distinction and skill as any other citizen." Both the *Norfolk Journal and Guide* and the *New York Amsterdam News* carried features on Rowan's appointment; the story in the *Amsterdam News* made the front page. *Ebony* featured a long photo essay on the "Youngest U.S. Ambassador." Rowan's appointment to Finland—the "hottest spot in the cold war"—had "confused" the Russians. Although Rowan claimed that he had come to Finland, not as "a specialist on racial problems and the Negro, but as the representative and ambassador of the people of the United States," he also noted that, "In a period when the American Negro is demanding greater opportunities and responsibilities, I could ill-afford to refuse to serve as chief representative in one of our most important diplomatic posts. I also felt that my coming to Finland would hasten the day when American Negroes are playing the role they ought to play in our foreign service."[31]

Rowan's steady march up the bureaucracy continued under President Johnson, when he was named as director of USIA in 1964. Once again, the precedent-setting nature of the appointment was played up in an article in *Jet*. Rowan was now the "new chief salesman for Uncle Sam and for millions of global inhabitants." Noteworthy was the fact that he would be following "in the footsteps of one of the country's ablest journalists, Edward R. Murrow." His new position meant that Rowan was set "to become the President's key Negro appointee." As director of the USIA, he would "become the first Negro to sit in on top secret security council sessions."[32]

Also attracting special attention was the appointment of the first African-American woman as a U.S. ambassador. Patricia Roberts Harris, a professor of law at Howard University, was selected by President Johnson in 1965 to serve as ambassador to Luxembourg. In addition to the usual newspaper stories, *Ebony* ran a lengthy article, which, aside from some ridiculous comments about Marine embassy guards who "flipped" when they saw the "decidedly attractive" new ambassador, accentuated Harris's professionalism and people skills. The piece also noted that she was "raising a few eyebrows" with her invitation to NAACP Executive Secretary Roy Wilkins to be her first guest of honor at an embassy dinner. Harris explained that, "I just wanted certain people to know how I still feel about civil rights. I didn't want anybody to think that I'd divorced myself from the problems at home simply because I was a few thousands miles away. We've got racial problems and they're just as important as many of the problems we have to deal with in international diplomacy."[33]

Other newcomers to U.S. diplomatic ranks were heralded in the black press. Both the Kennedy and Johnson administrations took many of their African-American diplomatic appointees—such as Harris—from the academic world. One of Kennedy's first picks was Howard University professor of romance languages Mercer Cook, named as ambassador to Niger in 1961. Cook, one of the founding members of AMSAC, was on leave from Howard and working as director of the African Affairs Program at The Congress for Cultural Freedom in Paris when he was selected. Elliott P. Skinner, a professor of anthropology at Columbia University, was selected as ambassador to Upper Volta in 1966, a nation he knew well from his field research into the country's peoples and cultures. Hugh Smythe, who had had an on-and-off relationship with the Department of State for a number of years, was with the sociology department at Brooklyn College when he was tapped by President Johnson to be the first African-American to serve as an ambassador in the Middle East—Syria—in 1965.[34]

Other stories focused on the appointments of career FSO Clifton Wharton as ambassador to Norway in 1961; Barbara Watson, a New York lawyer, as acting administrator of the Bureau of Security and Consular Affairs in 1967; Chester C. Carter, a former Peace Corps official, as deputy chief of protocol in 1964; and John H. Morrow, who had served as ambassador to Guinea under Eisenhower, as an alternate delegate to the UN. Features, such as those about Department veteran David Bolen, who was made Officer in Charge of Nigerian Affairs in 1964; Franklin Williams, chief of the Peace Corps' Division of United Nations and International Agency Relations; and Zelma Watson George, who served on the UN delegation, were common.[35]

The optimism over the 1961 employment conference and the handful of well-publicized African-American appointments and promotions was, however, never unquestioned by some black leaders and media, and after a relatively brief "honeymoon" period after Kennedy's election in 1960, it began to fade very quickly. Indeed, the Kennedy administration had barely settled into office before questions and complaints regarding the use of African-Americans in foreign policy positions began to be raised. A January 1961 article in the *Afro-American* charged that, "Unless the Kennedy administration reverses the current policy of the U.S. State Department in selecting ambassadors and embassy personnel to new nations of Africa, no increase in the use of colored personnel is likely in the foreseeable future." That "current policy" was one that accentuated "experience," which, owing to the small number of experienced African-American diplomats, obviously worked against their appointment to the new posts in Africa. Just a few weeks later, the newspaper declared that, "It appeared this week that America's top echelon diplomatic representation in West Africa will be all white." The removal of John H. Morrow as ambassador to Guinea, and his replacement with a white—an editor for *Look* named William Attwood—meant that no black currently served as an ambassador to an African nation.[36]

At about the same time, Congressman Charles Diggs returned from a two-week tour of Africa and in a press conference lashed out at the notion that some nations would not accept African-Americans as diplomats. According to Diggs, "Negroes have a distinct advantage over white representatives." The stories about nations refusing African-American diplomats were "propaganda deliberately started by members of the State Department in an attempt to keep Negroes out of the service." As Diggs explained, "The State Department itself is very clannish and there are a number of Southern whites in the service. There has been evidence of an attempt to systematically eliminate Negroes from the service." Fellow congressman Adam Clayton Powell rapped the Kennedy administration for its refusal to put "some black faces" on the American delegation to the UN. Powell charged that Kennedy had named only one African-American (John H. Morrow) despite "repeated attack from several Negro groups."[37]

By mid-1961, the Kennedy administration was being pilloried for its lack of action in putting more African-Americans into diplomatic positions. An editorial in the *New York Amsterdam News* launched a slashing attack, arguing that, "The policy of the Government of the United States in the matter of barring Negroes from high posts in the Diplomatic Service is as indefensible a discrimination as is the act of a club-swinging policeman in Jackson, Mississippi, barring Negro youths from entering a 'white only' restaurant. Until both are corrected this country will never deservedly hold the position of world leadership it now claims." The United States currently had no African-American ambassador serving in Africa; out of the forty-five diplomatic appointees to America's UN delegation, only two were black. The reason was clear: "The principal reason they are barred is because certain people in the State Department decree it be so." African-American diplomats sent to Africa were sent "burdened with 'second class citizenship.'" An editorial in the *Afro-American* was equally as stinging. There was nothing less than "a determined, well organized effort on the part of State Department officials to embarrass colored officers and diplomats." That was how they undercut the effectiveness of John Morrow in Guinea: his suggestions were routinely "thrown into the wastebasket." Guinea certainly learned the lesson: Morrow's replacement was white, and "a white envoy can accomplish more for their country than a colored one." State's usual defense for not using outstanding blacks as ambassadors—used when it opposed the selection of John A. Davis as ambassador to Denmark—was that only professional FSOs should be awarded these posts. Yet, "State does not trot out this bromide when a white man is considered. Hence, Bill Blair, Adlai Stevenson's law partner, got the nod to Denmark." Clifton Wharton, appointed to Norway, was a career man, was "not racially militant, and will retire very soon"; he would not be "double-crossed as badly as other colored envoys will by State."[38]

In a special report to AMSAC in May 1961, Executive Director John A. Davis bluntly declared that, "There is still a dearth of Negro foreign service officers in the Department of State. There is no question but that the original cause of this dearth was discrimination in the past which the Department did not try to remedy." This very visible discrimination had also served to cause resentment in the "small Negro nations" to which most of the early African-American diplomats had been sent, "the more so because lack of United States interest in their countries usually went along with such an appointment." When a nation rose in status "the tendency has been to appoint the best white career officers." These African states were "undoubtedly encouraged . . . in this attitude" by Department officers. The appointment of Clifton Wharton to Norway was a welcome break with past tradition, but this "alone will not change the image of the American Foreign Service in the eyes of African and Asian nations." Only one African-American had been proposed as ambassador to Africa in the first months of the Kennedy administration (Mercer Cook, to Niger). "This," Davis concluded, "is indeed a sorry picture. Regardless of how it is explained, it must be extremely galling to the heads of African nations to be told that under the career rules of our Department of State only white men are qualified to represent this nation in Africa. This, in itself, says more about the American system in relation to the Negro than all of our propaganda says." Davis fumed that, "It is shameful that at this writing there is only one Negro ambassador—to Norway, and one proposed—to Niger. Negroes hold no rank in State above Deputy Assistant Secretary, of which there are 78. There is only one of these and he is in a propaganda post which as a matter of policy seems both lame and obvious. For the first time the American delegation to the UN is lily white." The Department of State needed to "take positive steps to put to rights past wrongs."[39]

Criticism seemed to dissipate somewhat in late 1961, perhaps as a result of the August equal employment conference, which suggested that the Kennedy administration was going to effectively attack the problem. It was not long, however, before many African-Americans were questioning whether that meeting had been worth the time it had taken to attend it. In a January 1962 article, Rayford Logan noted that Secretary Rusk seemed to be sincere, but "few Negroes in the State Department believe that he has time to check whether his subordinates will implement his determination." A February editorial in the *Afro-American* was even more explicit in condemning the futility of the 1961 conference. According to the piece, the Department of State had "made no honest effort yet to upgrade colored officers"; had made "no strong attempt to find colored candidates for openings which now exist"; had "not yet demonstrated that it fully understands or intends to carry out the full meaning of fair employment or fair promotion"; had "fought and continues to fight the appointment of qualified colored people for ambassador." "It's no secret," the editorial continued, "that the majority of colored leaders—and certainly the newspaper people—who attended that conference last August now consider it a complete waste of time." The Department's obvious "emphasis on beginning and entering positions (the lowest) rather than on the higher appointive positions which are continually available" was having an effect. Few African-Americans had taken the latest Foreign Service examination, and "this number will remain small until colored people all over America are convinced the State Dept. means business in the matter of fair hiring and promotion." Considering the almost complete lack of a black presence in the higher level positions in the Department, it was "little wonder that colored people are bypassing it." The editorial's conclusion was positively scathing: "As far as fair employment and equal opportunity is concerned, the State Dept.'s corporate image stinks. It is . . . an exclusive country club composed of white people who look upon the art of diplomacy as an indigenous blessing to the fortuitous accident which made them all white. When the image changes, the State Dept. will be flooded with colored applicants. Until then, we predict an eternal dribble of half-interested students who are simply curious."[40]

A year later, the *Afro-American* could find little significant improvement in the situation: "By now, it must be painfully apparent to colored Americans, Asians and Africans that the essential posture of the United States Department of State is boldly anti-colored. Despite the noble promises of the 'new frontier' . . . to alter a racist image, it nonetheless clings like tar to road on a hot summer day." Despite some "limited progress" on the issue, the real problem was in the Department itself where "people who are Southerners and who bitterly resent colored progress are able to impede, slow up and more often than not actually scuttle the new emphasis on integration to which the Kennedy administration is committed." There still was not "a single colored person in America in a policy-making position in the United States Department of State."[41]

By 1964, with Kennedy gone and three years since the 1961 employment conference, the second meeting of ANLCA surveyed the progress in terms of the integration of African-Americans into the Department of State and Foreign Service. While recognizing some improvement, this was judged to be far too little. A resolution declared that "the presence of a very few Negroes in the Foreign Service and especially in the Department of State does not constitute fair employment nor reflect the importance of the racial factor in world politics today." A report delivered by John A. Davis concurred, noting that the Kennedy and Johnson administrations had "made a start toward the fair employment of Negroes in the Foreign Service." Yet, he concluded, "Considering the amount of effort placed on the matter, the results are miserable." In three years, the number of black FSOs had increased from seventeen to nineteen. Until this matter was addressed more effectively "the Department can never hope to overcome the long term problem of the place of the American Negro in the Foreign Service." Furthermore, a smaller number of African-Americans had taken the Foreign Service exam in 1962 than in 1961. There had been a few "high level" appointments, but most of these had come in "sister agencies such as the Peace Corps, AID and USIA rather than in the State Department." Overall, the Department had "exhibited a considerable amount of motion without comparable results." Only two African-Americans served as ambassadors, both in Africa; this was a "meager record."[42]

The criticisms continued to mount during the Johnson years. Congressman Powell, in a letter to Chairman John Macy of the U.S. Civil Service Commission, happily noted the appointments of Patricia Roberts Harris and Mercer Cook. However, he took exception to Macy's statement that "quality" was the basic guideline in terms of appointments. Powell stated that "too often the factor of race is still a determinant in the concept of 'quality.'" C. Sumner Stone, one of Powell's special assistants, downplayed Assistant Secretary G. Mennen Williams's optimistic assessment of the success of the Department's efforts at greater integration. He was delighted to know that there were three African-American ambassadors, but noted that "the role of the Negro has diminished because there has been an *increase* of Ambassadors in two years." Furthermore, "Few Negroes are impressed with general increases. . . . No real, honest or significant progress will be made in the State Department until Negroes are hired as Assistant Secretaries, Deputy Assistant Secretaries, Assistant Legal Officers, Directors of Bureaus and Directors of Offices. The Africans know this, Negroes know this, and all of us can only hope and pray that one day the State Department and the Secretary will know it."[43]

In a 1969 article in the *Journal of International Affairs,* John A. Davis, who had been fighting the battle for integration of the Department of State since the 1940s, gave his impressions of eight years of plans, promises, and programs during the Kennedy-Johnson administrations. Despite "considerable effort," nothing much had changed: "three Negro ambassadors, two in

Africa; two Deputy Assistant Secretaries of State, none in African areas; nineteen Foreign Service Officers; eleven Junior Foreign Service Reserve Officers; and twenty-four Foreign Service Reserve Officers—a drop of twenty-seven since 1967. This picture is a disgrace, a monument to bureaucratic rigidity and an embarrassment to the United States everywhere in the world, especially in Africa and Asia."[44]

African-Americans began the decade of the 1960s with tremendous optimism about their ability to influence the new administration as regarded the idea of race and U.S. foreign policy. They were sure that the "new frontiers" of which Kennedy spoke extended into the realm of race relations, both at home and abroad. Perhaps the new president would understand that the civil rights movement in the United States and the struggles in Africa for independence and equality were closely connected; that race had become a worldwide issue; that racism in the United States was hurting America's foreign policy; and that African-Americans could, and should, provide a necessary and unique presence and voice in the foreign policy making bureaucracy.

After just a short time, however, the optimism of African-Americans had faded badly. While acknowledging that efforts on the part of the Democratic presidents had been made on many fronts, they were certain by the mid-1960s that those efforts had gone for naught. The United States did not seem to understand the problem of colonialism in Africa; did not fathom that its policy toward South Africa was unacceptable; did not seem to grasp the fact that race was an issue that had to be directly confronted, not obfuscated by fuzzy proclamations and vague rhetoric about the "rights of man" and "equality." It seemed blithely unaware that calling for liberty and justice abroad was ludicrous at best, and hypocritical at worst, when the civil rights of African-Americans were routinely violated at home. And on the issue of desegregating the Department of State and Foreign Service, the picture was, as Davis concluded, "a disgrace." Here again, the rhetoric had been loud and long, but aside from a few highly publicized appointments (and none of these to policy making positions) little had changed. Even with a great deal of effort, the "new frontiers in race relations" seemed unable to penetrate the old frontiers of discrimination and disinterest lodged securely in the nation's foreign policy bureaucracy.

∽ 7 ∽

New Frontiers and the
Old Boys' Club

Kennedy, Johnson, Foreign Policy,
and Race, 1961–1969

The initial optimism expressed by many African-Americans concerning the possibilities of a new official U.S. approach to issues of race—both at home and abroad—under the administrations of John F. Kennedy and Lyndon B. Johnson was based on more than simply hope. The moment did seem propitious for such a change. Abroad, particularly in Africa, colonialism was in eclipse. As Thomas Noer states, "By 1960 France, Britain, and Belgium were largely resigned to the end of colonization. The uprising in Angola in 1961 indicated that eventually Portugal also would be pushed off the continent."[1] At home, the civil rights movement was reaching its climax, with the help of leaders such as Martin Luther King Jr., and organizations such as the Student Non-Violent Coordinating Committee.[2]

As significant as these events were, their impact on U.S. policy would, to a large degree, depend on the men who sat in the Oval Office and their advisors. Here, again, there seemed to be a basis for optimism. At least publicly, both Kennedy and Johnson evidenced a strong interest in civil rights at home and a new and intense interest in African affairs abroad. Yet, the two presidents' records are hardly conclusive. In terms of the former, there is little disagreement among historians that the two men oversaw the passage of some of the most far-reaching civil rights legislation in the nation's history. Their commitment to the issue, however, has been questioned. As Mark Stern argued in his 1992 book, *Calculating Visions,* both Kennedy and Johnson were "political schemers. They maneuvered, made promises, and again maneuvered as political necessity dictated. . . . In their drive for power the politicians moved to where the votes were, and they moved to where the idealists led them." Neither man had a sparkling record on civil rights issues before coming to the White House. Driven by presidential politics, by the 1960s they made stronger gestures toward black voters.[3]

On the issue of Africa, there seemed to be even less substance to the rhetoric. Kennedy had made Africa a very public issue in his 1960 campaign, but, as Richard D. Mahoney argues, "Kennedy's handling of the Africa issue in the 1960 campaign—his pitch to the liberal and black vote—was a minor classic in political exploitation of foreign policy. . . . The strategy was to use concern for Africa as a means of wooing American blacks without alienating Southern whites." Thomas Noer agrees with this analysis, but feels that it was "more than just a campaign issue for him: he saw Africa as a major opportunity for gain in the Cold War." For Kennedy, Africa was "an arena of significant Cold War rivalry," yet he and his advisors "viewed Africa more as an area of symbolic significance and as a battleground for international prestige." The president's basic approach, therefore, was hardly a dynamic one: "Kennedy's goal in Africa was victory through denial, a defensive diplomacy that defined success as not losing." Johnson, despite promising to maintain Kennedy's "new" policy toward Africa, was even more reticent to take dramatic foreign policy steps. As Terrence Lyons explains, "Africa occupied a peripheral position on Johnson's list of priorities"; it "was best kept on the back burner."[4]

Not surprisingly, on issue after issue in Africa—particularly the continuation of Portuguese colonialism and apartheid in South Africa—both Kennedy and Johnson were willing to compromise their public statements about support for African self-determination, their intense distaste for colonialism, and their opposition to apartheid. As Noer explains, "Kennedy had repeatedly criticized Eisenhower for not supporting decolonization, and black Africa expected the Administration to put strong pressure on Portugal." However, Kennedy was also concerned about "a disruption in NATO, the loss of the Azores base, and instability resulting from too rapid a rush to independence by the seemingly unprepared Portuguese colonies." In terms of addressing apartheid in South Africa, "Economic and strategic considerations limited American actions against apartheid. . . . A direct confrontation with Pretoria risked the cut-off of gold, diamonds, manganese, platinum, and chrome." Thus, "the Administration was largely left with symbolic gestures to illustrate its opposition to apartheid." Gerald Thomas concludes that, "In the final analysis, Kennedy's approach proved to be not too different than that of Eisenhower before him," and "Johnson followed Kennedy's policies toward Africa to a large extent." Thus, "The actual performance of the Kennedy and Johnson administrations and the subsequent events leave a mixed record, and not one that recognized the human rights of black Africans in South and southern Africa to any commendable extent." For both Kennedy and Johnson, "their primary consideration was always the Cold War, Europe, and the Middle East . . . the 1960s, insofar as black freedom and progress in Africa is concerned, can be said to have come in like a lion but gone out like a lamb."[5]

Given such views, it is not hard to understand the frustration and disappointment of African-Americans concerning the Kennedy and Johnson policies in dealing with race, civil rights, and people of color around the world, particularly in Africa. A number of factors combined during the 1960s to make the Kennedy and Johnson approaches to those issues in the international arena little different in terms of substance and results from the 1940s and 1950s. First and foremost, it is evident that during the 1960s the U.S. government was neither well informed about nor very interested in black views on foreign policy. An April 1963 Department of State memorandum summarized the materials it had on hand "which might provide some basis for an assessment of current American Negro opinion." There was very little. Public Affairs kept track of the *Washington Afro-American* ("intermittently"), plus the *Chicago Defender, Jet,* and *Ebony.* The Department had tried to subscribe to the *Pittsburgh Courier* and the *Baltimore Afro-American,* but "these were received so infrequently in 1962 that we gave up for 1963." It was of little matter, since, "None of the above newspapers or magazines contains very much comment on foreign affairs."[6] The last claim was patently absurd: the *Courier, Afro-American,* and *Defender,* in particular, contained a wealth of information about foreign affairs.

The memorandum offered one hope for discovering more about "Negro opinion": ask the Gallup Organization if it had any information. A few months later, the results of several polls done since late 1962, in which the responses of "Whites" and "non-Whites" to twelve questions were listed, were sent to the Department. The usefulness of the information was debatable. Five of the questions dealt with U.S. policy toward Cuba; most of the others were extremely general queries. There were no questions dealing with the issues of greatest interest to African-Americans: nothing on Africa or Asia, colonialism, or apartheid. It was not altogether surprising, therefore, that the percentage of African-American respondents indicating "no opinion" varied from 25 to 65 percent.[7]

In addition to this lack of information, most officials in the U.S. government indicated their strong disinterest in a distinct black voice speaking out
on the nation's foreign policy. A series of White House memoranda from
late 1964 and early 1965 concerning the proper stance toward the ANLCA
illustrates this point. The debate began with a note from Lee White, an
advisor on civil rights matters, to President Johnson in December 1964. He
reported that he had just had a meeting with Roy Wilkins who, in speaking
about the latest meeting of the ANLCA, charged that "those who are shaping our African policy have missed a few opportunities and perhaps mis-
handled others." Wilkins wanted representatives of the group to meet with
Johnson to discuss the matter. White informed Wilkins that he "personally
saw some problems in the president meeting with a group of American
Negroes to secure from them their recommendations on what our African
policy should be." He suggested that Wilkins and some others from
ANLCA might meet with McGeorge Bundy and others "on a completely
informal and unscheduled basis." Johnson passed the note on to National
Security Council (NSC) staffer Robert Komer, who then contacted Bundy
in January. According to Komer, the president's position was clear: "He
doesn't think it at all a good idea to encourage a separate Negro view of
foreign policy. We don't want an integrated domestic policy and a segregated foreign policy. ... In short, I get loud and clear that the president
wants to discourage emergence of any special Negro pressure group (a la
the Zionists) which might limit his freedom of maneuver."[8]

Komer suggested that Bundy contact Secretary Rusk about the matter, and
Bundy immediately did so. He informed Rusk about the gist of Johnson's
comments, and then asked the secretary to speak with the "American Negro
leadership because you have a particularly high standing with them." At that
meeting, Rusk's main job would be to get Johnson's points across in an
effective manner: "the main impression that the president has left with us is
that he wants to discourage a Negro pressure group on African affairs and
that you are the man who can do it." Rusk's meeting with members of the
group, which took place a few weeks later, was, according to Rick Haynes
(an African-American member of the NSC staff), "quiet and friendly." While
it did not appear that Rusk bluntly informed the group of Johnson's views,
Haynes judged the meeting a success: it was "given minimal press coverage
and is not likely to give rise to any undesirable repercussions."[9]

Both Haynes and Komer were stunned, therefore, to discover that the
meeting had not had its intended impact. Haynes informed Komer in late
March that the ANLCA was meeting on 1 April "to create a *permanent
organization concerned with American Negro influence on U.S. foreign
policy in Africa*. This is an attempt to organize an 'ethnic lobby' out of a

heretofore relatively ineffective and loosely constituted interest group." He suggested that "we ought to be thinking of doing something to eliminate the raison d'etre of such a group ... like a high-level U.S. friendship tour of Africa!" Both Haynes and Komer were "quite concerned over the prospect of an imminent Negro leadership conference to *set up an organization to influence US policy on Africa.*" This was exactly what Johnson "*doesn't want.*" In a memorandum to McGeorge Bundy, they suggested that "we should guide this toward a non-racial outcome, i.e., it should include whites as well as Negroes." Clifford Alexander, one of Johnson's special assistants, also wrote to Bundy, indicating that he had the same concerns. One way of dealing with the situation would be to "ignore this specific group and hope they disappear." Part of this approach would involve telling African Affairs in the Department of State "not to give as much time and attention to representatives of the Conference as they have in the past, and also to stay away from various meetings held by the group. Another way would be to "talk to the major powers in the Civil Rights movement and indicate our feelings about racial lobbies." Of course, this approach would be "dangerous politically and could enhance the prestige of the group if they violated our confidence." When it became obvious that the group was not going to "disappear" as fast as desired, Haynes advised White that the best policy might be to just get along with it as best the White House could. He concluded, "the fact is that this particular group has proven itself to be a loose conglomeration of disparate organizations which lacks the expertise and background to be of any real help to us in formulating African policy."[10]

Despite the indifference (and even hostility) of the U.S. government toward anything resembling a distinct black voice in America's foreign policy, there were a few parallels between African-American views and those of many American officials. Most particularly, U.S. policymakers shared the belief that America's problems with race and civil rights had a detrimental impact on the nation's international status. An October 1962 USIA report summarized the problem. "Racial prejudice," it concluded, "is the chief blemish on the image of the American people abroad, even among the majority of citizens of non-Communist nations who hold the United States in high esteem." While there was no evidence that these perceptions had "caused any nation to align itself against us," they were "an added and explosive burden to carry in a world where 'white nations' are in a minority."[11]

Crisis situations, such as those which occurred in Oxford, Mississippi, in 1962 and Birmingham, Alabama, in 1963, only added to that "explosive burden." In the former instance, federal troops had been necessary to allow James Meredith to attend the University of Mississippi. In the latter, Birmingham police had brutally disrupted a peaceful protest led by Martin

Luther King Jr., and jailed the civil rights leader. As Deputy Director of the USIA Donald Wilson explained, "The picture of a dog attacking a Negro, of a police officer pinning a Negro woman to the ground—these pictures have dramatic impact on those abroad who listen to our words about democracy and weigh our actions against those words." And the problem would get worse before it got better: "by any honest reckoning, there will be more ugly pictures to come, there will be more awareness abroad of our problem of race relations, there will be more headlines calling our inequities to the attention of the world." America could no longer deal with such incidents as anomalies, for it was "no longer dealing with isolated incidents. Where the span between a Little Rock and an Oxford could be marked by months and years, now we are witnessing a massive effort throughout the nation, and there will be no long pauses which allow us to slip into apathy."[12]

A USIA survey of world media reaction to the events in Mississippi indicated the depth of the problem for the United States. In much of Western Europe, the view was that "U.S. prestige had been enhanced by the firm and prompt handling of the situation by the president"; however, there was also the feeling that "the incident could adversely affect U.S. prestige throughout much of the world." Especially in Africa and Asia that seemed to be the case: "The tenor of comment from the Far East clearly indicated that U.S. prestige had suffered as a result of the incident. Some African comment noted that education rather than law was required to liquidate racial prejudice and that America's role in Africa and in the world would be handicapped until such a change was achieved."[13]

African-Americans had often pointed out that America's race problems were of particular concern in Africa, and this belief was shared by many U.S. officials. Three Democratic senators who visited Africa in early 1961 came to the conclusion that "racial discrimination in the U.S. probably is the most important of all the natural barriers to a better understanding between Africa and America." USIA surveys substantiated that claim. According to a February 1962 study, "In African eyes the most serious blight upon the American image was the failure (so far) to guarantee the full implications of the American political philosophy to the colored ten percent of the population." In early 1963, USIA Director Edward Murrow informed President Kennedy about the opinions of nearly three hundred African students in Germany. Two-thirds of them viewed the "general esteem" of the United States in favorable terms. There was, however, one particular sore spot: "U.S. race relations are considered poor or very poor by 61 per cent. Only South Africa scored worse on this point, with 86 per cent." A follow-up report a year later, which focused on African students in the United States, came to the same dismal conclusion: "In contrast to attitudes toward

U.S. education and the American economic system, evaluations of the U.S. racial situation are overwhelmingly adverse." More troubling was the fact that "three times as many students say their opinion of the position of the American Negro has changed for the worse since they came to the U.S. as say it has changed for the better."[14]

Despite these reports, U.S. efforts during the Kennedy and Johnson years to deal with the issue of race in its international context differed very little from those undertaken during the previous fifteen years. To be sure, the propaganda was a bit more intense and sophisticated, but its themes and directions remained the same. The main line of thinking remained unchanged: the biggest problem facing the United States in underdeveloped regions such as Africa was communism, not racism; therefore, American propaganda should focus on the East-West, not black-white struggle. Part of that struggle involved "distortion" of race problems in the United States by communist propagandists. The goal of U.S. information efforts, therefore, should be to counter those distortions and get the "truth" out to the world's people. Africa was a special focus for those efforts.

Fear of communist penetration of Africa remained strong throughout the Kennedy and Johnson years, often overwhelming considerations of other issues—such as race—in the construction of U.S. policy toward that continent.[15] A 1964 study from the Bureau of Intelligence and Research in the Department of State outlined the dangers. "The Soviet Union developed an active interest in tropical Africa in the late 50s." Communist China was also working in Africa, and "the principal impact of the Sino-Soviet rift in Africa will be the acceleration of attempts on the part of each communist power to gain influence." Though their "influence in and access to Africa was close to zero at the outset of Africa's independence," this was no longer the case: "Starting thus virtually from scratch, communist advances in Africa seem dramatic." There was no danger of communists taking over the continent, but there was a "[d]anger of successful communist subversion of African nationalist regimes."[16]

Even when Assistant Secretary of State for African Affairs G. Mennen Williams developed a "New African Program" (which became the "Strengthened African Program") in early 1965, anti-communism dominated the analysis. In a draft memorandum Williams sent out in May 1965, the primary concern expressed was that, "Communist efforts to penetrate and control Africa are rapidly increasing." Two months later, as the "Strengthened African Program" continued to take shape, the number one "basic policy" of the United States in Africa was, "To help create a truly independent Africa, increasing in political and economic strength and resistant to Communist subversion." McGeorge Bundy, reviewing steps that might be taken to improve U.S. relations with Africa, agreed: "The broad U.S. policy aims in Africa are: (a) political stability for the new nations; (b) economic growth and development, and (c) the prevention of Soviet and Chicom penetration."[17]

In 1968, with the Johnson presidency coming to an end, the Department of State undertook a history of its accomplishments and goals during the period 1963 to 1968. When it came time to discuss U.S. policy in Africa, the document concluded that the primary political goal for America was that "the African states remain independent and free from excessive influence of blocs or power systems hostile toward us." Only at the end of analyzing U.S. interests in Africa did the history somewhat cryptically note that one goal was to "develop that kind of racial relationship which will enhance our own influence and head off international confrontations and hostile alignments on a racial basis." The document's conclusion, however, left no doubt about how the United States measured its successes in Africa: "As the United States surveyed the scene in 1968, it could be reasonably satisfied that, within the limits of the resources available, recent U.S. policies toward Africa had generally been effective. . . . In the main, the United States succeeded in limiting Communist expansion." How it had fared in developing "that kind of racial relationship" it desired was not addressed.[18]

There was also a widespread feeling among U.S. officials that many of the negative international criticisms of America's race problem were the result of serious distortions—often abetted by Communist propaganda. Deputy Assistant Secretary for Public Affairs Carl Rowan, in speaking to a gathering of U.S. chiefs of mission to Latin America in October 1961, noted that "there will continue to be race incidents in the U.S." The goal was to "put it in perspective. We must show that the picture is not one of whites vs. Negroes, as our enemies would depict it, but of the vast majority of whites and Negroes striving together for progress." Rollie White, who was deputy special assistant for psychological strategy, agreed that perspective was an important point. "Every instance of positive (constructive) action taken in the U.S. by local, state or federal authorities should be made available to our posts overseas in order that the negative aspects (racial demonstrations, violence, etc.) which 'grab the headlines' may be offset."[19]

Given the U.S. focus on anti-communism, it was not surprising to find American officials arguing that many of the "distortions" were Communist fabrications. Thomas Sorenson, who in 1964 was deputy director of USIA, expounded on this subject: "In many countries there are both damaging gaps in knowledge about the United States and widely held shibboleths which adversely affect the achievement of our objectives. Among these stubborn canards are that we are capitalists in the evil 19th century Marxist sense, that we are materialistic and without culture, that we are racist." USIA's 1968 administrative history also put forward this theory. It argued that the "increasing outbursts of racial violence and militancy captured the headlines and thus the attention of foreign audiences and tended to color their view of American society." This was exacerbated by the fact that "Communist propaganda focused ever more sharply on race problems in the United States," and "portrayed the race riots in the summer of 1967 as 'a civil war,' in which legitimate demands by Negroes were bloodily rejected."[20]

With these as the starting points from which U.S. propagandists considered the issue of race, it is little wonder that the information output of the 1960s—though greater in total mass and in its technical sophistication—took essentially the same approach as earlier American propaganda efforts in the 1940s and 1950s. This meant emphasizing the "progress" of African-Americans, the government's wholehearted commitment to civil rights, and the desire of U.S. officials to have close and equal relationships with people of color in Africa and elsewhere.

The overall approach of USIA was best summed up in a 1964 description of the agency's priority issues. "Racial and Ethnic Progress" was number one. The summary of USIA's general theme on this issue had a familiar ring:

> The United States has the most diverse population in the world. In the melting pot process, minorities have often suffered in the U.S., as they have historically and still do in many countries. But the U.S. democratic social, political, and economic system has provided a means for them to join and be absorbed into the main stream of American life, in all its richness and variety. The last large such minority—Negro Americans—are now actively in this process of full integration. Progress will not always be easy, but, with the support of the Federal Government and a majority of the citizenry, will continue until the process is complete.[21]

Various reports from the 1960s indicated the size and scope of the U.S. propaganda effort. A 1963 memorandum informed its readers that "a special planning task force is working with their world media output—wireless bulletin, radio, television, motion pictures, pamphlets, etc.—to assure proper treatment of the subject of civil rights being sought by Negroes." Films and copies of President Kennedy's addresses on civil rights were being distributed throughout the world, and VOA was "providing specialized coverage in its broadcasts of the civil rights situation in various languages and dialects." In addition, large amounts of written material was "being circulated abroad which will indicate the advances being made by

American Negroes in their struggle to obtain adequate civil rights." Rollie White provided an even more in-depth look at how the race issue was being handled. Both USIA and VOA were making every effort to "provide a continuing flow of materials showing hard evidence of week-in-and-week-out progress towards equality of rights and opportunities." The Public Affairs people were "making a concerted effort to feed background material which it has developed on racism in the Soviet Bloc and Red China to selected newsmen." The Division of Cultural Affairs had a "coordinated program with the Justice Department whereby all Americans going overseas under the Exchange Program are being briefed by a Department of Justice representative concerning the various considerations involved in the U.S. race relations situation." USIA had a "special 'monitor unit' to screen all events of significance in the civil rights field and to assure that the appropriate coverage is included in USIA media output."[22]

Since Africa was of special concern in regard to the racial issue, USIA gave a great deal of attention to the continent. As the USIA's administrative history pointed out, by 1963 it "operated in 34 countries through 50 mission and branch posts, 48 libraries, and 12 reading rooms." Donald Culverson, in a 1989 article about the USIA in Africa concludes that its primary job was to "project a positive image of the United States precisely at a time when Afro-American political activism was questioning the quality of America's commitment to democracy at home." He went on to describe the various programs: nearly 12,000 words of "background reports, commentaries, and news and editorials" to Africa every day; publication of the magazine *Topic;* an accelerated program to make motion pictures, television, and radio material available for the African audience; and strenuous efforts at public opinion gathering and poll taking. By 1964, USIA's budget for its African programs had doubled since 1960.[23]

The U.S. propaganda effort relied heavily on printed material to get its messages about American race problems across to an international audience. This ranged from news releases to information packets for U.S. missions to much larger and slicker publications. USIA continued to send special news stories to U.S. missions around the world, all spreading the news about racial progress in America. A typical example was a 1962 feature, "Tuskegee Institute: A Successful Experiment in Self-Help." Detailing the history and growth of the educational institution, the feature concluded that, "The saga of Tuskegee's growth from a one-room building with just 30 students to a 25 million dollar college with 2,300 students is an outstanding example of the social progress of the American Negro in the past three-quarters of a century." And when some of the landmark civil rights legislation was being enacted in the United States, USIA was quick to send out a packet of materials entitled, "The Great Society—New Goals for the USA." This included the document, "More Than Equality," which informed its readers that "in the 1960's Negro Americans know that the Great Society means them, too." The civil rights legislation was "an indication of how rapid have been the transformations in race relations in the United States in recent years." Equal opportunity was "now considered too small a goal for American society. The struggle against official discrimination can already be counted as won."[24]

Supplementing these efforts were larger and more technically sophisticated pieces. One example is the 1961 publication, "The Negro American: A Progress Report." Written by an African-American scholar, historian John Reuben Sheeler, the thirty-two-page booklet began with an effort to draw a "dispassionate account of the present-day status of Negro Americans."

> What America has given—both good and bad—to its nearly 19,000,000 Negro citizens can be viewed from different perspectives. There are those, for example, who want only to disseminate propagandist distortions of racial oppression. Thus, to people who have no better information, lurid descriptions of mob violence and slums may become the 'true' picture of the average American Negro's lot. Others, in answer to such distortions, are tempted to point to the prestige of Nobel Peace Prize winner Ralph Bunche or to great artists like the singer, Marian Anderson. The fact is that the truth lies in neither extreme.

Despite this rather promising beginning, the document quickly got to its main theme: "The long record of advances made by the Negro American in past years points to the fact that he is well on his way toward taking his proper place in America." After a few short pages detailing the history of slavery, Reconstruction, and the early twentieth century, most of the publication focused in on the 1950s and the tremendous progress African-Americans had made in the areas of economics, politics, society, the arts, education, and the military. Photographs portrayed biracial scenes at work, in social gatherings, at school.[25]

Three years later, USIA turned out "America's New Civil Rights Act," which celebrated the signing of the 1964 Civil Rights Act. This action indicated that "unlike totalitarian governments, the United States recognizes the denial of rights—because of race, color, religion, or national origin—as an aberration contrary to national policy." Again, pictures of racial harmony (including one in which "a Negro psychiatrist treats an emotionally disturbed white youngster") were prominently featured. The act was a "great step forward," and represented "the most comprehensive plan for the implementation of constitutional guarantees for members of minority groups ever adopted in the United States, or indeed in any nation."[26]

In addition to the sheer size of the written propaganda effort undertaken during the 1960s, USIA output was also characterized by more reliance on the use of more modern mediums. One sign of this was USIA's greater reliance on film. The use of this medium ranged from simple filmstrips to the production of Academy Award–winning documentaries. "Toward Equal Opportunity," was part of USIA's effort to "resume its filmstrip program, which had been discontinued in 1954 on economy grounds." In 1962 it was shown at a number of U.S. posts in Africa, to groups ranging from a handful to a few hundred viewers. The response was overwhelmingly favorable: "Filmstrips seem more flexible and adaptable for various levels of intellectual audiences from young students to and including top ministerial officials." More sophisticated efforts included the 1964 documentary film, "Nine From Little Rock," which won an Oscar; and "The March," also produced in 1964, which focused on the great civil rights march of the year before. Carl Rowan, in informing President Johnson about USIA's Academy Award–winning effort, explained that the film focused on the nine African-American students who broke the color barrier at Central High School in Little Rock in 1954, particularly "their progress to education at the college level, and the progress of Little Rock itself." The film had been sent to nearly one hundred nations, and translated into seventeen languages. The reception in Africa was particularly encouraging. "The March" zeroed in on the 1963 civil rights march on Washington, particularly Martin Luther King's famous speech. As noted by Edward Murrow, it was a response to distorted reports about violence and the civil rights movement: "I commissioned this film to counter that distortion."[27]

Greater technical expertise did not necessarily translate into a more sophisticated message. According to Richard MacCann, who has written a study of films produced by the U.S. government, both "Nine From Little Rock" and "The March" have to be watched with a critical eye. The former film did indeed show the African-American students' "faces ... full of courage," but "the narration made clear the step upward they had achieved—most of them had moved away from Arkansas." "The March" failed to show "Southern repression in all its harshness, the Northern ghetto with its cold segregation."[28]

It was an impressive outpouring of propaganda, but the evidence suggests that with the passage of the 1964–1965 civil rights legislation the United States steadily lost interest in dealing with civil rights and race as an international issue. As USIA Director Carl Rowan explained in mid-1964, even before much of the landmark legislation was passed, "The impact of racial happenings in the U.S. over the past year has been negative. However, now as before, generally adverse reactions to U.S. race relations are outweighed by other impressions of America which in the net produce a highly favorable overall opinion."[29]

After the 1964–1965 acts had been passed, U.S. officials went even farther, arguing that these successes meant that less time and energy needed to be devoted to propaganda on the issues of civil rights and race. A meeting of U.S. chiefs of mission in Africa addressed those issues, stating that, "The civil rights movement in the United States has attracted continuing attention in Africa. The strength and widespread criticism of us on this issue has waned in recent months as a result of the measures we have taken to resolve this problem. The group felt that because of this the intensity of VOA civil rights information broadcasts could be relaxed." Rick Haynes was more direct: "the Voice of America devotes too much of its African-oriented broadcasting time to race relations in the U.S."[30]

Perhaps in response to those suggestions and criticisms, a USIA report of several months later came to several definite conclusions. It began by echoing Rowan's assessment that, while world opinion about America's race problem was "unfavorable," it was "more conspicuous as a blot on our image, and galling to our self-esteem, than as a problem for our influence. *Awareness of and disapproval of treatment of the Negro seem to have comparatively little effect on general opinion of the US.*" That being the case, the report asked, "*Does the racial issue as a propaganda problem preoccupy us more than the facts warrant?* The answer seems to be, probably *Yes*." Race, as a propaganda issue, had always been "frustrating." If the propaganda were to "face up to problems 'fully and frankly,' " then it was seen as a "test of our candor." Yet, it could also be argued that stressing the issue meant that the United States was seeking to "put our worst foot forward, that we confused a kind of crusading masochism with freedom from hypocrisy, or that we were unfairly presenting a section of the US." Overseas opinion had changed during the last two years, with more favorable viewpoints concerning U.S. civil rights being expressed. The real challenge now was to shape the world's opinions as to *how* the changes had taken place.

Just as U.S. officials had expressed dismay over the possibility of a separate "black foreign policy," the USIA report made it clear that the civil rights legislation should not be seen as merely the result of pressure by the "Civil Rights movement and Negro leadership." To do so would "suggest that what has occurred or is occurring in the US is a successful War of People's Liberation. Emphasis should be on change, evolution, *not* dramatic revolution in our conscience, folkways, or political life." U.S. propaganda in the future should, therefore, lay "stress on the evolution of Negro progress in the context and framework of normal American life, rather than within the civil rights movement. The Negro needs to be perceived within a pattern of acceptance, rather than as conducting a separate social movement." In conclusion,

> we should avoid devoting massive sections of programming to the issue, and responding dramatically to drama. The unofficial media will carry all the drama and violence; we can obliquely acknowledge, but keep our emphasis on the response of the white community, not the fate of the Negro. We should avoid, in short, the black-and-white treatment, prefer[ring] the low key, mulatto, as it were coverage. And we should not dwell on the past; it probably serves better to remind of an unfavorable situation than to point up a more favorable one.[31]

Lawrence Rogers, who traveled to Africa in early 1967 to inspect USIA operations there, also felt that U.S. propaganda was focusing too heavily on the civil rights issue. He concluded that, "Heavy emphasis in USIA materials on the Negro-American and the 'civil rights struggle' is likewise a quixotic notion. These nations are virtually all military dictatorships in which civil rights are non-existent. . . . One can hardly blame an African for failing to comprehend such esoteric concepts as full enjoyment of civil rights or antidiscrimination." In his opinion, "Capitalism, communism; east, west; black, white; civil rights; poverty . . . these are abstract concepts totally lost on almost all Africans who just want to know . . . 'How do you get to be like an American'?" Therefore, "Preoccupation of USIA with the civil rights struggle in the United States is more damaging than helpful to our cause."[32]

Even when a dramatic event, such as the assassination of Martin Luther King Jr., occurred, USIA stuck to its assessment that the civil rights issue was now of little concern. Noting that world opinion consistently ranked the United States lower on the race issue than on any other, a report from April 1968 concluded, "These differences suggest that West Europeans tend to a considerable degree to see the race problem as a wart, so to speak, on the face of America rather than the image as a whole. There is thus grounds for believing that such a distinction will continue to be made and that the race problem with all its current very negative aspects will be perceived in correct perspective as only a partial element in the American image."[33]

Progress toward a more racially representative diplomatic corps during the Kennedy and Johnson years was similar to the efforts in the propaganda field: a great deal of action, but signifying little if any change. There was an initial surge of interest and activity, with new programs and various committees assigned to investigate the problem. By 1969, however, the racial make-up of the Department of State and Foreign Service looked little different from that left over from the Eisenhower administration.

The Department of State and Foreign Service inherited by the Democrats in 1961, it was painfully obvious, still suffered from severe problems of racial discrimination. The numbers did not lie. A June 1961 State Department report noted that there were only seventeen black FSOs and three black FSRs out of a total of 4,872; there were just fifty-eight black FSSs out of a total of 3,527—and all of those were in the five lowest ranks. Of the 12,680 employees of the Department of State, less than a thousand were African-Americans. Blacks accounted for just five of the 3,132 highest ranking employees.[34]

Early indications were that the new Democratic administration was going to take direct and forceful action to remedy the situation. Even before taking office, the Kennedy team was studying the problem and making recommendations for bringing more African-Americans into the diplomatic service. In September 1960, W. Averell Harriman offered the suggestion that, "Speaking to Negroes the Senator might refer to the difficulties placed in the way of Negroes in entering the foreign service and the important role American Negroes can play in representing our country in Africa." In December, former ambassador Edward Dudley, who was a member of Kennedy's Task Force on Sub-Saharan Africa, opined that "qualified Negroes" should be targeted for posts in Africa, but should also be "considered for other posts." Later that month, the Task Force on State Department Field Operations agreed that the "President should instruct the Department of State to adopt a vigorous program which would increase the rate of recruitment of Negroes into the Foreign Service." The Task Force on Africa, however, argued that blacks "should be recruited for general service abroad, not specifically for Africa. . . . No Negro should ever be assigned to Africa just because of his color."[35]

As William Crockett, who served as assistant secretary and then deputy under secretary for administration during the 1960s, explains, "the pressure for increasing minority representation in the Foreign Service came from the White House. It demanded that we have more black Ambassadors and more black Foreign Service officers. It started when Kennedy was president, but Lyndon Johnson certainly stressed it." Roger Jones, who was tapped to be the new deputy under secretary for administration, discovered that fact when he had a January 1961 meeting with Dean Rusk, who informed him that one of the "problems which the president requests be got into focus at once" was "the number of Negroes in the Foreign Service, the reasons why more Negroes have not applied and qualified, and possible means of increasing Negro input." Kennedy expressed that interest directly to his new under secretary of state, Chester Bowles: "As you know I have been deeply concerned at the small number of Negroes and members of other minority groups employed in the foreign service and throughout the foreign affairs operations of the government."[36]

Interest in increasing the numbers of African-Americans in the U.S. foreign policy bureaucracy was shared by many on the Kennedy team. Following his 1961 trip to Africa and Europe, Vice President Lyndon Johnson concluded that "we should make an effort to bring Negro talent into the foreign service and end the 'Jim Crow' consular service situation." G. Mennen Williams, who had been picked as the new assistant secretary for African affairs, was a consistent advocate for greater integration of the U.S. diplomatic corps. In his "Strengthened African Program" proposal of 1965, he claimed that one of the greatest weaknesses of the United States was its inability to provide "convincing evidence" to the African nations of its commitment to racial equality. "One credible and effective way to present this evidence," he argued, "and at the same time benefit both the United States and Africa would be to strengthen our efforts to recruit and retain qualified Negro Americans for assignment abroad."[37]

The most immediate reaction to this pressure was the August 1961 Conference on Equal Employment Opportunity held by the Department of State. In his letter of invitation, Secretary Rusk explained that his department "feels keenly the need for a Foreign Service Corps that is representative of the people of the United States," and asked the recipient to help "strengthen the efforts of the Department of State in this matter." The black leaders who attended heard Secretary Rusk greet them with the admission that "the United States ought to be represented by people who reflect our total population, and that is not yet the case to the extent that we would like it to be." This was followed by reports from Department officials such as Roger Jones, Carl Rowan, and Herman Pollack, as well as debates and comments from the African-Americans in attendance. The meeting ended with the establishment of the nine recommendations noted in the previous chapter.[38]

As a report from Chester Bowles two months after the conference suggested, the Department was making slow progress in meeting the recommendations. In terms of informing African-Americans that they were wanted by the Foreign Service, the only thing that had occurred was that conference attendees were being asked to provide the names of qualified African-American candidates. The proposal for the appointment of a black to a "high level policy position" was "under consideration." As soon as "suitable assignments occur for which we have qualified Negroes, the Department will not hesitate to make such appointments." The lack of African-American FSOs made it nearly impossible to meet the recommendation for black recruiters at more college campuses, though more visits were planned to black colleges. Three African-Americans had been made FSRs at the middle grades. The surveys of civil service employees and blacks in USIA, AID, and ICA were "underway," with no discernible results so far. Noted psychologist Kenneth Clark was currently studying the Foreign Service examination. Two African-American students were among the twenty summer interns for the next year.[39]

By early 1964, when the follow-up conference to the 1961 meeting was being planned, the picture seemed somewhat brighter. The "campaign" had expanded to include articles about the Foreign Service in magazines such as *Ebony* and *Jet*. Black FSOs had given over a dozen talks to different groups around the country. As for "high level policy positions," progress remained slow. Two blacks were currently serving as U.S. ambassadors; Rowan had been made director of USIA; and two African-Americans had accepted positions as deputy assistant secretaries. The small number of black FSOs was still crimping efforts to use more African-American recruiters, but other programs were going forward. One of these was the revision of the "Foreign Service career booklets": "they were given an integrated look for the first time. Pictures of Negro personnel in various work and social situations typical of the Department and of the Foreign Service were used to illustrate all three booklets." Twenty-five blacks had been brought aboard as FSRs, and the percentage of African-Americans at the lower levels of the civil service employees had been reduced by 15 percent. The question of lateral transfers from USIA and other agencies had "not been pursued vigorously." The rationale was that this would "not result in any net gain of Negroes to the foreign affairs complex." Nothing much had happened in regard to studies of the Foreign Service examination, but blacks were now serving on the oral examination panels and promotion boards. Black colleges had worked with the Department to develop new curricula, and African-American students had been in every group of summer interns since 1961.[40]

The most widely celebrated program, however, was the Foreign Affairs Scholars Program (FASP), instituted in 1963. The program was primarily the result of efforts by Herman Pollack, his Special Assistant Richard K. Fox (who went on to become director of the Department's Office of Equal Employment Opportunity), and Kenneth Clark. In 1963, they had written a proposal, which was eventually funded by the Ford Foundation to the tune of $600,000, for a plan to improve the skills of African-American college students in order that they might become suitable candidates for foreign policy work. At the end of their junior year in college, forty minority college students would be selected as participants in the summer intern program at the Department of State, USIA, or AID. These internships would include Saturday seminars conducted by representatives from all three agencies. Upon returning to their educational institutions for their senior years, the forty students would be required to take the Foreign Service examination. (They were under no obligation to join the Service if they passed.) As a further encouragement, twenty-five of the students would receive one-year fellowships to do graduate work in some area of the study of foreign affairs. By March 1967, over one hundred students had gone through the program. Three were already working for State or AID, and eight more were expected to take positions with one of those two agencies or USIA. Forty-four others had passed the Foreign Service written or entrance exams. In all, over sixty participants in the program would be qualified for appointment to State, AID, or USIA by June 1968.[41]

Yet, despite all of this activity, by the time the Johnson presidency was drawing to a close it was clear that the progress made toward better integrating the U.S. diplomatic corps simply did not correspond to the effort. By 1967, the overall results of over six years of initiatives to increase the number of African-Americans in the Department of State and Foreign Service were detailed in a study was prepared by Eddie Williams, who had replaced Richard Fox as director of the Office of Equal Employment Opportunity. Its opening observations set the tone for the report: "In terms of employing more Negroes in the Foreign Service, little has been accomplished, and under present circumstances the prospects for future achievements are quite bleak. . . . Six years and over a million dollars of Department of State and private Foundation money have been invested in this effort, but the resultant Negro employment picture is not strikingly different from what it was in 1961." The statistics bore out these gloomy appraisals. There had been a net increase of just two African-American FSOs since 1961. The written examination was a big problem. No African-American had entered the Foreign Service through the examination process since 1963. While an average of 25 percent of all persons taking the test since 1961 had passed, less than 4 percent of African-American candidates had passed. None had been a graduate of a predominantly black college, where 80 percent of all black graduates came from.

FASP, which had been designed to address this problem, had been disappointing. Less than one hundred participants had even taken the Foreign Service exam, and only fourteen had passed. As the study concluded, "It is clear . . . that the FASP did nothing to remedy the educational deficiencies of many Negro college students." The Ford Foundation was not renewing the program, having decided that it was "a good try, but it was very expensive indeed in the light of the limited results that were achieved." The irony in all of this was that the "Department does not know . . . whether this inability to pass the FSO examination also reflects an inability to perform the work of an FSO."

As for other efforts to increase the number of African-Americans in the Foreign Service, these, too, had been failures. Since 1961, only three blacks had been brought in the Service through lateral transfer. Having African-Americans brought aboard as FSRs had been a good idea, but by 1967, there were less than sixty black FSRs out of a total of nearly 1,900. Most of these had been recruited by Williams's own office.[42]

The reasons for this rather miserable record were not hard to discern. Overall, it was clear that many of the perceptions and biases that had stymied earlier efforts to integrate the Department of State and Foreign Service continued to exert a powerful influence during the 1960s. One of these problems left over from earlier years was that, despite the more sympathetic rhetoric of the Kennedy and Johnson administrations concerning black appointments to the diplomatic service, troubling suggestions of tokenism hung over many of the discussions and decisions concerning those appointments. When W. Averell Harriman suggested in 1960 that Senator Kennedy should address the issue of blacks in the Foreign Service, he went on to make it clear that he saw the issue as primarily a symbolic one: "I believe we should appoint some Negroes as ambassadors but only a few. At least a quarter of our personnel in our African missions should be Negro. Also, I would like to see the Senator suggest at an appropriate time and place, that he would appoint a Negro as ambassador not just to Africa but to a European country."[43]

Efforts to bring more African-Americans into the diplomatic service almost always carried with them the stigma that these were "special" appointments, done more for show than any real policy reasons. Kennedy special assistant Frederick Dutton argued in early 1961 that the president should "also obtain immediate *tangible (at least show-case) results in specific areas* like the Foreign Service" in order to demonstrate his commitment to civil rights. John Clinton, who served as a White House staff assistant dealing with recruitment, sent a memorandum to Kennedy aide Ralph Dungan in 1963 discussing his "special recruiting effort." As of yet, he noted, he and his associates had not "focused our attention on State although we are aware of and are assisting efforts to place one or two Negro economists in Grif Johnson's and/or Ed Martin's area." He was also busy "recruiting for a Negro staff man for Bundy" (the NSC). And, as during the Truman and Eisenhower years, there was the usual report about the token black for service on the UN delegation. An aide for Harlan Cleveland (who served as assistant secretary for international organization affairs) informed Secretary Rusk in 1961 that "Ambassador Stevenson's choice for the negro representation is Reverend James Robinson of New York who would be able to entertain African delegates at his home."[44]

An examination of three instances where an African-American appointment was discussed during the Kennedy period reveals the problem. In mid-1963, Edward Dudley was being mentioned as U.S. ambassador to Nigeria. A summary of the reasons for his appointment naturally focused on his previous success in Liberia, his skills as an administrator, and his knowledge of Africa. Yet, rather than end there, the report went on to note that, "The appointment of a distinguished American Negro with proven executive capacity and African experience to our most important African mission would be testament to American ideals and beneficial to American foreign policy." A few months later, Dudley having dropped out of consideration because of "political needs in New York," attention now turned to John H. Wheeler, an African-American from North Carolina. As a State Department memo observed, the department had been "attempting to find a Negro non-career candidate to be Ambassador to Nigeria." Unfortunately, Wheeler was now bowing out of the running. This decision "leaves us without an outstanding Negro candidate and the job will go by default to someone else, a non-Negro. This is not good." A black appointee would "be proof positive of the Administration's faith in civil rights." The memo suggested that the White House put friendly pressure on Wheeler to reconsider: "Top Negro talent is scarce. Does not that which exists have an obligation to their country as well as to their race?" (None of the pleading seemed to work—the position went to Elbert Mathews, a white.) Finally, near the end of the Kennedy presidency, discussions were raised about the possibility of an African-American for third deputy assistant secretary for African affairs. As a Department report indicated, "a Negro is sought." The "justifications" centered on the "extraordinary imbalance of Negro officers presently serving in the Foreign Service and the need of this Administration by deed to affirm its commitment to equal opportunity for all." The requirements began with the "prerequisite quality of being a Negro." The biggest problem was that the "class of Negroes who might qualify for this position is small."[45]

The taint of tokenism continued into the Johnson years. In January 1965, a list of African-American candidates for ambassadorial positions was circulated in the White House. As John Macy, who handled many of the personnel matters during the Johnson years, argued, "there is a strong desire to include a Negro among the first batch of new ambassadorial appointments." When it was time to consider a new ambassador for Afghanistan in 1966, seven non-career men were considered. Three categories for evaluation were listed: "Age," "NEA Experience," and "Negro." Only Jerome Holland fit the last category. Elliott Skinner, who was eventually made U.S. ambassador to Upper Volta in 1966, had been judged "a good candidate for a non-career, Negro ambassadorial appointment" by a panel of reviewers. And when it came time to pick an alternate representative to the UN, John Macy duly forwarded a list of "Negro candidates."[46]

In short, what the evidence suggests is that neither the Kennedy nor the

Johnson administration was able to completely divorce itself from the idea that a few high visibility selections of African-Americans would solve the basic problem facing the Department of State and the Foreign Service. The belief that one or two such appointments would give credence to the two administrations' rhetoric about equal rights is not, however, altogether surprising. The desire for political "quick-fixes" for sticky and delicate problems was not created during the 1960s, nor would it disappear in the years to follow.

Harder to understand was the tenaciousness of the argument, used throughout the 1940s and 1950s, that African-Americans were either (1) unwelcome as U.S. diplomatic representatives in certain parts of the world; or (2) suited only for service in black nations. African-Americans who had served overseas had fought these perceptions for years but had not been completely successful. In 1964, for instance, White House Special Assistant Jack Valenti informed President Johnson that *Jet* had just run an article suggesting that an African-American candidate for the ambassadorship to the Netherlands, Theodore Berry, had been rejected by that nation because he was black. Valenti was immediately directed to contact McGeorge Bundy to find out more about the situation. What came of this contact is not certain from the files, but one thing does seem clear: the suggestion that Berry would not be accepted by the Netherlands came not from that country but from Secretary Rusk. Just a few weeks before Valenti's memo to the president, Rusk had himself written to Johnson concerning the appointment of Berry to the Netherlands. He was "firmly convinced that it would be a mistake for the United States to appoint a Negro as Ambassador to The Netherlands." During his recent visit to that country he had noted that the "two Negro Ambassadors in The Hague (both from African countries) . . . are almost completely excluded from all but the most formal and ceremonial occasions." Rusk suggested that Berry be sent to work on Adlai Stevenson's staff at the UN.[47]

Ironically, however, by the 1960s another argument was gaining greater currency: that African-American diplomats were also not wanted by African countries. It did seem rather odd that just at the moment that dozens of opportunities for ambassadorships were opening up in Africa this argument should gain steam, but not entirely surprising. When there had been only a handful of African posts, Department officials had been more than happy to conclude that, due to the racism of other foreign countries, African-American diplomats could only be appointed to that continent. Now, with new posts in Africa (and, assumedly, dozens of veteran white diplomats looking for ambassadorial opportunities and any number of white political allies looking for a "thank-you for your support" in the form of an overseas appointment), the tune had changed. William Attwood, who had replaced

John Morrow in Guinea, was quite blunt in describing the situation in his book, *The Reds and the Blacks*. One of the advantages he had in Guinea, he reported, was that he did not "have the handicap of being a Negro, like my predecessor." Attwood had "discovered something which is still not fully appreciated in Washington—that Africans are generally suspicious of Negro American diplomats," because they believe that "Negroes are second-class citizens in the United States, and that Washington is being deviously patronizing, and clearly race-conscious, in sending them more or less dark-skinned ambassadors." Attwood conceded that, "We did have a Negro Public Affairs Officer—which was all right."[48]

Attwood's feelings were shared by others. An assistant informed John Macy that there was trouble with the appointment of an African-American candidate, Franklin H. Williams, as ambassador to Ghana. When news of the proposed appointment had reached the U.S. mission in Ghana, it had cabled back that it was "under the impression that the Government of Ghana had informed the Department that they did not desire a Negro representative." Though the Department had indicated that it had no official notification of this kind, "someone did recall an offhand remark by the Ambassador from Ghana to this effect." In the end, Williams got the post. That others might not have been so lucky is suggested by a letter from Ramsey Clark in the Justice Department discussing African-Americans who might be considered for ambassadorships: "The State Department would have to give careful consideration to the appointment of a Negro to a sub-Sahara nation. There are problems. Apparently appointments of Negroes to White nations involves fewer problems."[49]

This rather astounding turn of events caught even African-Americans by surprise. It also raised a serious question. For years, blacks had been arguing that African-American diplomats should not be confined to Africa. The results were minimal, at best. Yet, with the independence movements in Africa becoming more and more successful, a growing number of opportunities for American diplomats were opening up on that continent. For some African-Americans, it now seemed logical (and, given their virtual exclusion from other geographical areas, practical) to reverse the old arguments, and stress that blacks *should* be sent to African posts. In taking such a stand, however, they were opening themselves up to criticisms that they were supporting the old policy of de facto segregation of black diplomats to Africa. This quandary among African-Americans was captured best in a "debate" between Richard Fox and Rick Haynes of the State Department in late 1964. Fox, who was serving as special assistant to William Crockett, began the exchange by examining the assignment policy concerning African-American diplomats. The Department's official policy was that blacks were assigned to posts based on exactly the same criteria as any other diplomats. While Fox agreed in principle, he also felt that there was a "definite advantage in assigning more Negro officers to African posts." His position was based on his belief that "Negro Americans are likely to develop more effective and intimate relations with Africans"; that the "very fact of being a Negro makes for an entree and ease of communication which is attained only with greater difficulty by most white Americans"; and that "Negro Americans present the American position on the racial issue more effectively and convincingly." Of course, one disadvantage was that "Africans have the impression that the assignment of a Negro is contrived." He was quick to caution the reader that his plan was not "to overload any one area," and that, "Priority should be given to assigning Negro officers to posts in Western Europe and other areas where their appearance would be of definite advantage and where few have ever served." Immediately, however, he returned to his original point: "A conscious effort should be made to assign more Negro officers to African posts in political and economic jobs."

Haynes, who was then working in African Affairs, was quick to respond. In his opinion, Fox was arguing for "two mutually exclusive conclusions": that blacks should be assigned all around the world, and that blacks should be "concentrated in Africa *because of their race.*" His own discussions with black desk officers in African Affairs had convinced him that "the Negro FSO is *not* specially endowed by virtue of his race for service in Africa." Black FSOs should certainly not be given "major responsibility for explaining the USG position on the racial issue. . . . Whether or not the appellation is deserved, he would be labelled a 'stooge' or 'apologist.' " Fox's suggestion, Haynes argued, would simply intensify an already bad situation: "Because of the obvious concentration of Negroes in African Affairs at State, USIS, and AID, Africans *are* beginning to express bewilderment, suspicion, and even indignation, not against the Negro officer, but rather against the USG over the motives behind such a concentration." Haynes realized that, "Other Bureaus, particularly EUR (European Affairs), have not shown anything approaching the same measure of success" in employing African-Americans as had African Affairs. However, if the racial imbalance was ever to be solved, the "other regional Bureaus" would have to take primary responsibility.[50] Thus, even for African-Americans in the Department of State, questions of hiring and assignment were becoming more complicated. Both Fox and Haynes had the same goal in mind: greater integration of blacks into the Department and Foreign Service. Given that arguments were being floated that black diplomats were unwelcome in both Africa and elsewhere, it was not surprising that each man came to a different conclusion about how to accomplish that goal.

Despite the staying power of these old perceptions, it seems clear that the biggest impediment to further integration of the Department of State was the outlook of many officials in that bureaucracy. Simply put, most officials in the Department demonstrated little if any interest in reforms of their personnel selection system, especially if those reforms seemed to threaten their nearly sacred tradition of "professionalism." Without that support, initiatives from the White House, no matter how well intentioned, were almost always doomed to failure.

The lack of interest among State Department officials was in evidence in many shapes and forms. For those few, like William Crockett and Herman Pollack, who were committed to the notion of better integrating the Department, the problem started with Secretary Rusk. Rusk was well known for his relatively liberal views on civil rights, perhaps most dramatically in evidence during his July 1963 appearance before the Senate Committee on Commerce when he testified in support of an administration bill dealing with public accommodations. After his opening statement, Rusk was grilled by Senator Strom Thurmond, who tried to bait the secretary into some sort of tacit approval of violent demonstrations concerning race. Rusk took Thurmond on, stating that, "I would say this, Sir, if I were denied what our Negro citizens are denied, I would demonstrate." Yet, when it came time to apply his views to the personnel situation in his own department, his words spoke louder than his actions. William Crockett recalled that Rusk was merely "passively supportive of our efforts" to bring more blacks into the Foreign Service. The secretary "made his perfunctory appearance before each appropriation committee, but never took any initiative to support anything we tried. 'Full' support is not a phrase I would apply to either the Secretary of (sic) Undersecretary. The White House was much more supportive and in many cases, full hearted." Herman Pollack agreed with Crockett's assessment of Rusk's role in programs designed to increase the African-American presence in the Department, noting that "I have trouble recollecting that he [Rusk] had very much to do with it, except to let it proceed." Lee White, a Kennedy aide who specialized in civil rights issues, sent a memo to the president in 1962 criticizing State's slow movement in hiring more blacks. "Secretary Rusk," he admitted, "is not opposed to any increase in emphasis in this field; however, he does not give to it the same vigorous attention that a program of this type requires in order to break through existing recruitment and promotional patterns." More pressure would be exerted on Rusk to do better, and the situation could show improvement if "Secretary Rusk can be induced to give at least a little personal attention to the problem."[51]

Undoubtedly, a primary factor for Rusk's lack of initiative on this issue was his dedication to the "professionalism" of the Department and Foreign Service. As he proclaimed in his autobiography, "My constituency was the Foreign Service." Having inherited a Department of State that had had its morale badly shaken during the 1950s by McCarthyism and budget cuts, Rusk was determined to restore confidence. When President Kennedy indicated a desire to "shake up" the diplomatic corps by bringing in "outsiders" to fill important foreign policy positions, Rusk fought back: "I felt that career officers had a leg up on another (sic) candidates and battled hard for them. Only when needing special talent was I inclined to reach outside the Foreign Service." One clear example of Rusk's efforts may be seen in the percentage of ambassadors who were career officers. Under Eisenhower, only 64 percent of U.S. ambassadors were career FSOs; during the Kennedy and Johnson years, that figure rose to nearly 75 percent.[52]

Rusk's emphasis on "professionalism" was understandable. The practice of having political cronies and incompetents appointed to diplomatic posts did no one credit. Yet, his position could also be use by some as a blanket defense against "outsiders"—including African-Americans. Any effort to better integrate the Department of State and Foreign Service, therefore, was likely to stir up resentment among some white members of the foreign policy bureaucracy who felt that "special treatment" was being meted out to African-American recruits and employees. Katie Louchheim, who served as deputy assistant secretary of state for educational and cultural affairs from 1966 to 1969, recalled in a 1969 interview her frustration when Barbara Watson, a black woman, was made assistant secretary for security and consular affairs the year before. As Louchheim put it, "I could also say to you, if I wanted to be caustic or bitter, that my name came up at a time when they were very much interested in blacks." When her interviewer laughed and exclaimed, "You were discriminated against the other way!" she responded, "I think if my face had been black, my chances would have been better." Henry S. Villard, a veteran of decades of service in the Department of State (who, in the 1940s, had supported the idea of rotating blacks out of Liberia—if suitable African-American replacements could be found), expressed the resentments of many of his colleagues in his book, *Affairs at State,* published in 1965. Secretary Rusk's stated desire to make the Foreign Service representative of "America as it is" seemed odd to Villard: "The fact is that the Foreign Service no longer prides itself on being an elite corps; it seems to pride itself on *not* being elite." Rusk's goal "could mean a motley crew indeed, composed of individuals from every walk of life." Efforts such as FASP, were "specifically designed, it would seem, to meet minority pressures." Villard concluded that "if Negroes have not hitherto had the qualifications, they must either be assisted in acquiring them, or the entrance hurdles must be lowered a few more notches."[53]

Deputy Director of the Office of Employment Opportunity Idris Rossell criticized these kinds of feelings among Department colleagues in a 1969 article in the *Foreign Service Journal*. She began the piece by recounting a conversation she had with a retired FSO. He had said, "Do you really think we need any more of this? I read the last NEWSLETTER and they had a full page of pictures showing the new junior officer class. It looked to me like half of them were minority." This kind of response, together with, "Corridor conversations and cryptic comments such as, 'You have to be a Negro these days to get hired,' also confirm that employees in general, and Foreign Service officers in particular, know next to nothing about the difficulties of recruiting and hiring Negroes and other minorities for officer level positions in the Foreign Service."[54]

Making the process even more difficult—and serving as another example of the Department hierarchy's lack of interest in any sustained effort at better integrating the diplomatic corps—was the fact that most Department officials who *did* show an interest in the matter did not last long at their jobs. Bowles lasted less than a year as under secretary of state before being removed. His replacement, George Ball, never took much interest in civil rights matters. Three men—Roger Jones, William Orrick, and William Crockett—served as deputy under secretary for administration, primarily responsible for instituting any changes dealing with personnel. Herman Pollack, who had been one of the moving forces behind FASP, was assigned to the War College in 1963. Kenneth Clark, commenting on this constant reshuffling, indicated in a 1963 letter that he was "terribly upset" about the departure of Pollack. Where this all left matters concerning equal opportunity employment in State was "confused, unclear, and in transition."[55]

All of this contributed to tremendous frustration, both from officials in the White House and from African-American diplomats already in the Department of State. Frederick Dutton, responding to a Department memorandum on the issue of minority employment, fumed that, "My personal reaction to the latest reply is that personnel officials in the State Department hope to outtalk us on this matter." When he finally did receive a more detailed response a short time later, Dutton's anger flared: "I particularly think that the State Department report is completely inadequate and suggest that a more specific and complete reply be prepared there. This is a concrete example of the disregard at the intermediate levels there on major projects."[56]

For the African-Americans who served in the Department and Foreign Service during the 1960s, all of these problems were painfully apparent. This was especially so for the newcomers—the "outsiders" brought in by Kennedy and Johnson; but veterans were certainly not immune. Mercer Cook, who was appointed as U.S. ambassador to Niger in 1961 and later went on to serve in Senegal (1964) and Gambia (1965), ran into the old argument about African-American ambassadors not being wanted by Africans. Just a few weeks after his appointment to Niger, an article in *U.S. News & World Report* had repeated the argument, claiming that "new Negro states of Africa are not at all enthusiastic about having Negroes assigned to serve in those countries. It is pointed out that Negroes from the U.S., if to serve in Africa, must be 'well adjusted' since they may not readily be 'accepted.' " Cook was stunned by the logic: "There was no mention of the obvious fact that any appointee—white or black—serving anywhere in the world, needs to be 'well adjusted.' " However, he was "not surprised that certain career officers should be reluctant to see the Foreign Service lose some of its country club exclusiveness." When a "New Frontier appointee" wondered whether Africans would "welcome Negro diplomats," Cook's response was that "would depend on the African and the Negro—*and* the kind of support the diplomat received from back home." As Cook soon discovered, "Support was my problem, not acceptance." Niger's ambassador to the United States had contacted Cook after his appointment and expressed "his delight that a Negro had been chosen to represent the U.S. in his country." Support from his own country, however, was slower to develop, since Niger was "a poor country with no resources likely to attract private American investment and no Communist presence to stimulate AID." It was frustrations such as these that led to his resignation as ambassador to Senegal and Gambia in 1965. In a letter to President Johnson, Cook complained that a letter from Senegal's president, Léopold Sédar Senghor, to Johnson had been forwarded to the Department months before. To Cook's "amazement, that friendly communication was prevented from reaching its destination." He was also dismayed that his efforts to secure an aid package for Senegal had been "as unsuccessful as my attempt to transmit a letter from one President to another." He blamed this failure for Senegal's decision to accept a multimillion-dollar credit from the Soviet Union. Based on all of this, Cook had decided that it was time to "return to teaching." He wanted Johnson to know, however, that in the "unlikely event that you ever see this letter," he was grateful for the opportunity to serve America.[57]

Franklin H. Williams was appointed as U.S. ambassador to Ghana in 1965; by mid-1967 he had resigned his position. Williams had come to the job with an impressive resumé: he had held positions off and on in the UN since 1961 and had been appointed the director of the African Regional Office of the Peace Corps in 1963. Despite his own appointment to Ghana in 1965, he consistently expressed the "frustrations some of us have had in recent years" in trying to "get the State Department more broadly representative of America." In 1966, he urged Lincoln University to grant William

Crockett an honorary degree, largely in recognition of the fact that he had "contributed to the little bit of integration that the Department has achieved. Frankly, without him it would be safe to say there would have been almost none." Williams's own unsuccessful efforts to gain lateral transfer into the Foreign Service eventually prompted him to resign his ambassadorship in 1967. In a letter to President Johnson's special assistant Bill Moyers, Williams indicated that he had applied for transfer but "my conversations with the head of the Foreign Service gave me little hope for success. The inbreeding is tremendous!" During their conversation, the director had commented that, "Mr. Ambassador, some of us have had to climb the ladder rung by rung while others come in at the top. This is hardly fair." Williams's response was that, "When some of you stepped onto the first rung of the ladder, men like myself were not admitted into the State Department." He was forced to conclude that "all of Kennedy's and Johnson's efforts to integrate the career Service have failed." In a letter to Richard Fox, Williams was even more pessimistic: "Frankly, I have grown terribly disillusioned about the Department and have just about concluded that this is finished for me. . . . My conversation with some people in Washington indicates to me that we need look for no improvement in the future."[58]

Elliott Skinner was made U.S. ambassador to Upper Volta in 1966. His correspondence with fellow African-American diplomats reveals incisive attacks on nearly all aspects of U.S. foreign policy dealing with race. In a letter to Hugh Smythe, who was in Washington awaiting reassignment, he offered his assessment as to how America should handle its racial image overseas. Such work should begin with the realization that, *"Americans are race-conscious* and in dealing with foreigners we should not deny it." It did not "make any sense for American whites or Negro Americans serving in foreign posts to pal around together if the object of such behavior is to enhance our country's image." The best approach was to "admit the truth of our problems and indicate the steps being taken to solve them." In addition, "Americans should not respond to our racial image abroad by saying: 'you have your problems too!' " While this was no doubt true, it was a terrible approach since, "The problems for Americans abroad is that *they* are the ones who are striving to sell their social order or win friends and influence people."[59]

Skinner also took a special interest in the appointment of more African-Americans to diplomatic positions. In his letter to Smythe, he argued that one of the best responses to America's racial image overseas was by "using more Negro Americans in all our overseas programs." He had heard the argument that African-American diplomats were not welcome in certain countries, but he believed that it was "often false and is used by whites to protect their own interest." Even if some foreigners believed that "sending

American Negroes as representatives indicates that America does not consider them as first-class people," this implied a "negative image of America," not of African-Americans. He particularly took William Attwood to task. Attwood's comment about Africans disliking African-American diplomats was "gratuitous." Elliott declared that, "I would never claim that the Negro Americans sent overseas are superior to *all* their white counterparts, but I would say that we are damn good. . . . What people must get out of their heads is that a Negro does not have to be twice as good to equal a white person." When Smythe complained about run-ins with the director general of the Foreign Service over the issue of black representation, Skinner tried to put the issue in perspective: "it is difficult to tell anyone over sixty about American race-relations since to them we are living in an 'age of revolution' with respect to the racial problem. How can persons who were born at the height of European and white domination understand that that period is over, gone, done with! You can never convince him that there are black people qualified to do anything but be porters." And he sympathized with Franklin Williams's resignation from his post in Ghana. His absence "thereby reduces the kind of reporting which I believe is unique and more nearly correct." Skinner suggested that Williams indicate in his letter of resignation to President Johnson that "his subordinates exhibit less attachment to his democratic ideals"; Johnson should know that "the Foreign Service is still archaic with respect to American ideals." Writing to Smythe about Williams's resignation, he agreed with the latter's pessimism about whether the Foreign Service "is ready for us." He understood Williams's frustration only too well: "I do not feel that I shall ever be given a challenging post and do not like the job so much that I would accept to remain in countries where our interests are minimal."[60]

Perhaps the most vociferous critic of the State Department among the African-American diplomats was Hugh Smythe. Smythe was a professor of sociology at Brooklyn College in 1965 when he was chosen by the Johnson administration to be the first African-American to serve as ambassador to a nation in the Middle East—Syria. Later, when Syria severed diplomatic relations with the United States, Smythe was reassigned to Malta. His rocky relationship with the Department of State went back to the 1940s, when he had unsuccessfully tried to secure a diplomatic post. He believed at that time that racism had cost him the job. Despite securing the ambassadorships in Syria and Malta, Smythe continued his attack on the hiring and placement policies of the Department. In February of 1968, he sent a long letter to Director General of the Foreign Service John M. Steeves in which he stated that he was "deeply concerned and extremely interested in correcting the unsavory reputation for bigotry in personnel matters for which the Department is so widely and for so long has been known." He then bluntly informed Steeves that "it is the strongly felt consensus among the four Negroes now serving as Ambassadors that so long as you remain the Director General none of us is ever going to be assigned to a really challenging post for which we are well qualified." Smythe suggested that Steeves consult the record: the present black ambassadors were "all in out-of-the-way posts looked upon as insignificant by the Department"; no African-Americans had served as under secretary or deputy under secretary; no black had ever served in "the inner circles in a high level position on the Seventh Floor, in spite of the fact that there are Negroes as qualified or even better prepared than some white officers now occupying or who have occupied such positions." Furthermore, "this racism continues in the Department" despite the strenuous efforts by President Johnson in the area of civil rights.[61]

Like Williams, Smythe was also frustrated by his attempts to gain lateral entry into the Foreign Service. Responding to an optimistic letter from the Department's Equal Employment Opportunity Program that stated that the policy on lateral entry was not "immune to review," Smythe caustically remarked that this was "nothing but bureaucratese that is absolutely meaningless and has been used down through the years to forestall action and to prevent real integration in the Department." Writing to Elliott Skinner a few months later, Smythe was still fuming. He had spoken to some officials in Washington about the situation and was convinced that they were "well aware of the fact that persons of our background, experience, reputation, and caliber are what might be called 'under-positioned.' " Changing the situation would not be easy since "the Department is a jungle and we still have a difficult fight ahead to get a lot of just opportunities in it." He agreed with Skinner's position that he would "stay on in the Foreign Service if I felt that I could do much more than I am doing here." He also wrote to Franklin Williams, who had since taken a position at Columbia University. Optimistic reports were emanating from the Department of State about new programs to attack the employment problem. Smythe was skeptical: "I am sure you are well aware of the arch conservatism that still besets many high positions in the Department and so we will simply have to wait and see whether there will be any action taken to rectify the great wrong of racism which has plagued the Department almost since its inception."[62]

Even Patricia Roberts Harris, who viewed her appointment to Luxembourg as simply a small step in her impressive career, could not completely contain her skepticism about her selection in 1965. When asked whether she had been offered a selection of posts, she replied in a 1969 interview, "I was offered Luxembourg. Gad, there had been all kinds of debate about, you know, 'isn't there a smaller or less significant post we can find for a woman who is also black,' but that's only rumor. There had been discussion, I gather, of Switzerland and Malta, along with Luxembourg." She also "found the Foreign Service . . . from the point of view that I had to deal with it, a pain in the neck."[63]

Carl Rowan was another newcomer to the Department of State who had been recruited by the Kennedy administration in 1961. Though he had no desire to make diplomacy his career, he came face to face with the same frustrations and obstacles confronted by other African-American diplomats. According to Rowan, "the State Department was a virtual plantation. There were many blacks in State, but they were the messengers, the janitors, the low-paid secretaries." It was a "hostile environment" inhabited by too many "southern elitists who in 1961 still carried the mental baggage of the Civil War era." Efforts to correct the situation ran into a brick wall: "Rusk, Bowles, Ball, Crockett, and others began 'bold' moves to make the State Department and foreign service something better than a lily-white enclave of relatively privileged Americans. But nothing much changed, no matter the lip service, the meetings, the memos."[64]

Rowan had been joined in the Department by his friend from Minnesota, Richard Fox. Fox was assigned to work with Herman Pollack on personnel matters. Unlike Rowan, he looked forward to a career in the Foreign Service. He understood the daunting prospects: the lack of African-Americans in the Foreign Service "really said something about the interest and the intentions of the department in trying to develop a career service that reflected the diversity of this country. . . . My impression was that the department was, in fact, an 'old boys' club." Working with Pollack and William Crockett, Fox had made some significant efforts to change that situation, particularly through the FASP initiative, but it was an uphill struggle: "The Foreign Service was always interested in protecting itself from invasions from the outside. Therefore, it looked upon any effort to infuse a large number of people, some above the entrance level, as a potential threat to the Service."[65]

Terence Todman had already served in the Department and Foreign Service for nearly a decade when the Kennedy administration came to power. As one of the few African-American insiders, he instantly perceived that the 1960s were "a difficult time, because many of my colleagues in the State Department saw themselves as caretakers of the good of the United States. . . . And they were going to insist that things be done in a certain way; that you look at the historical precedents and you respect them." He understood the resentments of some of his white colleagues toward efforts to integrate the Department: "it's an elite group and one of the ways to insure that you maintain that sense of elitism is to not have too many people in who'll be different."[66]

Perhaps Eddie Williams, in his 1967 report on minority hiring, had gotten to the crux of the matter. As his report concluded, "The Department cannot avoid the minority employment issue simply by supporting outside efforts to improve educational opportunities for Negroes." What had to be faced was the fact that the "Department's negative image in some minority communities—whether imaginary or real—adversely affects one's choice of foreign affairs as a career." That image was hardly helped by the fact that, "There has never existed an organized Department-wide EEO program which enjoyed the support of all available resources and professional expertise." The end result was a stalemate: "Because there are few Negro officers in the Department, it is difficult for the Department to attract more qualified Negroes, and thus a vicious circle is produced."[67]

And so, the decade of the 1960s had ended just about where it had begun in terms of the Department of State and its dealings with the issues of race and civil rights. Nearly a quarter-century of thinking about the matters had led the Department to dead ends and "vicious circles." Edward Dudley, in presenting his view about why qualified African-Americans were best suited for service in Africa, also made it clear what would change that situation: "The very fact that the world atmosphere has been poisoned during the past 100 years by representing anyone less than white as second class or something to be shunned, ipso facto, gives a decided advantage to a qualified Negro in Africa today. Only when the white world ceases to consider race as a factor will this not be so."[68] By 1969, that time seemed as far away as ever.

~ 8 ~

Conclusion

For a quarter century after World War II, both African-Americans and the Department of State struggled with the issues of race and civil rights. For the former, these matters were of grave concern. Many blacks clearly grasped the notion that international affairs—especially those concerning people of color in underdeveloped nations in Africa and Asia—were inseparably intertwined with their own battles for equal rights and an end to discrimination in America. Thus, their fights against colonialism and apartheid, for example, were seen as merely overseas extensions of the civil rights struggle at home. They also realized quite clearly the damage being done to America's status and prestige around the world by the racial problems dividing the nation. How could the 75 percent of the world's people who are not white ever really trust the United States and its professions of democracy and freedom when the treatment of African-Americans belied those lofty ideals? One way of winning back their trust would be to appoint more blacks to positions in the Department of State and Foreign Service; the unique perspectives provided by African-American diplomats might give those organizations—long decried for their lily-white composition—a new and deeper understanding of the issue of race.

The Department of State and Foreign Service, however, were never comfortable in confronting race as an international problem. Their history, traditions, sense of mission, and personnel make-up made it difficult for them to come to terms with the new significance of race in the world arena. The overall reaction to this development was to treat race and civil rights as propaganda issues, which, if given the proper treatment, would redound to America's favor or, perhaps more hoped for, simply go away. In terms of bringing more of a black presence—and voice—into the halls of the U.S.

foreign policy bureaucracy, the Department of State and Foreign Service failed miserably. Disinterested in, and sometimes aggressively opposed to, broadening the racial composition of their organizations, officials in both made sure that few African-Americans were able to break into the "old boys' club."

Considering these twenty-five years of futility, it is not surprising to find that the frustrations continued into the 1970s, 1980s, and 1990s. During the Nixon-Ford years, newspaper and journal articles voiced the same criticisms (and unwarranted optimism) that had resounded throughout the 1940s, 1950s, and 1960s. A *Saturday Review* article in 1971, entitled, "Is the State Department Color-blind?," sounded like it could have been written by Rayford Logan in 1950: "A black American may not feel close to U.S. foreign policy. But he can count. He can make some judgments—by the numbers. And if he—indeed, if anyone—counts the number of black Americans who hold important foreign policy posts in our government, the conclusion is as obvious as it is brutal. There might as well be a sign outside the State Department reading NO BLACKS NEED APPLY." It was a simple equation: "if you are black you don't get to represent the president and the people of the United States very often." And despite the shopworn arguments trotted out by the Department of State to explain the situation— few "qualified" blacks, black disinterest in foreign policy—it was clear that, "At some point, regrettably, one must conclude that the absence of top-level blacks in our foreign affairs hierarchy is no accident. It is the result of purposeful discrimination—which is no more forgivable because it is subtle and even sometimes unconscious." While the appointment of a few more African-Americans to such positions would not be a solution in and of itself, it would "demonstrate the vigor of movement at a time when lethargy is less and less an acceptable response in our commitment on questions of race relations."[1]

An article in the *New York Times* the next year indicated that African-Americans were still trying to make an impact on U.S. policy toward Africa. Here again, the language was strikingly similar to that used ten or twenty years before. In arguing for more black influence in the nation's African policy, the organizers of a recent conference "reason that adversity affecting Africans will eventually affect black Americans, that there is a universality of racism and oppression, and that there is much that can be done inside the United States to affect Africans' lives because of the economic links between the two continents." Dr. Hugh Smythe, who had served as U.S. ambassador to Syria and Malta during the Johnson years, urged African-Americans to become more involved in U.S. foreign policy in a 1972 speech. While arguing that the "millions of Black Americans and the existence of Africa . . .

have together brought pressure for change in racial attitudes," he also noted that "Blacks have since their arrival in America been excluded from the national elite." This meant that they had "special difficulty in relating to United States foreign affairs, even over issues of vital concern to them." It was especially important that African-Americans be given a voice in those affairs, for, "If America is to change its image as one of the most disliked nations in the world by nonwhite peoples, a major transformation in her racial posture and priorities for international action is needed."[2]

From inside the State Department bureaucracy, African-Americans continued to raise many of the old concerns. A 1974 news story reported that, "There is a growing fear among black Americans in United States Government service abroad that the concentration of their senior members in African assignments could lessen their effectiveness in Africa and around the world." All five of the current black ambassadors were in Africa, as were the seven African-Americans who headed AID operations abroad. Seven of the ten blacks who directed overseas USIS offices were also in Africa. The problem, as one unidentified black diplomat put it, was that these officials were "beginning to face the same problem as blacks in American industry who are executives in charge of urban or minority affairs, and special markets. Both are restricted to low-priority areas where their black skins are supposed to count."[3]

By 1976, however, a new optimism concerning blacks in the Department of State was seen. An article in *Sepia* noted that a recent "showdown" between Secretary of State Henry Kissinger and a black ambassador (in which Kissinger was seen to have backed down) "represents a turning point in what has traditionally been the most lily-white branch of the government." There were, of course, still problems. The Foreign Service had "much to redress in making itself representative of the racial composition of the nation at large. For all its advances Foggy Bottom still hearkens back to the days when blacks in striped trousers were a sparse breed." The lack of more African-Americans in overseas duties "continues to reflect racism here at home." Nevertheless, the article ended on a hopeful note: "perhaps the view of one news columnist will really come to pass. 'Henry Kissinger is on the verge of yet another diplomatic miracle,' he wrote. 'He is about to discover black Africa.' To that might also be added black America." A 1976 report from State's Equal Employment Opportunity Office was also hesitantly optimistic. It began by citing the Department's "historical image as a 'lily white' all male organization." The report then went on to list the many achievements in equal opportunity employment during the last decade. Still, the numbers suggested that progress was incremental. Four percent of FSOs were black, an increase of just 0.4 percent in the past five years. The number of African-Americans in the civil service side of State had gone up just 4 percent in the same time.[4]

That optimism increased during the Carter presidency. An article in *Black Enterprise* declared that, "The foreign service, perhaps the last bastion of international elitism, is finally becoming a feasible career choice for black Americans." The piece noted that under Carter, twelve blacks currently served as U.S. ambassadors, and Terence Todman had been made the first African-American to hold the post of assistant secretary for Latin American affairs. Yet, questions remained. Another article in *Encore American & Worldwide News* in 1979 flayed the Nixon-Kissinger team for its failure to bring more blacks into diplomatic service, but asked, "has the current administration done any better?" It was difficult to say with precision, though it was evident that the Carter administration was taking more vigorous action to address the issue. Secretary of State Cyrus Vance seemed genuinely committed to the idea, a new task force to investigate the problem had been established, and the EEO office had been reactivated. Still, it was "not difficult to see that tradition has weighed heavily against Blacks being significantly represented in the 'semi-private club.' " Any efforts to change that situation would "meet with resistance," especially from the Association of Foreign Service Officers, which "wields tremendous clout within the department." One State Department official claimed that the association "blatantly disregards the views of female and minority officers." Overall, the situation was tenuous: "Despite the gains won and the support of the Secretary of State, some among the affirmative action advocates fear that their advantage may deteriorate in the face of the counterpressures from conservatives from within the department."[5]

As the article had feared, things went downhill quickly after the departure of the Carter administration. A 1983 story in *Black Enterprise* reported on the angry war of words between the State Department and TransAfrica, a lobbying group focusing on influencing U.S. policy in Africa. The organization's criticisms of the Reagan administration's new and friendlier policy toward South Africa was the issue provoking the rift. The Congressional Black Caucus was also firing away at the Reagan policy on South Africa and condemning its actions in regard to Angola. The piece concluded that, "The struggle over American foreign policy has not only excited the wrath of the State Department over TransAfrica, it has born positive results for black Americans. . . . It proved the effectiveness of collective efforts by black organizations and individuals and points up the importance of grass-roots input affecting issues that otherwise seem distant. Together it all goes to show that the black agenda goes far beyond events within the American shores."[6]

The issue of blacks in the Department of State and Foreign Service, however, brought forth even heavier attacks during the Reagan years. A 1983 article in *Ebony* bluntly asked, "Why Aren't There More Blacks in Foreign Service?" The number of black ambassadors, for example, had fallen from a high of fourteen during the Carter years to only six at present. The reason for this was clear to Franklin H. Williams, who had served as U.S. ambassador to Ghana during the Johnson presidency: "When American governmental leadership thinks of who speaks for America, or who represents America, or what is an American spokesperson, they never think of a Black person." Rick Haynes, who had been on the NSC staff under Johnson and appointed ambassador to Algeria by Carter, echoed those thoughts: "The Foreign Service has traditionally been a closed club. It is, in part, dominated by wealthy southern families and northeastern Ivy League educational establishments." Part of the problem, too, were the perceptions of American society at large: "The media are prepared to accept the notoriety of a Black who distinguishes himself in crime, the civil rights arena, entertainment, or sports. Since Blacks in the Foreign Service do not fall into any of those categories, we tend to become the 'invisible man.' "[7] Just a month later, a *New York Times* article reported on the sad state of affairs concerning minority hiring at State. Terence Todman recalled his "deep sadness" five years earlier when he had left Washington to serve as ambassador to Spain. This action "meant that at the important high-level functions here, there simply would be no blacks to let the world know that our nation is truly multiracial. It's distressing to think that five years later, that's still the case." Donald McHenry, who had been U.S. ambassador to the UN under Carter, claimed that there was a "massive problem" in minority hirings at State, and that there had been a "clear setback under the Reagan Administration." The Department's rather vague response was that "it takes time before affirmative action programs will impact at the top." This did not make sense to Michigan Representative George Crockett, who charged that, "We now have about five black Ambassadors wandering around the corridors of the State Department. Until the Reagan Administration came into office, all of them had served honorably, but one by one, they were recalled to Washington. And while other career officers have been given assignments comparable to their grade level in the State Department, the blacks have been passed over."[8]

By 1986, the criticisms had become so heavy that Secretary of State George Shultz felt compelled to more forcefully address the issue. In a letter to senior State Department officials, Shultz noted that he was concerned about "the small number of blacks in senior positions 'because' it is of fundamental importance that the Service represent the cultural and ethnic diversity of our society. This is not simply a personnel issue. It is a foreign policy problem which affects our image as a nation." Under Secretary Ronald Spiers agreed, arguing that the problem "must be addressed not 'for cosmetic reasons' but because we cannot represent our country overseas if we do not reflect our society at home."[9]

Matters did not improve, however. By the time of the Clinton administration, lawsuits were being brought both by African-Americans and by women against the State Department's hiring practices, and resentments among Department "professionals" were rising. A *Washington Post* article from 1994 observed that President Clinton's desire for "a government 'that looks like America' is causing controversy in the Foreign Service, with some white males charging that they are the victims of reverse discrimination and women and minorities countering that the service's dominant male character remains fundamentally unchanged." Senior officials in the Department were complaining about "checking with the White House about whether the proper racial and gender balance is being attained." A lawsuit brought by black FSOs "charged that they are discriminated against in promotions and ratings and are 'ghettoized' by being assigned in disproportionate numbers to Africa and the heavily black areas of Latin America, which are less prestigious areas in which to serve." Complaints had arisen over a rumor that posts in the European bureau were to be "set aside" for minorities. The response of Richard Moose, who was under secretary of state for administration, was clear: "If there was a plot to give European slots to minorities, it's a shame it wasn't more successful. The demographics of our representation there show that some people—blacks and other minorities—have been treated unfairly." The article opined that, "The old image of the Foreign Service as a bastion of tennis-playing Ivy Leaguers—what some called 'a club for WASPs with two last names'—has waned since World War II. Since then, the service has widened the talent pool in order to maintain America's superpower role. Each new shift has shaken morale."[10]

Just how "shaken" things were at State became clear in a 1996 article in *The Nation*. It quoted from a memorandum from the U.S. political counselor in Bolivia charging that the Department's efforts at diversity were "contradictory, deceptive, condescending in the extreme." In the letter, he called minorities in the Department "'unscrupulous race and ethnic jumpers' trying to 'con' their way to the top." At the same time, the president of the American Foreign Service Association had informed Secretary of State Warren Christopher that further efforts to diversify the Foreign Service "can only engender further resistance by officers who feel disadvantaged by them." "The State Department," the article charged, "long a bastion of prep-school patronage where change has come harder and slower than in any other Cabinet-level department—is in the midst of an internal war over racism in its ranks." The piece cited the case of two black FSOs who were part of a suit against the Department. They recounted "a daily racial humiliation in the workplace that belies that atmosphere of restraint; years spent being shuffled from one low-authority assignment to another while white peers are escorted by patrons up the power track." As the article noted, "Repeated Congressional investigations through the eighties proved conclusively that African-Americans and women were assigned in radically disproportionate numbers to the consular and administrative cones—assignments having nothing to do with their objective qualifications." It was clear that "the tradition of discrimination has persisted more stubbornly at State than at any other federal department." Terence Todman charged that State had avoided any deeper investigation of the problem through a "long track record of cooking the books to avoid the necessity of change." And, as Rick Haynes noted, the problem had wide-reaching implications. "The marginalization of African-Americans in the Foreign Service is part and parcel of this country's problem in dealing with dark-skinned people around the world."[11]

Finally, in 1996, there seemed to be some closure on the issue, as a settlement was reached whereby the Department of State agreed to pay compensation to hundreds of African-Americans "who alleged they were denied advancement and career opportunities because of their race." Nearly $4 million was to paid out to thirty plaintiffs. Yet, even then, the issue seemed far from settled. Twenty of the thirty plaintiffs objected to the settlement, which they claimed failed "to meet their demands." The Department, for its part, vigorously denied that "it had discriminated against the black diplomats because of their race." Without admitting any real guilt, the Department nevertheless pledged that it would be "carrying out some really substantial reforms in the personnel system so we can train our supervisors to manage a diverse work force."[12]

Those with perhaps the best vantage point from which to understand why so little has changed since 1945 are the handful of African-Americans who managed, against numerous obstacles, to make a career for themselves in U.S. diplomacy. One of the most enjoyable aspects of this study was the time spent with some of these individuals. Here, near the close of this study, their conclusions should have special value.

Terence A. Todman served in the Department of State and Foreign Service from the 1950s into the 1990s. He was U.S. ambassador to six nations during those years. Despite his own personal success, he was always well aware that his career was in many ways exceptional. Commenting on the efforts during the 1960s to improve the number of blacks in the diplomatic service, his opinion was that "nothing significant" had been accomplished.

This did not surprise him, for the "record of the State Department has been horrendous, it's been horrendous throughout." At various times, he admitted, attempts had been made, but none had gone very far:

> You get senior leadership which says, "yeah, we're committed to change." But the commitment never involves any follow-through of a personal nature . . . with that rare exception, people come in and make a lovely statement; you know, "This is what I believe in, this is what I'm going to do." And I wouldn't question the sincerity of the top people in making those statements. But I will state with absolute certainty, there was never any follow-up to insure that it took place. And if you don't have that follow-up, you have a built-in, protective group that wants its own kind and is able to ensure that it goes that way.

The impact on America's foreign policy, according to Todman, is immense. "We need as a country," he declares, "the very best input that we can into policy formulation and policy implementation. There are sensitivities that people bring into a meeting that you can't get otherwise. . . . We're denying ourselves of this by not bringing in minorities." The Department of State, unfortunately, is "really very, very shortsighted." He is pessimistic about the future, arguing that "they really don't care about it there." The argument for bringing more diversity to the Department is only vaguely perceived by its officials: "in the case of black Americans, it's not even on the screen. It's important to make a strong statement at first coming in, because the problem is there. But following up would take a certain amount of time and they just don't give priority to it. And because the establishment, the ones who actually run the things, have no particular reason to want to change it, unless they're forced to, it never will change."[13]

Horace Dawson, who also joined the Department in the 1950s and eventually went on to serve as U.S. ambassador to Botswana, shares some of Todman's concerns. For him, the issue is not the programs and proposals that have been suggested and implemented in the past. It is, instead, "what happens when these suggestions about programs reach the Department, and then also what happens when there are people who present themselves who are qualified to be officers. . . . In my view, the State Department has never come to grips with the point that it needs to make extraordinary efforts to recruit. It always says that we . . . do not want to compromise the examination process with quality service; the examination determines quality, therefore you must pass the examination." The Department, "in its corporate role . . . was not all that interested. Some individuals, from time to time, have been, but in its corporate sense, the obstacles are thrown up right and left at all times."[14]

John Reinhardt joined the USIA in the 1950s, eventually becoming a

Foreign Service Information Officer and serving as ambassador to Nigeria in the 1970s. His insider's perspective left him with the belief that, "There is a certain culture in the Foreign Service which emphasizes tradition, status quo, proper schools, proper religion, proper breeding, and all else that we associate with exclusivity and elitism. Certainly there have been changes in recent years, but only as few as have been made as the Service can manage." The obstacles to change are immense: "instructions move slowly, are changed, are resisted, and simply are not acted on in many instances. No one has to order a slowdown, it just happens for the good of the Service." To cite one example of how little has changed, Reinhardt referred to the retirement of Terence Todman when the Clinton administration came to power. That administration "inherited an extraordinary black Foreign Service Officer in Terence Todman but, somehow, managed to allow him to retire, probably without the President even knowing that he ever had him. The 'needs of the Service,' antiquated rules of the Service, and probably prejudice of the Service simply dictated that he should retire after a long and distinguished career. The one black Career Ambassador would seem to have been needed even if he were named Methuselah. Terence Todman was 67 when he retired." His hopes for the future, too, are dim. More talented African-Americans are looking elsewhere for employment, "rather than enter a Service where career advancement at best is slow and uncertain and where a demonstrable history of tokenism seems unchangeable."[15]

Richard Fox came into the Department in 1961, and was one of the leading forces behind the FASP. He later served as U.S. ambassador to Trinidad and Tobago. In 1974, he had been appointed deputy director of personnel. After a nearly ten-year absence from dealing with personnel affairs, Fox was disturbed by how little things had changed. "I found that we had not done very much over that ten or twelve year period. That the initial impetus that was there had slowly begun to tail off, and that the department was giving support to it in name only but there was not much active effort being exerted, except on the part of a few people." He was particularly discouraged by the inaction on the part of the geographical bureaus. Here Fox saw a "collision between the bureau's interest on the one hand—its self-serving interest, I would call it—and the absence of any real commitment and willingness to undertake the effort to support the department's objectives by reaching out to find people or minorities for these jobs." Cracking the Foreign Service was also still a problem; it had "not been deeply committed to this process" of selecting more minorities. "Foreign Service Officers feel insulted these days. They feel that this diversity issue is beginning to cost them assignments and promotions. . . . I notice now in talking to some people in the department that there is real

concern. They feel that their livelihood and their profession is threatened."
Despite the lack of concrete results, "The efforts that have been made over
the last thirty years have certainly been in the right direction. I think that
getting a broader based Foreign Service—that is, culturally, and ethnically,
and sexually—would certainly strengthen the Foreign Service. There's no
question about that in my mind."[16]

For twenty-five years after World War II, both African-Americans and
the Department of State and Foreign Service had done a great deal of
thinking about race. By 1969, however, there seemed to be little change in
the initial positions and perceptions of both sides. It is now nearly thirty
years since the end of the 1960s, and the old charges and countercharges,
the old wounds and the old denials are still being aired. For over five
decades of American history, years in which international relations often
dominated the thoughts and the resources of the nation, the black voice and
presence were virtually excluded from the national debate over foreign
policy and the bureaucracies that implemented that policy. And as the
twenty-first century approaches, it seems unlikely that matters will change
to any great degree, as the Department of State and Foreign Service continue to think about race in essentially the same ways they did half a century
ago. To return to a question raised earlier in this volume, would that voice
and presence have made for a different foreign policy; a different—a better—world? The exclusionary nature of American foreign relations prohib-
ited the nation from answering those questions. Whether those questions
remain unanswered into the next century will depend on how much rethinking about race the Department of State—and America as a whole—is willing to undertake.

Notes

Notes to Introduction

1. S. L. Washburn, "Thinking About Race," *Annual Report of the Smithsonian Institution* (1946): 363.
2. Michael H. Hunt, *Ideology and U.S. Foreign Policy.*
3. Ibid., chs. 3 and 5 (passim). The other two components of the U.S. ideology cited by Hunt are a deep and abiding belief in America's "national greatness" and an equally deep fear and distrust of revolutionary political and social change.

Notes to Chapter 1

1. For African-American responses to U.S. intervention in the Philippines, see Willard B. Gatewood Jr., "Black Americans and the Quest for Empire, 1893–1903," *Journal of Southern History* 38 (November 1972): 545–566; for their interest in the Boer War, see his 1976 article, "Black Americans and the Boer War, 1899–1902," *South Atlantic Quarterly* 75 (Spring 1976): 226–244. For Haiti, see Brenda Gayle Plummer, "The Afro-American Response to the Occupation of Haiti, 1915–1934," *Phylon* 43 (Spring 1982): 125–143. A general overview of the responses of U.S. ethnic and racial minorities to the nation's foreign policy during these years is found in Alexander DeConde, *Ethnicity, Race and American Foreign Policy: A History,* ch. 4.
2. A good brief analysis of the work of Du Bois and Garvey is found in Brenda Gayle Plummer, *Rising Wind: Black Americans and U.S. Foreign Affairs, 1935–1960,* 16–22. For more detailed studies, see Ben F. Rogers, "William E.B. Du Bois, Marcus Garvey, and Pan-Africa," *Journal of Negro History* 40 (April 1955): 154–165; Immanuel Geiss, *The Pan-African Movement;* George Padmore, *Pan-Africanism or Communism;* Theodore G. Vincent, *Black Power and the Garvey Movement;* Amy Jacques Garvey, *Garvey and Garveyism;* and Judith Stein, *The World of Marcus Garvey.*
3. See Plummer, *Rising Wind,* ch. 2. For more on the African-American response to the Ethiopian crisis, consult William R. Scott, *The Sons of Sheba's Race: African-Americans and the Italo-Ethiopian War, 1935–1941,* as well as his 1978 article, "Black Nationalism and the Italo-Ethiopian Conflict, 1934–1936," *Journal of Negro History* 63

173

(April 1978): 118–134; Joseph E. Harris, *African-American Reactions to War in Ethiopia, 1936–1941;* Robert G. Weisbord, "Black America and the Italian-Ethiopian Crisis: Episode in Pan-Negroism," *Historian* 34:2 (1972): 94–104; and Red Ross, "Black Americans and Italo-Ethiopian Relief, 1935–1936," *Ethiopia Observer* 15:2 (1972): 122–131.

4. Walter White, *A Rising Wind;* W.E.B. Du Bois, *Color and Democracy: Colonies and Peace;* Rayford W. Logan, ed., *What the Negro Wants;* Logan, *The Negro and the Post-War World.* For articles in the various African-American newspapers, the best place to start is *The Kaiser Index to Black Resources, 1948–1986,* 5 vols. While hardly exhaustive, the topical index is an extraordinarily helpful aid in finding articles on a number of foreign policy subjects. Also useful is Charles A. Simmons, *The African American Press: A History of News Coverage During National Crises, with Special Reference to Four Black Newspapers, 1827–1965,* which has chapters on the *Chicago Defender* and *Pittsburgh Courier,* as well as chapters on coverage of World War II and the Civil Rights Movement in the black press. The best secondary sources for African-Americans and U.S. foreign policy during the 1930s and World War II are Plummer, *Rising Wind,* ch. 3; Penny M. Von Eschen, *Race Against Empire: Black Americans and Anticolonialism, 1937–1957,* chs. 1 and 2; Richard M. Dalfiume, "The 'Forgotten Years' of the Negro Revolution," *Journal of American History* 55:1 (June 1968): 90–106; James L. Roark, "American Black Leaders: The Response to Colonialism and the Cold War, 1943–1953," *African Historical Studies* 4:2 (1971): 153–158; Mary L. Dudziak, "Desegregation as a Cold War Imperative," *Stanford Law Review* 41 (November 1988): 61–73; Alfred O. Hero, "American Negroes and U.S. Foreign Policy, 1937–1967," *Journal of Conflict Resolution* 8 (June 1969): 220–251; and Mark Solomon, "Black Critics of Colonialism and the Cold War," in *Cold War Critics: Alternatives to American Foreign Policy in the Truman Years,* ed. Thomas G. Paterson, 205–213.

5. For the best introduction to African-American attitudes toward U.S. foreign policy during the Truman years, see Plummer, *Rising Wind,* chs. 4–6. Also consult Von Eschen, *Race Against Empire,* chs. 4 and 5; and Gerald Horne, *Black and Red: W.E.B. Du Bois and the Afro-American Response to the Cold War, 1944–1963,* passim; Thomas Borstelmann, *Apartheid's Reluctant Uncle: The United States and South Africa in the Early Cold War,* passim; and Dudziak, "Desegregation," passim.

6. Cited in Paul Gordon Lauren, *Power and Prejudice: The Politics and Diplomacy of Racial Discrimination,* 1.

7. Du Bois to Lester Walton, 24 July 1946, Papers of Lester Walton, Box 16, W.E.B. Du Bois, 1944–1946 file, Schomburg Center for Research in Black Culture, New York.

8. White to Rayford Logan, 24 October 1951, Papers of the National Association for the Advancement of Colored People, Group II, Box A404, General Office File, Logan, Rayford, 1950–1951 file, Library of Congress, Washington, DC (hereafter Papers of NAACP, group and box number, file designation, LC).

9. "What Will San Francisco Conference Mean to Africa?" *The African* 3:1 (April 1945): 6; "Human Relations and Human Rights," *Race Relations* 5:9–12 (June–December 1948): 208.

10. "Address by Edith Sampson," at the United Negro College Fund Symposium "Color in Democracy," 18 November 1952, Papers of the United Negro College Fund (microfiche edition), frame no. 3179, LC; "Charley Cherokee," *Negro Digest* 8 (October 1950): 36.

11. See previously cited works by Von Eschen, Plummer, Horne, and Dudziak.

12. Copy of letter to Stettinius found in NAACP, "Minutes of the Meeting of the Board of Directors," 12 March 1945, Papers of Arthur Spingarn, Box 41, Minutes and Reports, Board of Directors, 1945 file, LC; "San Francisco," *The Crisis* (June 1945): 161; "Resolutions Adopted by the Forty-Third Annual Convention of the NAACP at Oklahoma City, Oklahoma, June 28, 1952," *The Crisis* (August–September 1952): 457.

13. The best study of the CAA is Hollis Lynch, *Black American Radicals and the Liberation of Africa: The Council on African Affairs, 1937–1955.* This must be supplemented, however, with Von Eschen, *Race Against Empire,* which discusses the activities of the CAA from its formation to its eventual demise within the context of African-American protest against colonialism. Plummer, *Rising Wind,* also mentions the CAA at several points.

14. Letter contained in Robeson and Yergan to Roy Wilkins, 29 November 1944; *New Africa* 3:4 (April 1944), Papers of the NAACP, Group II, Box A3, Africa-General-1944–1945 file, LC.

15. Walter White to Clement Attlee, 15 November 1948; "Comments by NAACP on ex-Prime Minister Winston Churchill's Address on March 5th at Westminister College, Fulton, Missouri," 7 March 1946, Papers of NAACP, Group II, Box A616, State Department, 1941–1947 file, LC; George Padmore, "The Sudanese Want Independence," *The Crisis* (June 1947): 178–180; Harold Preece, "Africa Awakes," *The Crisis* (December 1945): 348–350, 363; Herman P. Osborne, "The Road to West Indian Federation," *The Crisis* (January 1946): 14–15, 27–28; W.E.B. Du Bois, "The Freeing of India," *The Crisis* (October 1947): 301–304, 316–317.

16. Emile Faure, "French Terror in Negro Africa," *The Crisis* (April 1947): 108–110, 124; George Padmore, "Madagascar Fights for Freedom," *The Crisis* (December 1948): 365–367; George Padmore, "The Vietnamese Struggle for Independence," *The Crisis* (March 1948): 78–79, 91–92; John R. Andu, "The Indonesian Struggle for Independence," *The Crisis* (February 1948): 49–50, 62; "Review of the Month," *Race Relations* 4:12 (July 1947): 363. *Race Relations* was a monthly publication put out by the Social Science Institute at Fisk University.

17. George W. Westerman, "Canal Zone Discrimination," *The Crisis* (April 1951): 235–237; "Navy 'Democracy' in Guam," *The Crisis* (October 1946): 297.

18. "Confusion for Christmas," and "Byrnes and the Balkans," *The Crisis* (December 1945): 345.

19. "Democratic Elections—in Poland," *The Crisis* (March 1947): 73; "Democracy Defined at Moscow," *The Crisis* (April 1947): 105.

20. "As We Look to the Japanese," *The Crisis* (July 1949): 201; "Korean War," *The Crisis* (October 1950): 594.

21. "Charley Cherokee," *Negro Digest* (March; September 1950): 30; 38–39.

22. Charles S. Johnson, "Human Relations and Human Rights," *Race Relations* 5:9–12 (June–December 1948): 204–209.

23. "Symposium: Are Negroes Winning Their Fight for Civil Rights?" *Harlem Quarterly* 1:1 (Winter 1949–1950): 24–25.

24. Walter White, "Time for a Progress Report," *The Saturday Review of Literature* (September 22, 1951), 9–10, 38–41.

25. "The Church and Race, Official Statement Approved by the Federal Council of the Churches of Christ in America, at a Special Meeting, Columbus, Ohio, March 5–7, 1946," Papers of Ralph Bunche, Box 107, Commission on the Church and Minority Peoples—1944–1946 file, Special Collections-University Research Libraries, UCLA, Los Angeles (hereafter Bunche Papers, box and file designation, SC-URL); "Equal Justice Under the Law," reprinted from *The Survey,* March 1951, Anson Phelps Stokes Papers, Box 102, folder 1702, Yale University Library (YUL).

26. "Bunche Accuses Byrnes of Bigotry and Defaming Democracy Abroad," *New York Times,* (1 April 1951): 1, 71.

27. "Can Negroes Make Diplomats?" *Ebony* 4:7 (May 1949): 60.

28. "Minutes of the Meeting of the Board of Directors, March 12, 1945," Spingarn Papers, Box 41, Minutes and Reports, Board of Directors, 1945 file, LC. For a good

discussion of the NAACP's negotiations with Stettinius over the issue of African-American representation at the San Francisco conference, see Carol Anderson, "From Hope to Disillusion: African Americans, the United Nations, and the Struggle for Human Rights, 1944–1947," *Diplomatic History* 20:4 (Fall 1996): 531–563.

29. Walter White to Harry S. Truman, 18 August 1947, Papers of David Niles, Box 27, Civil Rights/Negro Affairs, July 1947–1948 file, Harry S. Truman Presidential Library, Independence, MO (HSTL).

30. Memo, Wilkins to White, 9 May 1951, Papers of NAACP, Group II, Box A617, State Department, General, 1951 file, LC.

31. Du Bois to Mr. Jackson, 6 January 1947, Papers of NAACP, Group II, Box A8, Africa-Channing Tobias, 1947–1948 file, LC.

32. "U.S. Told to Hire Negroes for Asia," *Pittsburgh Courier* (31 May 1952): 14; "Charley Cherokee," *Negro Digest* (October 1950): 36.

33. For more on Rayford Logan, see Kenneth R. Janken, *Rayford W. Logan and the Dilemma of the African-American Intellectual.* Janken, unfortunately, gives but a brief mention of the *Courier* articles and Logan's efforts to desegregate the Department of State.

34. "Courier Urges Review of Employment Policy in State Department," *Pittsburgh Courier* (15 April 1950): 1, 5.

35. "Negroes in Foreign Service Assigned to 'Colored' Countries," *Pittsburgh Courier* (22 April 1950): 1, 4.

36. "President Shows Signs of Ending Government Bias," *Pittsburgh Courier* (29 April 1950): 1, 5.

37. "It Employs Few Negroes, But Deserves Credit for Opening Some Doors to Us," *Pittsburgh Courier* (6 May 1950): 1, 4.

38. "School of Foreign Service at Georgetown U. Denies Negroes Are Not Wanted," *Pittsburgh Courier* (13 May 1950): 1, 5.

39. "5 Get Foreign Service Jobs Hiking Total to 34," *Baltimore Afro-American* (28 February 1948): 18.

40. "Appointment of Fisk Professor as Attache in Haiti Approved," *Baltimore Afro-American* (27 December 1947): 10; "Gets Indian Post," *New York Amsterdam News* (6 May 1951): 8; "America's First Negro Ambassador," *Ebony* (October 1950): 79–82.

41. Lester Walton, "Negroes in the U.S. Diplomatic Service," *New York Amsterdam News* (10 December 1949): 33, 49; Alice A. Dunnigan, "40 Serve in Diplomatic Service Field," *Baltimore Afro-American* (18 August 1951): 3. A much-revised version of Dunnigan's article was reprinted in the *Foreign Service Journal* (December 1951): 50 ("U.S. Sends Negro Personnel Into Foreign Countries, Nearly 40 Serving Abroad in State Department Posts").

42. "Can Negroes Make Diplomats?," *Ebony* (May 1949): 60; "School of Foreign Service at Georgetown U. Denies Negroes Are Not Wanted," *Pittsburgh Courier* (13 May 1950): 1, 5; Logan to Robert Oliver, 18 December 1950, Papers of Rayford Logan, Box 10, Folder 11, Moorland-Spingarn Research Center, Howard University, Washington, DC (hereafter Logan Papers, box and folder number, M-SRC).

43. Elmer Henderson to Acheson, 8 September 1950, Logan Papers, Box 6, Folder 2, M-SRC.

44. For background works on Bunche, see Brian Urquhart, *Ralph Bunche: An American Life;* Peggy Mann, *Ralph Bunche: UN Peacemaker;* Benjamin Rivlin, ed., *Ralph Bunche: The Man and His Times;* and Charles P. Henry, ed., *Ralph Bunche: Selected Speeches and Writings.* One small note: nearly all of these sources credit Bunche with being the first African-American to hold a professional (or "desk") position in the Department of State. In fact, Clifton Wharton Sr., who joined the Department in 1924 as a law clerk, holds that distinction.

45. Walter White to Dean Acheson, 25 October 1950; White to Senator Ralph E. Flanders, 11 January 1951, Papers of NAACP, Group II, Box A161, Bunche, Ralph-General-1950–1955 file, LC.

46. For discussion of this incident, see Urquhart, *Ralph Bunche,* 225; Rivlin, *Ralph Bunche,* 22; Mann, *Ralph Bunche,* 270; and Oral History Interview with Judge William H. Hastie, 5 January 1972, p. 69, HSTL; "Bunche Blasts D.C. Jim Crow," *Pittsburgh Courier* (11 June 1949): 1, 4, 13. While Bunche often took such principled stands, it is somewhat interesting to note that he seemed to show little interest in the issue of getting more African-Americans into the Department of State. Sometime in early 1952, for example, John A. Davis, who had been hired by the department as a consultant on minority hiring, wrote to Bunche asking for the names of individuals he might be able to suggest for diplomatic positions. Bunche's reply was terse: "I'm afraid that I cannot be of much help. For a long time, for our purposes here [in the UN], I have been seeking 'bright' young persons without too much success." (See John A. Davis to Bunche, n.d.; Bunche to Davis, 22 July 1952, Bunche Papers, Box 8, Correspondence D 1952 file, SC-URL).

47. Lester Walton to W.E.B. Du Bois, 8 September 1945, Papers of W.E.B. Du Bois (microfilm edition), Reel 58, Frames 163–164, LC. For a history of Walton, see Susan Curtis, *The First Black Actors on the Great White Way,* ch. 2.

48. Homer Calkin, "A reminiscence: Being black in the Foreign Service," *Department of State Newsletter* (February 1978): 25–28.

49. Author's interview with Terence A. Todman, 13 June 1995. The interview has been deposited with the Foreign Affairs Oral History Program at Lauinger Library, Georgetown University, Washington, DC.

50. Hugh Smythe to Logan, 16 April 1950, with attachments, Logan Papers, Box 20, Folder 15, M-SRC. Smythe continued his efforts to build a career in diplomacy, and during the presidency of Lyndon Johnson he finally broke through, with appointments as U.S. ambassador to Syria and, later, Malta. For more on Smythe, see Michael L. Krenn, "Hugh Heyne Smythe and Mabel Murphy Smythe-Haith," in *Notable U.S. Ambassadors Since 1775: A Biographical Dictionary,* ed. Cathal J. Nolan, 319–324.

Notes to Chapter 2

1. For a good overview of the racial content of U.S. foreign policy during the nineteenth and early twentieth centuries, see Michael H. Hunt, *Ideology and U.S. Foreign Policy,* ch. 3. Other works to consult include Reginald Horsman, *Race and Manifest Destiny: The Origins of American Racial Anglo-Saxonism;* Richard Drinnon, *Facing West: The Metaphysics of Indian Hating & Empire Building;* Arnoldo De León, *They Called Them Greasers: Anglo Attitudes Toward Mexicans in Texas, 1821–1900;* Ronald Takaki, *Iron Cages: Race and Culture in Nineteenth Century America,* 80–107; John J. Johnson, *A Hemisphere Apart: The Foundations of United States Policy Toward Latin America;* Thomas Hietala, *Manifest Design: Anxious Aggrandizement in Late Jacksonian America,* 132–172; Rubin Francis Weston, *Racism and U.S. Imperialism: The Influence of Racial Assumptions on American Foreign Policy, 1893–1946;* and John W. Dower, *War Without Mercy: Race & Power in the Pacific War.*

2. Robert K. Carr to Dean Acheson, 24 April 1947, Record Group 59 (RG 59), General Records of the Department of State, Decimal File, 501.BD-Human Rights/4–2447; Carr to George C. Marshall, 23 May 1947, RG 59, 811.4016/5–2347; Carr to Marshall, 5 June 1947, National Archives (NA). Interestingly, requests to other department officials, such as Walter Scott, director of the office of Departmental Administra-

tion (asking about minority hiring practices) and John M. Patterson, acting chief of the Division of Public Liaison (soliciting information about the civil rights content of overseas educational programs) were answered almost immediately: see Scott to Carr, 20 May 1947, and Patterson to Carr, 16 May 1947, Records of the President's Committee on Civil Rights, Box 6, State Department File, Harry S. Truman Library (HSTL).

3. Rusk to Marshall, 15 July 1947, RG 59, 501.BD-Human Rights/6–547, NA. Unfortunately, the attachments concerning the responses from the Policy Planning Staff, the UN Liaison Committee, and the geographic offices are not found in the file, and we must therefore depend on Rusk's summary. It is interesting to note, however, that the only geographic offices consulted were Eastern Europe, Europe, Inter-America, and Middle America. What their colleagues dealing with Africa and Asia (and not just the European colonies in those areas) would have said can only be conjectured. Rusk's personal feelings about the matter are equally obscure. In the 1990 publication, which was something of an "oral autobiography," *As I Saw It,* Dean Rusk (as told to Richard Rusk), ed. Daniel S. Papp, there is a large section on Rusk's involvement in civil rights issues, but no mention is made of the 1947 incident.

4. Marshall to Charles E. Wilson, 28 July 1947; Rusk to Carr, 29 July 1947, RG 59, 501.BD-Human Rights/6–547, NA; Allan Evans to Milton Stewart, 6 August 1947, Records of the PCCR, Box 6, State Department file, HSTL.

5. Carr to Rusk, 11 August 1947, RG 59, 811.4016/8–1147, NA.

6. "To Secure These Rights," 100–101, 146–148; "Statement by the President," 29 October 1947, Papers of Harry S. Truman, Official File (OF), Box 1509, File 596, HSTL.

7. James W. Ivy, "American Negro Problem in the Negro Press," *The Crisis* (July 1950): 416.

8. Frank M. Snowden Jr., "American Dilemma Seen from Abroad," reprint from the *Harvard Alumni Bulletin* (9 February 1952), in Papers of Ralph Bunche, Box 9, Correspondence 1952 Sl-Sz, Special Collections–University Research Libraries, UCLA (SC-URL); Robert L. Crowell to Representative Fred Marshall, 17 May 1951, Papers of Howard H. Sargeant, Box 4, Correspondence–Dep. Asst. for Public Affairs, 1951 file, HSTL.

9. "Quotations from the Foreign Press Concerning Racial Discrimination in the United States," 24 July 1947, contained in Dean Rusk to Robert Carr, 29 July 1947, RG 59, 501.BD-Human Rights/6–547; Margaret R. Parkin to Dept. of State, 3 December 1951, RG 59, 811.411/12–351, NA.

10. For a brief overview of the coverage of U.S. racial problems in the Indian press during this time, see Frenise A. Logan, "Racism and Indian-U.S. Relations, 1947–1953: Views in the Indian Press," *Pacific Historical Review* 54 (February 1985): 71–79.

11. Robert B. Streeper to Dept. of State, 20 June 1950; Evan M. Wilson to Dept. of State, 9 February 1951, RG 59, 811.411/6–2050, /2–951, NA.

12. "Comment in the Latin American Press on Alleged Violations of Civil Rights in the United States," enclosed in Willard F. Barber to Philip Levy, 14 March 1950, RG 59, 811.411/12–852, /3–1450, NA.

13. "Foreign Radio Commentary on U.S. Civil Rights," enclosed in L.K. White to Harold J. Krould, 18 June 1947; John H. Ottemiller to Krould, 19 June 1947; "Foreign Radio Comment on American Civil Rights," enclosed in L.K. White to Milton B. Stewart, 5 August 1947, Records of PCCR, Box 6, State Department file, HSTL.

14. J.W. Halderman, "Motivation of Propaganda on Civil Rights," 17 July 1947, Records of PCCR, Box 6, State Department file, HSTL.

15. Dean Rusk to Walter White, 18 January 1951, Papers of the NAACP, Group II, Box A284, Foreign Affairs, Asia, 1950–1952 file, Library of Congress (LC).

16. Bowles had been active in the civil rights issue long before his appointment to India. As indicated in Howard B. Schaffer, *Chester Bowles: New Dealer in the Cold War,* Bowles had been a strong advocate for African-American employment in the Office of Price Administration during his years there (1943–1946), had fought hard for a strong civil rights plank at the 1948 Democratic National Convention, and had been the first governor (Connecticut, 1949–1951) to order the integration of National Guard units. In 1960, he again played a key role in supporting a powerful civil rights stance at the Democratic National Convention (144–145, 174–175, 198, 445–446). Bowles makes mention of all of these activities in his autobiography, *Promises to Keep: My Years in Public Life, 1941–1969.*

17. Chester Bowles to Walter White, 15 November 1951 and 9 July 1952, Papers of Chester Bowles, Box 92, file number 212; Bowles to Frances Williams, 3 January 1952, Bowles Papers, Box 93, file number 217; Bowles to Howland Sargeant, 24 December 1951, Bowles Papers, Box 96, file number 280, Yale University Library, New Haven, CT (YUL). Not surprisingly, Bowles had responded enthusiastically to the letter he received in 1947 from the PCCR's Robert Carr. Indeed, his comments dealing with the international repercussions of America's racial discrimination were exactly the kind Carr had unsuccessfully sought to wring from George Marshall. (See Carr to Bowles, 26 February 1947, and Bowles to Carr, 19 March 1947, Bowles Papers, Box 49, file 542, YUL.)

18. Francis H. Russell to Mr. Perry, 11 October 1947, Papers of NAACP, Group II, Box A616, State Department, 1941–1947 file; Margaret R.T. Carter to Arthur Spingarn, 31 August 1949, Papers of NAACP, Group II, Box A617, State Department, 1949 file; State Department, General, 1951 file, LC.

19. F.H. Russell, "The flow of information on American Foreign Policy to Negro Americans," 28 February 1950, RG 59, Records of the Assistant Secretary of State for Public Affairs, 1947–1950, Box 4, Public Information Committee, 1950 (Sargeant File) file, NA.

20. Ibid.

21. Harry S. Truman, "Remarks to a Delegation From the National Emergency Civil Rights Mobilization Conference," 17 January 1950, *The Public Papers of the Presidents of the United States: Harry S. Truman, 1950,* 115; News Release, 13 June 1952, Papers of George Elsey, Box 20, 1948–February 2, Civil Rights Message-Press Releases, etc. file, HSTL.

22. See Kenneth O'Reilly, *Black Americans: The FBI Files.*

23. Philip Raine to Mr. Haden, 20 October 1952; John Ordway to Mr. Reid, 30 December 1952, RG 59, 811.411/9–3052, /12–3052, NA. For an excellent and detailed analysis of Josephine Baker and the State Department's campaign against her, see Mary L. Dudziak, "Josephine Baker, Racial Protest, and the Cold War," *Journal of American History* 81 (September 1994): 543–570.

24. See Edward W. Barrett, *Truth is Our Weapon,* chs. 5 and 6. Barrett was assistant secretary of state for public affairs, 1950–1952. Also consult Randolph Wieck, *Ignorance Abroad: American Educational and Cultural Foreign Policy and the Office of Assistant Secretary of State,* 13–18; and Thomas C. Sorenson, *The Word War: The Story of American Propaganda,* 21–30.

25. "The Truth About America," United States Cultural Cooperation and Information Program, Office of Public Affairs, Department of State, May 1947.

26. Gene Caprio, "View of America," *Foreign Service Journal* (July 1952): 20–21, 53; Bowles to Sargeant, 7 November 1951, Bowles Papers, Box 96, file 280; Bowles to Sargeant, 10 October 1951, Bowles Papers, Box 49, file 542, YUL. The USIE had been established in 1948 with the passage of the Smith-Mundt Act. It greatly expanded on the already existing Fulbright Exchange Program. See Wieck, *Ignorance Abroad,* 14–17.

27. Sampson to Roosevelt, 26 January 1952; Acheson to Roosevelt, 13 February 1952, RG 59, 811.411/1–2852, NA.

28. Marguerite Preston to Frances Barry, 5 February 1952, RG 59, Records Relating to International Information Activities, 1938–1953 (Records of IIA), Box 86, Negroes file, NA.

29. Charles Arnot to Melvin Weightman, 7 February 1952, RG 59, Records of IIA, Box 86, Negroes file, NA.

30. Mr. Fisk to Frances Barry, 7 February 1952, RG 59, Records of IIA, Box 86, Negroes file, NA.

31. USIS Feature, 24 December 1952; USIS Feature, 11 December 1952, Record Group 306, Records of the United States Information Agency, Air Bulletins, Box 3, USIS Feature, December 24, 1952 and USIS Feature, December 11, 1952, NA.

32. "Americans of Negro Descent: An Advancing Group," June 1950, RG 59, Records of IIA, Box 86, Negroes file, NA.

33. "The Negro in American Life," contained in Edward Barrett to Howland Sargeant, 21 January 1952, Sargeant Papers, Box 4, Correspondence-Asst. Sec. of State for Public Affairs, 1952 file, HSTL.

Notes to Chapter 3

1. For a brief but interesting discussion of African-American diplomats who served from 1869 through 1949, see Jake C. Miller, *The Black Presence in Foreign Affairs,* ch. 1.

2. Richard Bardolph, *The Negro Vanguard,* 72.

3. Office of Equal Employment Opportunity, Department of State, "A Chronology of Key Negro Appointments in the Department of State and the Foreign Service, 1869–1969," May 1969, furnished to author from the Personal Papers of Ronald D. Palmer; also see, U.S. Department of State, *United States Chiefs of Mission, 1778–1982.* The "Chronology" turned out by the Department of State cites a few interesting deviations. George H. Jackson served as consul at Cognac, France (1897); Henry W. Furniss was appointed as consul to Bahia, Brazil (1898); Richard T. Greener was made consul and commercial agent to Vladivostok (1898); Jerome B. Peterson served as consul at Puerto Cabello, Venezuela (1904); and William J. Yerby was appointed consul to Sierra Leone (1906).

4. Homer L. Calkin, "A Reminiscence: Being Black in the Foreign Service," *Department of State Newsletter* (February 1978): 26.

5. Andrew L. Steigman, *The Foreign Service of the United States: First Line of Defense,* 16–21. Also consult Robert D. Schulzinger, *The Making of the Diplomatic Mind: The Training, Outlook, and Style of United States Foreign Service Officers, 1908–1931,* chs. 1–3; and Martin Weil, *A Pretty Good Club: The Founding Fathers of the U.S. Foreign Service,* chs. 1 and 2.

6. Schulzinger, *Making of the Diplomatic Mind,* 107–108. For a good study of women in the Department of State, see Homer L. Calkin, *Women in the Department of State: Their Role in American Foreign Affairs.*

7. See "Chronology," 2–5; Schulzinger, *Making of the Diplomatic Mind,* 110; Calkin, *Women in the Department of State,* 69–70; Calkin, "A Reminiscence," 25–26; Memorandum, "Policy of the Department of State with reference to the assignment and transfer of Negro personnel of the Foreign Service," prepared by Harold Sims, 10 May 1949, contained in George McGhee to John Peurifoy, 19 January 1950, Papers of Edward R. Dudley, Box 1, Folder 8, Amistad Research Center, Tulane University, New

Orleans (ARC). In addition to women and blacks, Grew and others also sought to bar naturalized citizens. Weil, *A Pretty Good Club,* chs. 1–3, has some excellent material on the social make-up of the Department of State during these important years. The evidence cited by Calkin in *Women in the Department of State* relating to the biases of Grew and others came from the files of the Personnel Library of the Bureau of Personnel in the Department. The Personnel Library, unfortunately, was terminated in the early 1990s. Some of the more recent publications in the library were dispersed to other offices in the Department; the older, primary documents were, apparently, destroyed. Calkin had been working on a separate volume dealing with minorities in the Department prior to his death. Sadly, his notes and data for that study are also gone.

8. Weil, *A Pretty Good Club,* 47.

9. Memorandum, "Policy of the Department of State with reference to the assignment and transfer of Negro personnel of the Foreign Service," 10 May 1949, prepared by Harold Sims and contained in McGhee to Peurifoy, 19 January 1950, Dudley Papers, Box 1, Folder 8, ARC.

10. Wharton was a very private individual and not given to much self-promotion. Details of his life before serving in the Department of State are sketchy. See Calkin, "A Reminiscence," 26; Michael L. Krenn, "Clifton Reginald Wharton, Sr.," in *Notable U.S. Ambassadors Since 1775: A Biographical Dictionary,* ed. Cathal J. Nolan, 365–369; and a short biographical piece found in the Papers of Clifton Wharton, Box 2, Biographical Materials folder, Special Collections, Mugar Memorial Library, Boston University, Boston (MML). There is not much to be found in this collection; it is two boxes made up mostly of memorabilia and some press clippings. His son, Clifton Wharton Jr. (who also served in the Department of State), has indicated that he is currently at work on an autobiography in which he will discuss his father at length.

11. "A Short History of the U.S. Department of State, 1781–1981," *Department of State Bulletin* (January 1981): 538.

12. Calkin, *Women in the Department of State,* 72.

13. Calkin, "A Reminiscence," 27.

14. Biographical sketch, Wharton Papers, Box 2, Biographical Materials folder, MML; Calkin, "A Reminiscence," 27–28; Krenn, "Wharton," 365–369; Memorandum, "Policy of the Department of State . . . ," 10 May 1949, Dudley Papers, Box 1, Folder 8, ARC.

15. Memorandum for the President, 8 January 1945; Grew to Truman, 9 May 1945, Record Group 59, General Records of the Department of State, Decimal File, 121.4/1–845, National Archives (NA).

16. Miller, *The Black Presence,* 11. Apparently, not long after his appointment, Lanier made an effort to upgrade his position to ambassador. A note from Stanley Woodward in the Department of State to one of Truman's aides stated, "In regard to Mr. Lanier's suggestion that he be made an ambassador, it might be suggested that the President would not consider such a move desirable at this time." (Woodward to Connelly, 27 June 1946, Papers of Harry S. Truman, White House Central Files [WHCF], Official Files [OF], Folder 476–Misc., Harry S. Truman Library [HSTL].) Exactly why it was not desirable, given the fact that in 1949 the U.S. mission in Liberia *was* upgraded to embassy status, was not explained.

17. For background on Dudley, see "America's First Negro Ambassador," *Ebony* 5:12 (October 1950): 80–84; Krenn, "Edward R. Dudley," *Notable U.S. Ambassadors,* 88–93; Author's interview with Edward R. Dudley, 15 January 1995, on deposit with the Foreign Affairs Oral History Program (FAOHP), Lauinger Library (LL), Georgetown University.

18. Kenneth Birkhead, Oral History, 69–70, HSTL. For more on Truman, the African-American vote, and the 1948 election, see William C. Berman, "Civil Rights and Civil Liberties," in *The Truman Period as a Research Field,* ed. Richard S. Kirkendall,

192–193; Mary L. Dudziak, "Desegregation as a Cold War Imperative," *Stanford Law Review* 41 (November 1988): 78–80; and Donald R. McCoy and Richard T. Ruetten, *Quest and Response: Minority Rights and the Truman Administration,* 145–146.

19. Memorandum for the President from Edward Stettinius, 16 April 1945, Truman Papers, WHCF, President's Secretary's Files (PSF), Box 159, Subject File-Cabinet, State, Secy. of—policy manual, April 16, 1945 folder, HSTL; Charles E. Saltzman to Secretary of State, 8 October 1947, RG 59, 882.00/10–847, NA; Memorandum, "Subject: The Interest of the United States Government and Peoples in the Republic of Liberia," 12 August 1948, Truman Papers, OF, Box 1356, File 476–Misc., HSTL. For a good firsthand account of this U.S. activity in Liberia, see the article by Earl P. Hanson, who served as chief of the Foreign Economic Administration's mission to Liberia until 1946: "The United States Invades Africa," *Harper's Magazine* (February 1947): 170–177.

20. Dudley interview, 2; "America's First Negro Ambassador," *Ebony,* 80.

21. Lovett to Truman, 19 January 1949, Truman Papers, WHCF, Confidential File (CF), Box 39, State Dept. Correspondence, 1948–49 file, folder 5, HSTL.

22. *Baltimore Afro-American* (26 March 1949): 2. News of Dudley's elevation to ambassador was buried deep in the *New York Times* (15 March 1949): 16; the fact that Dudley was the first African-American to hold that title was not even mentioned. Dudley's appointment was front-page news in the *New York Amsterdam News* (19 March 1949) and the *Pittsburgh Courier* (26 March 1949).

23. Together with the records from the Personnel Library, which, as noted earlier, have been lost or destroyed, the lot file records of Deputy Under Secretary for Administration John Peurifoy, who served first as assistant secretary of state for administration, 1947–1949, and then as deputy under secretary for administration, 1949–1950, were also destroyed.

24. For overviews of Truman's civil rights activities, see Berman, "Civil Rights and Civil Liberties"; McCoy and Ruetten, *Quest and Response;* and Dudziak, "Desegregation."

25. Department of State, "Discrimination in Transfer and Reemployment of Government Employees," 15 January 1946; "Principles and Policies of Departmental Personnel Administration," 3 May 1944, Records of the President's Committee on Civil Rights (PCCR), Box 6, State Department file, HSTL.

26. Data enclosed in Arch Jenn to Robert Carr, 22 August 1947, Records of PCCR, Box 5, Government Departments and Agencies: Replies to Letters from the PCCR re Federal Government Employment of negroes (including working papers) file, HSTL. Responses from other agencies concerning minority employment can be compared to that from the Department of State (figures indicate percentage of workforce which is African-American): Department of Commerce: about 12 percent; Federal Security Agency: 21 percent; Civil Service Commission: 22 percent; Department of Interior: about 8 percent; Department of Agriculture: about 8 percent. Figures from a 1946 memorandum by Truman aide Philleo Nash indicated that in 1944, African-Americans made up 12 percent of employees in "Federal War Agencies" and 11.6 percent of employees in "all other Federal Government Agencies." (Philleo Nash to Ed Brown, 28 October 1946, Papers of David Niles, Box 26, Civil Rights/Negro Affairs, 1945–June 1947 file, HSTL.) In Department of State employment reports, there were occasional references to Asian-Americans, Hispanics, and "others." Department records do not reveal any effort to pursue the issue of employment for members of these racial categories with anything approaching the intensity of the interest directed toward African-Americans. In general, most reports from the federal government dealing with "minority employment" had as their focus African-American employment.

27. Villard to Bunche, 25 January 1946, Papers of Ralph Bunche, Box 101, Misc. Memoranda, Letters, 1946 file, University Research Libraries-Special Collections, UCLA (URL-SC).

28. Ralph G. Martin, "So You Want To Be a Diplomat," *New Republic* (27 October 1947): 17–19; Lanier to Secretary of State, 2 January 1948; Donald W. Smith to Lanier, 16 February 1948, both attached to McGhee to Peurifoy, 19 January 1950, Dudley Papers, Box 1, Folder 8, ARC.

29. "Policy of the Department of State with reference . . .," 10 May 1949, Dudley Papers, Box 1, Folder 8, ARC. Sims had only been in the Foreign Service four years when he prepared the report. Later that same year he was sent as a U.S. representative to the International Conferences on Land Utilization and Indigenous Rural Economy in Nigeria. In 1951, he was briefly officer in charge of West, Central, and East African Affairs, and then was sent to Salisbury, Rhodesia, to serve as consul general.

30. Ravndal to Peurifoy, 23 May 1949, Truman Papers, WHCF, CF, State Department Correspondence series, Box 39, 1948–1949 folder, no. 5, HSTL. For more on this memorandum, see Michael L. Krenn, "Outstanding Negroes and Appropriate Countries: Some Facts, Figures, and Thoughts on Black U.S. Ambassadors, 1949–1988," *Diplomatic History* 14 (Winter 1990): 131–141. The difference in citation for the memorandum is due to the fact that the papers in the Truman Library were reorganized between the publication of the 1990 research note and this present study. Peurifoy's memorandum to Ravndal has not been located; it may have been in the papers of the assistant secretary of state for administration, which have been destroyed.

31. Author's interview with Ronald Palmer, 28 September 1995, 23; Author's interview with Terence A. Todman, 13 June 1995, 18. Also consult the other interviews conducted by the author with Richard K. Fox, Horace Dawson, and Edward R. Dudley. All interviews are in the FAOHP, LL.

32. Department of State, "Black American Chiefs of Mission," March 1993; Krenn,"Outstanding Negroes."

33. Jessup to Rusk, 29 October 1949, RG 59, 121.3/10–2949, NA; Javits to Clement, 28 December 1951, Papers of the NAACP, Group II, Box A617, State Department, Qualified Negroes for, 1950–1954 file, LC.

34. Dudley to Peurifoy, c. 18 May 1950, Dudley Papers, Box 1, Folder 8, ARC. The original memorandum was not found in the papers. Dudley undoubtedly received his copy of the memorandum from George McGhee, a consistent proponent of getting more African-Americans into the Foreign Service.

35. Ravndal to Peurifoy, 23 May 1949, Truman Papers, WHCF, CF, State Department Correspondence, Box 39, 1948–1949 (5) file, HSTL; Sims to McGhee, 12 January 1950, Dudley Papers, Box 1, Folder 8, ARC; Memorandum of Conversation, 1 March 1951, attached to McGhee to Bourgerie, 8 June 1951, RG 59, Records of the Assistant Secretary of State for Near East, South Asia, and African Affairs, 1946–1951, Box 2, NA.

36. Daniel Brantley, "Black Americans as Participants in the Foreign Service," *The Crisis* 93:9 (November 1986): 32–33; Dudley to Richard P. Butrick, 14 July 1950; John W. Jago to Dudley, 19 July 1950, Dudley Papers, Box 1, Folder 8, ARC. Dudley, in a 1995 interview with the author, gave much of the credit for the "silent revolution" (and even the decision to raise the U.S. legation to embassy level) to the work done by the African-American FSOs in Monrovia, particularly Rupert Lloyd. (Dudley Interview, FAOHP, LL.)

37. Brantley, "Black Americans," 32–33.

38. Dudley to Truman, n.d. [1953], Dudley Papers, Box 1, Folder 12, ARC.

39. Bowles to Frances Williams, 20 August, 23 October 1951, Papers of Chester Bowles, Box 50, folder 584; Bowles to Williams, 14 November 1951, Bowles Papers, Box 96, Folder 290, Yale University Library (YUL).

40. Bowles to Sargeant, 24 December 1951; Bowles to Gerald Drew, 2 January

1953; Bowles to Allen, 22 March 1953, Bowles Papers, Box 96, Folder 280; Box 94, Folder 242; Box 93, Folder 229, YUL (emphasis in original).

41. George McGhee, "United States Interests in Africa," *Department of State Bulletin* 22:572 (19 July 1950): 1001; "Regional Policy Statement on Africa South of the Sahara," *Foreign Relations of the United States, 1950,* 5:1598. For more on McGhee's views on U.S. relations with Africa, see his 1983 memoir, *Envoy to the Middle World: Adventures in Diplomacy;* Brenda Gayle Plummer, *Rising Wind: Black Americans and U.S. Foreign Affairs, 1935–1960,* 235–238; Thomas Borstelmann, *Apartheid's Reluctant Uncle: The United States and South Africa in the Early Cold War,* 158–159. On p. 115, Borstelmann offers another side of McGhee's attitudes toward race, noting that he was "a white oil executive from Texas who acknowledged later that his Southern roots inclined him to sympathy with white South Africans and 'their extremely difficult racial problem.'"

42. McGhee to Dudley, 7 April 1950, RG 59, Records of AS/S for NE, SA, and AA, Box 2, NA. McGhee also spoke highly of Dudley in his 1983 memoir, recalling both his trip to Liberia in 1950, as well as an event that took place while they were traveling together to the Lourenço Marques conference in 1950. Stopping in Johannesburg, McGhee insisted that Dudley stay at the U.S. consulate (where McGhee would normally be housed) to "avoid the indignity of not being able to use the common rooms of the hotel, because he was black." (McGhee, *Envoy to the Middle World,* 120, 135–136)

43. Alice Dunnigan, "40 Serve in Diplomatic Service in Foreign Field," *Baltimore Afro-American* (18 August 1951): 3. The article also cited Harold Sims, Andrew Lynch (who had served as assistant chief and then acting chief of the Division of African Affairs, 1946–1948, and gone on to serve at Tripoli and in Jordan), Henry Villard, Garland Farmer, Clare Timberlake (who had served as assistant chief and then chief of the Division of African Affairs, 1946–1947, and had gone on to serve in India and Germany), and Ruth C. Sloan as having "sought to break up the solid colored staff in Liberia."

44. Sims to Dudley, 21 June 1951, Dudley Papers, Box 1, Folder 8, ARC. Sims also noted the work of others in the Department to bring about better opportunities for African-Americans: Andrew Lynch, Clare Timberlake, George McGhee (all of whom had been cited in Dunnigan's article), and Joseph Palmer II (who had served as acting assistant chief, assistant chief, and acting chief of the Division of African Affairs, 1947–1948, and had then gone on to serve in London).

45. "Statement to President Truman at the White House Conference on February 28, 1951," Papers of A. Philip Randolph, Box 31, Subject File, White House Conference, Truman, Correspondence, M-W 1951 (2) folder, LC.

46. Gerald Horne, *Black and Red: W.E.B. Du Bois and the Afro-American Response to the Cold War, 1944–1963;* Plummer, *Rising Wind;* Borstelmann, *Apartheid's Reluctant Uncle.*

47. Henderson, memorandum to Members of the National Board of Directors of the American Council on Human Rights, 1 March 1951, Papers of A. Philip Randolph, Box 31, Subject File, White House Conference, Truman, Correspondence, A-L 1951 (1) folder, LC.

48. Randolph to Logan, 5 April 1951, Randolph Papers, Box 31, Subject File, White House Conference, Truman, Correspondence, A-L 1951 (1) folder, LC. Originally, anywhere from ten to thirteen African-American leaders were to meet with Acheson. In the end, those present were Logan, Clarence Mitchell, Elmer Henderson, William T. Bell (Bishop, Colored Methodist Episcopal Church, South Boston, Virginia), Theodore Brown (Brotherhood of Sleeping Car Porters, replacing an ailing Randolph), and Jeanette Welch Brown (National Council of Negro Women, representing Bethune). See the original list, "Members of Committee of Negro Leaders who will attend conference with C.E. Wilson, Director of Mobilization and Dean Acheson, Secretary of State," n.d.; and

the list attached to the "Statement to the Honorable Dean Acheson, Secretary of State," 13 April 1951, both found in Randolph Papers, Box 31, Subject File, White House Conference, Truman, Correspondence, M-W 1951 (2) folder, LC. For the list of those who actually attended, see the memorandum prepared by one of Acheson's assistants of "Meeting of Negro Leaders with Secretary Acheson on April 13, 1951," 16 April 1951, Papers of Dean Acheson, Box 66, Secretary of State: Memos of Conversations File, April 1951 folder, HSTL.

49. "Statement to the Honorable Dean Acheson, Secretary of State," 13 April 1951, Randolph Papers, Box 31, Subject File, White House Conference, Truman, Correspondence, A-L 1951 (1) folder, LC.

50. Patrick Condon, "Meeting of Negro Leaders with Secretary Acheson on April 13, 1951," 16 April 1951, Acheson Papers, Box 66, Secretary of State: Memos of Conversations file, April 1951 folder, HSTL.

51. Diary entry, 14 April 1951, Papers of Rayford Logan, Diaries, Personal File, Box 5, 1950–1951 folder, LC.

52. Randolph to Martin, 20 April 1951, Randolph Papers, Box 31, Subject File, White House Conference, Truman, Correspondence, M-W 1951 (2) folder, LC.

53. McCoy and Ruetten, *Quest and Response,* 259. Much of the evidence for the section of their book dealing with State Department hiring of African-Americans comes from records of the Office of Personnel. Requests to the Department of State as to the whereabouts of these records went unanswered. Unfortunately, they might have been part of the records from the Personnel Library of the Bureau of Personnel, which were destroyed after that bureau was phased out.

54. Tobias to Randolph, 8 May 1951, Randolph Papers, Box 31, Subject File, White House Conference, Truman, Correspondence, M-W 1951 (2) folder, LC.

55. "Report to Board of Directors," June 1951; Arch K. Jenn to White, 16 July 1951, Papers of NAACP, Group II, Box A617, State Department, General, 1951 file, LC. The name of the individual hired was not specified. It may have been Herbert H. Tate, who was appointed to the Foreign Service in April 1951 and assigned as assistant attaché to Karachi. Lawrence B. Wilson was appointed as a vice consul to Bombay (with USIE) in May 1951.

56. Randolph to Acheson, 28 March 1952, Randolph Papers, Box 31, Subject File, White House Conference, Truman, Correspondence, A-W 1952 folder, LC.

57. Randolph to William Bell, 14 July 1952, Randolph Papers, Box 31, Subject File, White House Conference, Truman, Correspondence, A-W 1952 folder (a copy of the same letter to Walter White, dated 17 July 1952, is found in the Papers of NAACP, Group II, Box A617, State Department, General, 1952–1954 file); Mitchell to White, 19 November 1952, Papers of NAACP, Group II, Box A617, State Department, General, 1952–1954 file, LC.

58. Mitchell to White, 6 April 1953, enclosing State Department report, Papers of NAACP, Group II, Box A617, State Department, General, 1952–1954 file, LC (emphasis in original).

59. "Chronology," 5–6.

Notes to Chapter 4

1. "Rising Tide of Color," *The Crisis* (May 1960): 306–307.

2. James L. Roark, "American Black Leaders: The Response to Colonialism and the Cold War, 1953–1953," *African Historical Studies* 4:2 (1971): 266–270.

3. Gerald Horne, *Black and Red: W.E.B. Du Bois and the Afro-American Response to the Cold War, 1944–1963,* 57 (see chs. 6 and 7 for more details); Penny M. Von Eschen, *Race Against Empire: Black Americans and Anticolonialism, 1937–1957,* 110

(see ch. 5 for more on the "leftist"/"liberal" split); Thomas Borstelmann, *Apartheid's Reluctant Uncle: The United States and South Africa in the Early Cold War,* 67 (see ch. 4 for more information).

4. Brenda Gayle Plummer, *Rising Wind: Black Americans and U.S. Foreign Policy, 1935–1960,* 210–212 (see ch. 5 for more details).

5. "NAACP Stand on Colonialism and U.S. Foreign Policy," *The Crisis* (January 1955): 23–26; William Worthy, Jr., "Our Disgrace in Indo-China," *The Crisis* (February 1954): 77–83; "Portuguese Colonialism," *The Crisis* (February 1956): 102–104; "Unrest in Angola," *The Crisis* (June–July 1960): 383–385.

6. Randolph to Eisenhower, 17 June 1953, Record Group 59, General Records of the Department of State, Decimal File, 770.00/6–1753, National Archives (NA); P.L. Prattis, "New Look at the World," *The Crisis* (April 1953): 201–204, 255.

7. Wilkins to Dulles, 1 April 1954, Papers of the NAACP, Group II, Box A617, State Department, General, 1952–1954 file, Library of Congress (LC); George W. Westerman, "American-Panamanian Relations," *The Crisis* (March 1953): 147–153, 187–188; "Panama Friction," *The Crisis* (November 1960): 594–595.

8. Barnett to Allen, 15 May 1956, RG 59, 611.70/5–1556, NA.

9. Worthy, "Our Disgrace in Indo-China," 77–83; Horace Cayton, "World At Large," *Pittsburgh Courier* (10 September 1960): 14.

10. Horace Cayton, "A New Black Nation on the World Scene," *Pittsburgh Courier* (9 February 1957): 7 (magazine section); George Padmore, "The Press Campaign Against Ghana," *The Crisis* (December 1957): 607–612; "The Return of Saturday's Child," *Ebony* (August 1958): 19–26.

11. Roy Wilkins to five of the prime ministers in attendance, 15 April 1955, Papers of NAACP, Group II, Box A97, Bandung Conference, 1955 file, LC; Cumming to Department of State, 26 April 1955, RG 59, 670.901/4–2655, NA.

12. Borstelmann, *Apartheid's Reluctant Uncle,* has a number of references to the African-American interest in South Africa throughout; also see, Plummer, *Rising Wind,* 231–233.

13. For examples of stories in *The Crisis,* see "More Apartheid" (January 1955): 35; "South African Censorship" (March 1956): 157; "South Africa 'Treason Defendants' " (June-July 1959): 344; "South African Apartheid" (December 1960): 649–650; Wilkins to Herter, 22 March 1960, Papers of NAACP, Group III, Box A35, Africa, South Africa, 1956–1965 and undated file, LC.

14. Horace R. Cayton, "World At Large," *Pittsburgh Courier* (28 December 1957): 10.

15. "Our Ill Will Ambassadors," *Chicago Defender* (4 January 1958): 10; P.L. Prattis, "Horizon," *Pittsburgh Courier* (15 February 1958): 13; George S. Schuyler, "Views and Reviews," *Pittsburgh Courier* (12 April 1958): 12.

16. Horace R. Cayton, "World At Large," *Pittsburgh Courier* (February 15, 1958): 14; Du Bois to Membership of the Third Committee, United Nations General Assembly, 10 October 1957, Papers of W.E.B. Du Bois, Reel 72, Frame 1044, LC.

17. John E. Owen, "U.S. Race Relations—A World Issue," *The Crisis* (January 1954): 19–22; Otto Leichter, "The Negro Problem—Interpreted for Europeans," *The Crisis* (April 1955): 215–220.

18. J.A. Rogers, "History Shows," *Pittsburgh Courier* (April 12, 1958): 13.

19. "Discrimination Hurts Democracy, Speaker Says," *Norfolk Journal and Guide* (1 November 1958): 2.

20. Saunders Redding, *An American in India: A Personal Report on the Indian Dilemma and the Nature of Her Conflicts,* 34–36, 66–67, 114, 172.

21. Carl T. Rowan, *The Pitiful and the Proud,* ch. 10, and 191–192, 224–225, 378–379.

22. White to editor, *New York Times Magazine* (8 February 1954), Papers of Chester

Bowles, Box 147, Folder 461, Yale University Library (YUL); White to Dulles, 17 March 1954, Papers of NAACP, Group II, Box A617, State Department, General, 1952–1954 file, LC.

23. Horace R. Cayton, "World At Large," *Pittsburgh Courier* (December 21, 1957): 10.

24. "Little Rock Still International Issue, U.S. Learns," *Baltimore Afro-American* (24 May 1958): 3; Horace R. Cayton, "World At Large," *Pittsburgh Courier* (17 May 1958): 14.

25. Robert G. Spivack, "Faubus and U.S. Enemies," *Norfolk Journal and Guide* (4 October 1958): 8.

26. "A Statement to President Dwight D. Eisenhower," 23 June 1958, Dwight D. Eisenhower, Papers as President of the United States, 1953–1961, (Ann Whitman File), DDE Diary Series, Box 33, June 1958–Staff Notes (2) folder, Dwight D. Eisenhower Library, Abilene, KS (DDEL); "Suggested draft of resolution for Board Action, September 8, 1958," Papers of Arthur Spingarn, Secretary's File, Board of Directors of NAACP, Box 27, 1917–1963 and undated file, LC.

27. William P. Robinson Sr., "The Impact of Discrimination Upon American Foreign Policy—The Problem," *Negro History Bulletin* (October 1957): 19–21.

28. Alice A. Dunnigan, "Washington Inside Out," *Pittsburgh Courier* (2 July 1960): 6.

29. Rayford W. Logan, "Courier's 4-Point Program for New Secretary of State," *Pittsburgh Courier* (6 December 1952): 1, 5.

30. Barnett to John W. Davis, 9 April 1953, Dudley Papers, Box 1, Folder 12, ARC.

31. Mitchell to White, 1 May 1953, Papers of NAACP, Group II, Box A617, State Department, General, 1952–1954 file, LC; Scott McLeod to Donald Lourie, 5 May 1953, RG 59, Records Relating to Equal Opportunity Employment and Minority Employment in the Department of State, 1943–1966, Box 3, FEPC-Department's Policy Procedures file, NA; McLeod's memo begins with a typographical error, stating that the meeting was held on "May 28"—three weeks *after* he wrote the memo.

32. "Secretary's Report," April 1953, Papers of NAACP, Group II, Box A617, State Department, General, 1952–1954 file, LC; McLeod to Lourie, 5 May 1953, RG 59, Records Relating to EOE, Box 3, FEPC-Department's Policy Procedures file, NA; "Secretary's Report," May 1953, Papers of NAACP, Group II, Box A617, State Department, General, 1952–1954 file, LC.

33. Mitchell to McLeod, 26 May 1953, RG 59, Records Relating to EOE, Box 2, FEPC Correspondence-General file, NA; "Secretary's Report," July and August 1953; Memo of conversation, Herbert L. Wright to Harriet Mitchell, 17 June 1953, Papers of NAACP, Group II, Box A617, State Department, General, 1952–1954 file; State Department, Qualified Negroes for, 1950–1954 file, LC.

34. Powell to Eisenhower, 10 June 1953, Eisenhower Papers, White House Central Files, 1953–1961 (WHCF), Official File (OF), Box 731, 142–A-4 (1), DDEL; Powell to George Wilson, 8 April 1954, RG 59, Records Relating to EOE, Box 2, FEPC Correspondence-General file, NA.

35. "Appointment of Congressman Adam Clayton Powell, Jr. With the President—May 11, 1955," Eisenhower Papers, Whitman File, Whitman Diary, Box 5, ACW Diary May 1955 (5) file, DDEL; "Powell hits Dulles, State Department," *Baltimore Afro-American* (5 April 1958): 5; "Powell Criticizes State Dept. for Rejecting Negro Personnel," *Jet* (10 April 1958): 10–11.

36. "Diggs hits barrier in foreign service," *Baltimore Afro-American* (31 December 1960): 8.

37. Granger to Maxwell Rabb, 29 September 1953, RG 59, Records Relating to EOE, Box 1, Employment of Negroes in the Department file, NA.

38. Randolph to King, Granger, and Wilkins, 23 June 1958, Papers of A. Philip

Randolph, Box 31, Subject File, White House Conference, Eisenhower, Correspondence, E-S, 1958–1959 and undated file, LC.

39. Farmer and Odom to Wilkins, 7 December 1960, Papers of NAACP, Group III, Box A147, Government-National-USIA-1956–1965 file, LC.

40. Ethel L. Payne, "U.S. Diplomacy Not Diplomatic Where Race is Concerned," *Chicago Defender* (4 May 1957): 11.

41. Louis Lautier, "U.S. 'token' representation policy raked over the coals," *Baltimore Afro-American* (14 December 1957): 5; Lautier, "Say Diplomatic Policy of State Department in Need of Revision," *Baltimore Afro-American* (4 July 1959): 5.

42. "Ticker Tape U.S.A.," *Jet* (13 November 1958): 10; (27 August 1959): 10.

43. "Merit Hiring in Foreign Policy," *New York Age* (19 September 1959): 6.

44. "Ready to Appoint Tan Diplomats," *Baltimore Afro-American* (21 May 1955): 1, 2; "Seek More Negroes in State Department," *New York Amsterdam News* (6 August 1955): 3; Ollie Stewart, "Chances good for foreign service job assignments in Europe, Africa, Asia," *Baltimore Afro-American* (21 April 1956): 13.

45. William Worthy, "Diplomatic Service in the Far East," *Baltimore Afro-American* (2 July 1955): 7 (magazine section).

46. Marguerite Cartwright, "Charles H. Mahoney: Our First Permanent Delegate to the UN," *Pittsburgh Courier* (8 January 1955): 3 (magazine section); "Do-It-Now Diplomat," *Ebony* (March 1958): 43–44, 46–47. Cartwright also wrote, "The United Nations and the U.S. Negro," *The Negro History Bulletin* (April 1955): 164–167, which focused on Mahoney and Archibald Carey, a Chicago politician and lawyer. As for Jones, his four-year stay in Liberia (1955–1959) was the only position he ever served with the Department of State.

47. Ollie Stewart, "Rudy Aggrey directs U.S. center in Paris," *Baltimore Afro-American* (9 November 1957): 11; "Dr. Snowden new attaché to U.S. Embassy in Rome," *Baltimore Afro-American* (28 August 1954): 1, 2; also see, "Top Diplomatic Post for Howard U. Prof," *New York Amsterdam News* (21 August 1954): 3; "Morocco's Big American Family," *Ebony* (November 1958): 87–88; and "Morrow is sworn in as ambassador," *Baltimore Afro-American* (4 July 1959): 5.

48. "Clifton Wharton Gets New Job in France," *Baltimore Afro-American* (28 November 1953): 1, 12; "U.S. Sends 1st Negro Consul General to France," *Jet* (3 December 1953): 3–4.

49. "Negro Named U.S. Minister to Rumania," *New York Amsterdam News* (1 February 1958): 1, 7; "Ace in the Race," *New York Amsterdam News* (1 February 1958): 6; "Bostonian is Nominated Ambassador [sic] to Roumania [sic]," *Baltimore Afro-American* (1 February 1958): 1; "Wharton bolstering U.S. prestige abroad," *Baltimore Afro-American* (12 April 1958): 3; "Name Negro Diplomat to European Post," *Jet* (6 February 1958): 3; "Wharton First Colored Envoy," *Norfolk Journal and Guide* (15 February 1958): 2; "Breaking the Diplomatic Pattern," *Pittsburgh Courier* (15 February 1958): 12.

Notes to Chapter 5

1. Robert F. Burk, *The Eisenhower Administration and Black Civil Rights*. Also see Harvard Sitkoff, *The Struggle for Black Equality, 1954–1980*, chs. 1–3; Richard Polenberg, *One Nation Divisible: Class, Race, and Ethnicity in the United States since 1938*, 153–163; J.W. Anderson, *Eisenhower, Brownell, and the Congress: The Tangled Origins of the Civil Rights Bill of 1956–1957;* Daniel M. Berman, *A Bill Becomes Law: The Civil Rights Act of 1960;* Foster Rhea Dulles, *The Civil Rights Commission, 1957–*

1965. Somewhat more positive views are found in Michael S. Mayer, "With Much Deliberation and Some Speed: Eisenhower and the *Brown* Decision," *Journal of Southern History* 52 (February 1986): 43–76; and James C. Duram, *A Moderate Among Extremists: Dwight D. Eisenhower and the School Desegregation Crisis.*

2. "Telephone Calls, March 30, 1960, 4:20," Papers of Dwight D. Eisenhower, Ann Whitman File, DDE Diary Series, Box 48, Telephone Calls March 1960 file, Dwight D. Eisenhower Library (DDEL).

3. "Dulles Told Cayton U.S. Race Prejudice Hurting Us Abroad!," *Pittsburgh Courier* (6 December 1952): 1; Bob Houston to Dulles, 19 February 1956; Dulles to Houston, 24 March 1956, Papers of John Foster Dulles, Box 104, Houston, Robert E., Jr., 1956 file; Houston to Dulles, 26 September 1957; Dulles to Houston, 1 October 1956, Dulles Papers, Box 121, Re: Racial Integration, 1957 file, Seeley Mudd Library, Princeton University (SML).

4. Lodge to Dulles, 15 February, 23 March 1956; Dulles to Lodge, 3 April 1956, John Foster Dulles Papers, Box 4, General Correspondence and Memoranda Series, Miscellaneous Correspondence March 3, 1956–May 7, 1956 file; Powell to Eisenhower, Eisenhower Papers, White House Central Files (WHCF), Confidential File (CF), Subject Series, Box 70, State, Department of (November–December 1955) file, DDEL.

5. Untitled report, c. mid-1953, Eisenhower Papers, Whitman File, Name Series, Box 3, Byrnes, James (2) file; Morrow to Sherman Adams, 4 June 1957, Files of E.F. Morrow-Administrative Office-Special Projects, Box 10, Civil Rights-Office Memoranda, 1957–1960 file, DDEL; "Negro Leaders Say President 'Lacks Grasp' of Race Problem," *Jet* (10 July 1958): 8–10. The untitled report has a handwritten notation at the top, "Memorandum for James E. Byrnes," but the numerous citations from South Carolina newspapers suggests that the report may have been *from* Byrnes. The mid-1953 dating is suggested by the fact that the last date for a newspaper citation in the report is June 27, 1953. For Morrow's account of his years with Eisenhower, see E. Frederic Morrow, *A Black Man in the White House.*

6. For a good introduction to the Eisenhower administration's propaganda program, see Walter L. Hixson, *Parting the Curtain: Propaganda, Culture, and the Cold War, 1945–1961.* In particular, see pp. 129–132 for how the U.S. government dealt with the issue of race. As Hixson concludes, up to the Little Rock crisis of 1957, the Eisenhower administration basically "exercised damage control" (131).

7. USIS Feature, "Louis Armstrong: American Musician," April 1953, USIS Youth Packet #1; "The American Negro in Baseball," July 1953, USIS Youth Packet #4; "Men of Action," August 1955, USIS Youth Packet #28, all in Record Group 306, Records of USIA, Feature Packets (FP), Recurring Subjects (RS), boxes 1–4, National Archives (NA).

8. "Wilkins' Appointment Highlights Progress of American Negro," April 1953, USIS Labor Packet #13; "Fair Employment Legislation in the United States," November 1954, USIS Labor Packet #20, all in RG 306, FP, RS, boxes 1, 8, 10, NA.

9. "Equal Education for All," June 1954, USIS Youth Packet #15, RG 306, FP, RS, box 2, NA.

10. Lodge to Eisenhower, 28 March 1956; Eisenhower to Dulles, 30 March 1956, Dulles Papers, White House Memoranda Series, Box 4, Meetings with the President, January 1956–July 1956 (4) file; Dulles, memo to Eisenhower, 12 April 1956, Dulles Papers, Chronological Series, Box 13, April 1956 (3) file, DDEL.

11. Program, "Color in Democracy: A Symposium," 18 November 1952, Papers of UNCF (microfiche edition), fiche 3791, LC.

12. Lindsley F. Kimball to Jackson, 20 October 1954, Papers of UNCF, fiche 3217, LC; Jackson to Dulles, 14 January 1955, Papers of C.D. Jackson, Box 88, Time Inc. File-United Negro College Fund 1955–1956 file, DDEL.

13. John D. Silvera, "Color—A Factor In U.S. Psychological Warfare: An Appraisal and Approach to the use of the Negro as PsyWar Themes," Eisenhower Papers, WHCF, OF, Box 673, 142–B, DDEL.

14. "Africa: Problems of United States Policy," c. 1956, enclosed in John Hoover to Various American Missions, 17 February 1956, RG 59, 611.70/2–1756, NA; "The Vice President's Report to the President on Trip to Africa, February 28—March 21, 1957," White House Office (WHO), Office of Special Assistant for National Security Affairs (NSA), Special Assistant Series, Subject Subseries, Box 10, Vice President (1) January 1954–April 1957 file; Memorandum, "Discussion at the 335th Meeting of the National Security Council, Thursday, August 22, 1957," 23 August 1957, Eisenhower Papers, National Security Council Series (NSC), Box 9, 335th Meeting of NSC, August 22, 1957 file, DDEL.

15. "Chronology"; Giles Hubert to Rufus Clement, c. August/September 1953, Papers of Giles Hubert, Box 1, Folder 16, Amistad Research Center (ARC).

16. Memorandum for the president, "Chief of Mission Appointments," enclosed in Sherman Adams to John Foster Dulles, 19 June 1953, Eisenhower Papers, WHCF, CF, Subject Series, Box 67, State, Department of (through September 1953) (8) file, DDEL; Department of State, *United States Chiefs of Mission, 1778–1982*, 145.

17. "Do-It-Now Diplomat," *Ebony* (March 1958): 43–44, 46–47; "Richard Lee Jones," n.d., WHO, Office of Special Assistant for Executive Appointments: Records, 1952–1961, Box 35, Jones, Richard Lee file, DDEL.

18. Davis to A.E. Weatherbee, 23 June 1953, Record Group 59, Records Relating to Equal Opportunity Employment and Minority Employment in the Department of State, 1943–1966 (Records of EOE), Box 3, FEPC-Department's Policy Procedure, NA.

19. John W. Roxborough II to George P. Wilson, 31 January 1955, RG 59, Records of EOE, FEPC Publicity file, NA; Ethel L. Payne, "U.S. Diplomacy Not Diplomatic Where Race is Concerned," *Chicago Defender* (4 May 1957): 11. Efforts to find a copy of Roxborough's report have been unsuccessful.

20. Davis to A.E. Weatherbee, 23 June 1953; Roxborough to George Wilson, 23 August 1956, RG 59, Records of EOE, Box 3, FEPC-Department's Policy Procedures file; Box 2, Employment Policy, 1959–1960 file, NA.

21. John W. Hanes to Donald Lourie, 6 March 1953, Dulles Papers, Special Assistant Chronological Series, Box 2, Chrono. O'Connor and Hanes March 2–18, 1953 (5) file, DDEL. Race entered into the Haitian appointment in another way. As Hanes explained, the person under consideration for Haiti was "a Floridian and hence a southerner." This posed a problem since "the Haitians, whatever they may think of themselves, are persons of decidedly dusky hue." It was, therefore, "desirable to pay our debt to Florida with some other of the South or Central American countries and not send a southerner to a colored country."

22. "Ike's Missing the Boat," *Chicago Defender* (18 July 1953): no page number, enclosed in William C. Hueston to Leonard Hall, 31 July 1953, Records of the Republican National Committee, Chairman (Hall), Box 114, Minority Groups, 1953 file, DDEL; "GOP Explains Why Envoy To Haiti Is White," *New York Amsterdam News* (15 September 1953): 3.

23. John E. Reinhardt, written response to questions from author, 15 June 1994, in possession of author.

24. "Telephone Conversation with Leonard Hall," 6 May 1953, Dulles Papers, Telephone Calls Series, Box 1, Telephone Memoranda (May-June 1953) (2) file, DDEL; W.K. Scott, Memorandum for the Secretary, 8 July 1953, Dulles Papers, Box 77, White, Walter, 1953 file, SML.

25. "The Communist Party and the Negro," n.d., enclosed in J. Edgar Hoover to

Robert Cutler, 18 February 1953; "The Communist Party and the negro, 1953–1956," n.d., enclosed in Hoover to William H. Jackson, 24 October 1956, WHO, NSA, FBI Series, Box 1, The Communist Party and the Negro (February 1953) file; Box 10, The Communist Party and the Negro (October 1956) file, DDEL. In addition, there is a report entitled, "Communism versus the Negro," found in the Papers of C.D. Jackson. Prepared either by or for Jackson in 1952, it came to the same conclusion as the FBI reports: "so long as the party continues to put Russia first, communist propaganda among American Negroes will not succeed." African-American membership in the Communist Party comprised "less than one tenth of one percent of Negro population." (Jackson Papers, Box 88, Time Inc. File-United Negro College Fund-Basic 1952 file, DDEL.)

26. Author's interview with Ronald D. Palmer, 28 September 1995, 7–15, 17–19, Foreign Affairs Oral History Program (FAOHP), Lauinger Library (LL), Georgetown University.

27. Author's interview with Terence A. Todman, 27 June 1995, 49–51, FAOHP, LL.

28. Department of State, "A Chronology of Key Negro Appointments in the Department of State and Foreign Service, 1869–1969," May 1969.

29. "Telephone Conversation with Gov. Adams," 17 July 1953, 1:56 P.M.; "Telephone Conversation with Gov. Adams," 17 July 1953, 5:25 P.M., Dulles Papers, Telephone Calls Series, Box 10, White House Telephone Conversations-May to December 31, 1953 (2) file, DDEL.

30. "Telephone Conversations Re: UN Delegation," 20 July 1953, 12:30–12:36; "Telephone Conversation with Gov. Adams," 22 July 1953, 2:10 P.M., Dulles Papers, Telephone Calls Series, Box 1, Telephone Memoranda (July-October 31, 1953) (5) file; Box 10, White House Telephone Conversations-May to December 31, 1953 (2) file, DDEL.

31. "Telephone Conversation with Gov. Adams," 8 July 1954, 2:44 P.M., Dulles Papers, Telephone Calls Series, Box 10, White House Telephone Conversations-General-July 1, 1954– October 30, 1954 (2) file, DDEL.

32. William R. Ming to Eisenhower, 5 September 1957, Eisenhower Papers, WHCF, OF, Box 732, 142–A-5–A (1), DDEL. The National Advisory Council of the AVC was a mixed bag indeed: Senator Paul Douglas, Clark Eichelberger, Abe Fortas, General Telford Taylor, Thornton Wilder, and Ronald Reagan.

33. "World Reaction to US Racial Integration Incidents," 12 September 1957; "Staff Notes No. 193," 13 September 1957, Eisenhower Papers, Whitman File, DDE Diary Series, Box 27, September 1957 Toner Notes, DDEL. For an interesting contemporary reading of the impact of Little Rock on U.S. foreign relations, see Harold R. Isaacs, "World Affairs and U.S. Race Relations: A Note On Little Rock," *Public Opinion Quarterly* (Fall 1958): 364–370. The most important and comprehensive study of the foreign policy implications of the Little Rock crisis is Mary L. Dudziak, "The Little Rock Crisis and Foreign Affairs: Race, Resistance, and the Image of American Democracy," *South California Law Review* (September 1997): 1641–1716.

34. "Reaction to US Integration Incidents Increases," 13 September 1957; "Staff Notes No. 199," 24 September 1957, Eisenhower Papers, Whitman File, DDE Diary Series, Box 27, September 1957 Toner Notes, DDEL.

35. "By phone from Wayne Hawks, Newport, 1:45 P.M., September 17, 1957," Papers of Bryce Harlow, Pre-Accession Collection, Box 11, Integration file; Lodge to Eisenhower, 25 September 1957, Eisenhower Papers, Whitman File, Administration, Box 24, Lodge, Henry Cabot 1957–1958 (3) file; "Telephone Call to Attorney General Brownell," 24 September 1957, 2:15 P.M., Dulles Papers, Telephone Calls

Series, Box 7, Memoranda Telephone Conversations-General-September 1957 to October 1957 (3) file, DDEL.

36. Foreign Broadcast Information Service, "Daily Report: Foreign Radio Broadcasts Supplement," 27 September 1957, Harlow Papers, Box 11, Integration file, DDEL.

37. "The World Looks at Little Rock," 2 October 1957, RG 306, Office of Research, Box 14, Special Reports, 1953–1963 file, NA.

38. USIA, Office of Research and Intelligence (ORI), "Public Reactions to Little Rock In Major World Capitals," 29 October 1957, Morrow Files, Box 11, Little Rock clippings and data file, DDEL.

39. USIA, ORI, "Post–Little Rock Opinion on the Treatment of Negroes in the U.S.," January 1958, Eisenhower Papers, WHCF, CF, Subject Series, Box 99, USIA (3) file, DDEL.

40. Lodge to Eisenhower, 15 October 1957, Eisenhower Papers, Whitman File, Administration, Box 24, Lodge, Henry Cabot 1957–1958 (3) file, DDEL; W. Mallory-Browne to Department of State, 30 October 1957, RG 59, 811.411/10–3057, NA.

41. Christian Herter to various missions in Eastern Europe, 10 October 1957; Herter to U.S. Missions in Africa south of the Sahara, 10 October 1957, RG 59, 811.411/10–1057, NA.

42. Editorials are found in USIA, ORI, "The World Looks at Little Rock," 2 October 1957, RG 306, Office of Research, Box 14, Special Reports, 1953–1963 file, NA.

43. John E. Reinhardt, written response to author's questions, 15 June 1994, in possession of author.

44. For the best introduction to the U.S. participation at the 1958 World's Fair, see Robert W. Rydell, *World of Fairs: The Century-of-Progress Expositions*. Though it focuses on the fairs of the 1920s and 1930s, it concludes with a chapter on the Brussels fair. Also consult Hixson, *Parting the Curtain*, 141–150; and Robert H. Haddow, *Pavilions of Plenty: Exhibiting American Culture Abroad in the 1950s*, chs. 2–7. For detailed analysis of the "Unfinished Business" exhibit, see Michael L. Krenn, " 'Unfinished Business': Segregation and U.S. Diplomacy at the 1958 World's Fair," *Diplomatic History* 20:4 (Fall 1996): 591–612; and Haddow, *Pavilions of Plenty*, ch. 7.

45. William Tyler to Charles Ebrick, 3 October 1956, RG 59, 855.191–BR/10–356; Judith Murphy, "*Fortune*'s Pavilion at Brussels: What It Is, How It Came About, and Why," 10 February 1958, Record Group 43, Records of International Conferences, Commissions, and Expositions, Records Relating to United States Participation in the Brussels and International Exhibition of 1958, Box 12, EXH-414 Unfinished Business file, NA.

46. Brussels Fair Theme Committee, interview with Walt Rostow, 10 January 1957, Max Franklin Millikan Papers, Box 4, Folder 119, Institute Archives and Special Collections, MIT Libraries, Cambridge, MA. There is a list of the members of the group, "Elting E. Morison to Members of the Study Group for the Brussels Universal and International Exhibition, 1958," 8 April 1957, in the same location. Quote is from "Subcommittee Reports Presented at the Final Meeting of the Cambridge Study Group for the Brussels Universal and International Exhibition, 1958," 28 April 1957, Millikan Papers, Box 4, Folder 120. Jackson's role is discussed in Murphy, "*Fortune*'s Pavilion at Brussels," RG 43, Brussels, Box 12, EXH-414 Unfinished Business file, NA.

47. This description is compiled from several sources: John J. Slocum to Gerson Lush, "Operations Memorandum," 2 June 1958, and "Captions for 'The Unfinished Work'," n.d., RG 43, Brussels, Box 12, EXH-414 Unfinished Business file, NA; and "Fair Gets Exhibit on United States Problems—Private Display at Brussels Deals with Segregation, Slums, and Resources," *New York Times* (11 March 1958): 12.

48. For Johnson, see *Congressional Record*, 85th Cong., 2d sess., 104, pt. 5:5541–42; for Talmadge, see Talmadge to John Foster Dulles, 26 March 1958, RG 59,

855.191–BR/3–2658; for Rivers, see Rivers to Gerson Lush, 25 April 1958, RG 43, Brussels, Box 12, EXH-414 Unfinished Business file; and for Thurmond, see Thurmond to Dulles, 25 April 1958, RG 59, 855.191–BR/4–2558, NA.

49. "Unfinished Business Exhibit—Description as of April 21," enclosed in Burke Wilkinson to Andrew Berding, 28 April 1958, RG 43, Brussels, Box 15, Brussels, Brussels Fair-1957 General file; Herter to Howard Cullman, 5 May 1958, RG 59, 855.191–BR/8–858, NA.

50. Folger (for Cullman) to Herter, 14 May 1958; Abbott Washburn to George V. Allen, 17 June 1958, RG 59, 855.191–BR/5–958, /5–1458; /6–1758, NA; "Preston Raps U.S. Exhibit at Fair," *Washington Post* (24 June 1958); "Brussels Exhibit on Bias is Decried," *New York Times* (23 June 1958), both stories found in "Exhibits and Fairs (Brussels, 1958)" file, USIA, Historical Collection, Washington, DC; "Memorandum of Conference with the President, 24 June 1958," 25 June 1958, Eisenhower Papers, DDE Diary Series, Box 33, June 1958–Staff Notes (2) file; "Memorandum of Conversation with Mr. James S. Plaut from Washington, D.C., Thursday, July 10, 4 P.M. (Brussels time)," Papers of Katherine Howard, Box 25, Confidential—Mrs. Howard file, DDEL. (Howard was one of the deputy commissioners for the U.S. exhibit.)

51. Doxometrie S.P.R.L., "Survey on Visitors of the Brussels 1958 World's Fair to know their opinion about the U.S. and U.S.S.R. and Czech Pavilions," September 1958, Exhibits and Fairs (Brussels 1958) file, USIA, Historical Collection. Also see the USIA summary of the survey, "Follow-Up Study of Visitor Reaction to the U.S. Versus Major Competing Exhibits at the Brussels International Fair," June 1959, same location. As the summary indicated, the poll on the "Unfinished Business" exhibit was sketchy. Due to the short and sporadic life span of the exhibit, only forty-two visitors recalled having seen it.

52. Homer L. Calkin, "A Reminiscence: Being Black in the Foreign Service," *Department of State Newsletter* (February 1978): 28; "Clifton R. Wharton Gets Ready for Rumania," *U.S. News & World Report* 44:22 (21 February 1958): 22. Despite the obvious racial overtones of Wharton's selection, he faced a tough assignment in Romania and handled matters in such a way that U.S.-Romanian relations did show improvement. See Michael L. Krenn, "Clifton R. Wharton, Sr.," *Notable U.S. Ambassadors Since 1775: A Biographical Dictionary*, ed. Cathal J. Nolan, 365–369.

53. "Wharton Sworn as Minister to Rumania After Mix-Up Results in 2 Ceremonies," *New York Times* (8 February 1958): 5.

54. John H. Morrow, *First American Ambassador to Guinea*, 8; Henderson to Herter, 17 March 1959, Papers of Christian Herter, Box 21, Personal H-K file, DDEL.

55. One of the loose ends in all of this was what to do with Richard Jones. In a letter to Herter from Eisenhower's Special Counsel David Kendall, the latter reminded the acting secretary of state that "this is always a sensitive problem," and suggested that "the appropriate political bases be tagged before Ambassador Jones is notified." Perhaps Jones could be offered a place on the U.S. delegation to the UN; "it is always difficult to find a qualified Negro Republican to serve." As Kendall put it, "This would keep him occupied until next year and would provide a graceful exit from the government." Kendall to Herter, 27 March 1959, Eisenhower Papers, WHCF, CF, Name Series, Box 2, Jones, Richard Lee file, DDEL.

56. Herter to Martin Sommers, 20 October 1960, Herter Papers, Box 9, Chronological File October 1960 (1) file, DDEL.

57. Reinhardt, response to author.

58. Memorandum, "International Repercussions of U.S. Race Incidents," 16 October

1958, enclosed in Marks to Karl Harr, 26 December 1959; Kenneth Landon to Colonel Coffey, 4 February 1960, WHO, NSA, OCB Series, Subject Subseries, Box 4, Misc. (9) (November 1959–February 1960) file, DDEL.

Notes to Chapter 6

1. Carl T. Rowan, "New Frontiers in Race Relations," *Interracial Review* 34 (October 1961): 259–262.

2. All from *The Crisis:* Juan René Betancourt, "Castro and the Cuban Negro," (May 1961): 270–274; "Vatican and Racism," (March 1964): 156; "Double Diplomacy," (October 1962): 472–473; Leonard W. Malone, "A Negro Reports from Denmark," (August–September 1961): 451–454; August Meier and Elliot M. Rudwick, "Come to the Fair?," (March 1965): 146–150, 194–198; William Bunge, "Racism in Geography," (October 1965): 494–497, 538.

3. David J. Garrow, *Bearing the Cross: Martin Luther King, Jr., and the Southern Christian Leadership Conference,* 453, 556. Also see Adam Fairclough, "Martin Luther King, Jr. and the War in Vietnam," *Phylon* 45:1 (1984): 19–39.

4. James E. Westheider, *Fighting on Two Fronts: African Americans and the Vietnam War.* Also see Peter B. Levy, "Blacks and the Vietnam War," in *The Legacy: The Vietnam War in the American Imagination,* ed. D. Michael Shafer, 209–232.

5. Martin Staniland, *American Intellectuals and African Nationalists, 1955–1970,* 193–213; for the impact on African-American culture, see Robert G. Weisbord, *Ebony Kinship: Africa, Africans, and the Afro-American,* ch. 6; John A. Davis, ed., *Africa from the Point of View of American Negro Scholars;* John A. Davis and James K. Barker, eds., *Southern Africa in Transition.* For AMSAC, see Brenda Gayle Plummer, *Rising Wind: Black Americans and U.S. Foreign Policy, 1935–1960,* 253–256, and Peter Duignan and L.H. Gann, *The United States and Africa: A History,* 341.

6. "Action Against Apartheid," *The Crisis* (June–July 1965): 359–361, 396.

7. Dennis Hickey and Kenneth C. Wylie, *An Enchanting Darkness: The American Vision of Africa in the Twentieth Century,* 289–290.

8. George Houser to James Farmer, Martin Luther King, A. Philip Randolph, et al., 14 December 1962, Papers of the American Committee on Africa (microfilm edition), Reel 1; all articles from *The Crisis:* "Portuguese Colonialism," (April 1961): 226; "Angolan War," (June–July 1962): 335–338.

9. John A. Davis, "Black Americans and United States Policy Toward Black Africa," *Journal of International Affairs* 23 (Summer 1969): 236–249.

10. Jonathan Zimmerman, "Beyond Double Consciousness: Black Peace Corps Volunteers in Africa, 1961–1971," *The Journal of American History* (December 1995): 999–1028.

11. Ethel L. Payne to Louis E. Martin, 3 August 1960, Records of the Democratic National Committee, Box 145, 1960 Campaign, Civil Rights Division (Louis Martin), Foreign Policy (Africa) 8–3–60—10–25–60, undated file, John F. Kennedy Library (JFKL).

12. James Reston, "Copper Sun, Scarlet Sea, What Is Africa to Me?" *Pittsburgh Courier* (28 February 1961): 3; Langston Hughes, "American Interest in African Culture," Address at opening of new USIS Center and Library, Accra, 29 June 1962, Papers of Hugh Smythe, Correspondence File, Hughes, Langston file, no box, LC. (The manuscript collections of both Hugh Smythe and Mable Smythe-Haith in the Library of Congress had only recently been deposited and were not completely cataloged when Dr. Smythe-Haith kindly gave her permission for me to be the first researcher to use the

collections. Many of the citations, therefore, will be incomplete; some may have been changed by the staff of the Manuscript Collection Division after my visit. I apologize for any inconvenience this may cause future researchers.)

13. Roy Wilkins to Frank Ferrari, 10 February 1966, Papers of the NAACP, Group IV, Administrative, General Office File, Leagues and Organizations, African-American Institute, 1966–1967 file, Library of Congress (LC).

14. Roy Wilkins to Dean Rusk, 21 March 1961, Papers of NAACP, Group III, Box A146, Govt.-Natl.-Department of State, 1956–1965 file, LC; Rayford Logan, "Discrimination: Weakness of Our African Policy," *Current History* (January 1962): 28–35, 48.

15. "Guinea Diplomat Says U.S. Bias Hurts Nation," *Norfolk Journal and Guide* (25 August 1962): 11; "Race Issue Hurts U.S. in Africa," *New York Amsterdam News* (4 September 1965): 31.

16. List of members and sponsors is found in "The Role of the American Negro Community in U.S. Policy Toward Africa," 23–25 November 1962, Papers of NAACP, Group III, Box A198, ANLC on Africa, 1962 file, LC. For more on the ANLCA, see Davis, "Black Americans and United States Policy Toward Black Africa," 241–243; Plummer, *Rising Wind,* 307–308, 310–311; and Duignan and Gann, *United States and Africa,* 341–342.

17. Randolph, Wilkins, Height, Young, Farmer, and King, form letter, 21 August 1962, Papers of NAACP, Group III, Box A198, ANLC on Africa, 1962 file, LC.

18. "Remarks of Roy Wilkins of New York City, Executive Secretary of the National Association for the Advancement of Colored People at the opening of the American Negro Leadership Conference on Africa, Arden House, Harriman, New York, Friday, November 23, 1962, 8 P.M.," Papers of NAACP, Group III, Box A198, ANLC on Africa, 1962 file, LC.

19. ANLCA, "Resolutions," 23–25 November 1962, Record Group 59, Papers of G. Mennen Williams, Subject Files, 1961–1966, Box 16, American Negro Leadership Conference file, National Archives (NA); "U.S. Negroes Link Aid to Sub-Sahara African Nations with Rights Struggle," *New York Times* (25 November 1962): 8.

20. Theodore Brown to Conference Participant, 21 December 1962, Papers of the NAACP, Washington, DC, Bureau, Box 4, ANLCA, 1962–1963 file, LC; Farmer, Height, King, Randolph, Wilkins, and Young to Kennedy, 17 December 1962, Papers of John F. Kennedy, White House Central Files (WHCF), Subject File (SF), Box 360, HU2 12–26–62—6–20–63 file, JFKL.

21. ANLCA, "Resolutions," 24–26, 27 September 1964, Papers of NAACP, Group III, Box A199, ANLC on Africa, 1964–1965 file; Adelaide Cromwell Hill, "How the American Negro Relates to Africa," paper presented at 2nd National Conference, ANLCA, 24–27 September 1964, Papers of NAACP, Group III, Box A34, Africa-General-1960–1965 file, LC.

22. For the collapse of the ANLCA, see previously cited works by Davis, Plummer, and Duignan and Gann.

23. Harold L. Keith, "Where Do Negroes Fit in State Department Hiring Policies?," *Pittsburgh Courier* (November 26, December 3, 10, 17, 24): all articles appeared on p. 4. The quotes are taken from the first and last articles.

24. "Mr. Kennedy Chooses Well," *Baltimore Afro-American* (24 December 1960): 4.

25. "Williams Favors 'Qualified' Negroes in State Department," *Pittsburgh Courier* (14 January 1961): 1; "A new day in foreign policy–JFK may name 3 as diplomats," *Baltimore Afro-American* (18 February 1961): 5. There is little evidence to support the rumors about Bunche and Mays as ambassadors. Bunche certainly had little interest in such posts by this time in his career. It is also interesting to note that Wharton, considered for Denmark and then sent to Norway, was not exactly breaking with Department

history: Ravndal's 1949 memorandum had noted that in Europe, the most likely spot to send an African-American ambassador would be to the Scandinavian region.

26. "Conference on Equal Employment Opportunity," 16 August 1961, RG 59, Williams Papers, Administrative-Office Series, Box 3, EEO 3.-Meetings file, NA.

27. "Negroes and Foreign Service," *Pittsburgh Courier* (9 September 1961): 9, 28; "State Dept. Seeks More Negro Foreign Service Officers," *Jet* (9 November 1961): 52–53; "Top State Dep't appointment urged by fair job consultant," *Baltimore Afro-American* (26 August 1961): 8; "New Search for Diplomats," *Ebony* (October 1962), contained in undated brochure, "New Search for Diplomats': The United States Department of State Seeks Talent for the Foreign Service," Papers of Kenneth Clark, Professional File, Subject File, Box 46, EEO Conferences, Federal Government, 1961–1964 file, LC. (Please note that the staff of the Manuscript Division at the Library of Congress kindly allowed me to do research in the Clark papers while they were still being processed. Box numbers and file designations, therefore, may have changed in the interim.)

28. "Russia Can't Match USA's Ace in the Hole: 18 Million Negroes," *Norfolk Journal and Guide* (24 September 1960): 9; John W. Davis to Philip H. Coombs, 13 March 1961, Papers of John W. Davis, Box 10, Folder 12, Moorland-Spingarn Research Center, Howard University (M-SRC).

29. "Dawson's Refusal," *Pittsburgh Courier* (14 January 1961): 13; Roger Wilkins to Ralph Dungan, 19 November 1962, Kennedy Papers, WHCF, SF, Box 358, HU 1–1–62 file, JFKL; Diggs to Lyndon Johnson, 4 March 1966, John Macy Files, Box 644, Williams, Franklin H., D-Calif. file, Lyndon B. Johnson Presidential Library, Austin, TX (LBJL).

30. ANLCA, "Resolutions," 23–25 November 1962, RG 59, Williams Papers, Subject Files, 1961–1966, Box 16, American Negro Leadership Conference file, NA; Farmer et al. to Kennedy, 17 December 1962, Kennedy Papers, WHCF, SF, Box 360, HU2, 12–26–62–6–20–63 file, JFKL; Brown to Conference Participants, 21 December 1962; Brown to Conference Participants, 25 January 1963, Papers of NAACP, D.C. Bureau, Box 4, ANLCA, 1962–1963 file, LC.

31. "Carl Rowan Named Deputy Asst. Secretary of State," *Jet* (2 February 1961): 13; "Rowan, 37, looks at appointment as real challenge," *Baltimore Afro-American* (2 February 1963): 3; "Rowan to be Diplomat," *New York Amsterdam News* (19 January 1963): 1, 2; "Rowan Packs for U.S. Ambassador Post in Finland," *Norfolk Journal and Guide* (16 March 1963): 16; "Youngest U.S. Ambassador," *Ebony* (January 1964): 52–54, 56–58, 60.

32. "Former Ambassador Carl Rowan Becomes U.S. Voice for Millions," *Jet* (6 February 1964): 46–49.

33. The *New York Amsterdam News* ran two front-page stories about the Harris appointment: 8 and 29 May 1965; *Ebony* (January 1966): 23–26, 28, 30, 32.

34. For Cook: "Being Ambassador a Tough Job and Dr. Cook Is Doing It Well," *Norfolk Journal and Guide* (13 September 1962): 8; "H.U. Prof Ambassador to Niger," *New York Amsterdam News* (3 June 1961): 7; "Ambassador Mercer Cook," *The Crisis* (December 1963): 603–605; "Ambassador Mercer Cook," *AMSAC Newsletter* (Summer 1961): 2; "Resume," Papers of Lyndon B. Johnson, White House Central Files (WHCF), Name File, Cook-ME, LBJL. For Skinner: "Skinner to Upper Volta," *New York Amsterdam News* (21 May 1966): 1, 2; "Dr. Skinner to Take on Ambassador's Role," *New York Amsterdam News* (2 July 1966): 16; "Skinner Ambassador to Volta," *New York Amsterdam News* (30 July 1966): 3. For Smythe: "Our Man in Damascus," *Ebony* (December 1966): 29–34.

35. "Envoy to Norway," *Jet* (23 March 1961): 5; "Top Gov't Post for N.Y. Woman," *Pittsburgh Courier* (13 May 1967): 2; "C.C. Carter a 'First' in Protocol Post,"

Norfolk Journal and Guide (9 May 1964): 2; "Carter Given High State Dept. Post," *Baltimore Afro-American* (9 May 1964): 1, 2; "J.H. Morrow New Alternate UN Delegate," *Baltimore Afro-American* (11 March 1961): 1; "Ex-Olympian Stars in Foreign Service," *New York Amsterdam News* (5 March 1966): 33 (article dealing with Bolen); "Franklin Williams, One of Peace Corps' Most Valued Aides," *Pittsburgh Courier* (24 March 1962): sec. 2, p. 2; "Lady Diplomat Scores Hit at UN," *Baltimore Afro-American* (7 January 1961): 12.

36. "Questions raised regarding new ambassador for Africa," *Baltimore Afro-American* (14 January 1961): 3; "U.S. is sending all white envoys to West Africa," *Baltimore Afro-American* (18 February 1961): 7.

37. " 'U.S. Must Change Approach to African Problem'-Diggs," *Pittsburgh Courier* (7 January 1961): 17; "U.S. Hit on its UN Mission," *New York Amsterdam News* (11 March 1961): 5.

38. "United Nations," *New York Amsterdam News* (1 July 1961): 13; "Capital Heartbeat," *Baltimore Afro-American* (3 June 1961): 5.

39. "Report on the Utilization of Negroes in the State Department and USIA as Overseas Representatives, Especially in Africa," 27 May 1961, enclosed in John A. Davis to G. Mennen Williams, 6 July 1961, RG 59, Williams Papers, Administrative-Office, Box 4, Organizations—American Society of African Studies file, NA.

40. Logan, "Discrimination," 30–31; "State Dept. is Still Racist," *Baltimore Afro-American* (3 February 1962): 4.

41. "Anti-Colored U.S. State Dept.," *Baltimore Afro-American* (4 May 1963): 4.

42. "Resolutions," ANLCA, 24–27 September 1964; John A. Davis, "The Employment of Negroes in the Foreign Service of the United States," Papers of NAACP, Group III, Box A199, ANLC on Africa, 1964–1965 file; ANLC on Africa, 2nd National Conference, September 1964 file, LC.

43. Powell to John Macy, 5 August 1965, Johnson Papers, WHCF, Human Rights HU2–1, Box 45, HU2–1 Employment 5/8/65–11/11/65 file, LBJL; Stone to Williams, 13 April 1965, RG 59, Williams Papers, Subject Files, Box 164, NA.

44. Davis, "Black Americans," 238.

Notes to Chapter 7

1. Thomas J. Noer, *Cold War and Black Liberation: The United States and White Rule in Africa, 1948–1968,* 129.

2. Harvard Sitkoff, *The Struggle for Black Equality, 1954–1980;* David Lewis, *King: A Biography;* Clayborne Carson, *In Struggle: A History of SNCC.*

3. Mark Stern, *Calculating Visions: Kennedy, Johnson, and Civil Rights,* 232–233. For a selection of studies that support or contradict this thesis, see James C. Harvey, *Black Civil Rights During the Johnson Administration;* James L. Sundquist, *Politics and Power: The Eisenhower, Kennedy, and Johnson Years,* 254–255, 283–286; Irving Bernstein, *Promises Kept: John F. Kennedy's New Frontier,* chs. 2 and 3; Steven F. Lawson, "Civil Rights," in *Exploring the Johnson Years,* ed. Robert A. Divine, 93–125; Carl M. Brauer, *John F. Kennedy and the Second Reconstruction;* and Richard D. Mahoney, *JFK: Ordeal in Africa,* 28–31.

4. Mahoney, *Ordeal in Africa,* 30–31; Thomas J. Noer, "New Frontiers and Old Priorities in Africa," in *Kennedy's Quest for Victory: American Foreign Policy, 1961–1963,* ed. Thomas G. Paterson, 256–258; Terrence Lyons, "Keeping Africa Off the Agenda," in *Lyndon Johnson Confronts the World: American Foreign Policy, 1963–1968,* 245.

5. Noer, "New Frontiers," 269–274, 275–278; Gerald E. Thomas, "The Black Revolt: The United States and Africa in the 1960s," in *The Diplomacy of the Crucial Decade: American Foreign Relations During the 1960s*, ed. Diane B. Kunz, 326, 350–355. Also see, Lyons, "Keeping Africa,"; Mahoney, *Ordeal in Africa;* and Noer, *Cold War and Black Liberation.*

6. H. Schuyler Foster to Mr. MacKnight, 11 April 1963, Record Group 59, Papers of G. Mennen Williams, Subject Files, Box 16, Civil Rights-Africa file, National Archives (NA).

7. James L. Greenfield to Mr. Williams, 27 June 1963, RG 59, Williams Papers, Subject Files, Box 16, Civil Rights-Africa file, NA.

8. Lee White to President Johnson, 28 December 1964, Papers of Lyndon Johnson, White House Central Files (WHCF), Confidential Files (CF), CO 1–1, Box 6, Africa (11/23/63–3/29/66) file; Robert Komer to McGeorge Bundy, 6 January 1965, Johnson Papers, National Security File (NSF), Vol. II (7/64–6/65), Country File: Africa, Box 76, Africa-General Memos and Misc. [1 of 2] folder, Lyndon B. Johnson Library (LBJL).

9. McGeorge Bundy to Rusk, 7 January 1965; Rick Haynes to McGeorge Bundy, 4 March 1965, Johnson Papers, NSF, Vol. II (7/64–6/65), Country File: Africa, Box 76, Africa-General Memos and Misc. [1 of 2] folder, LBJL.

10. Haynes to Komer, 25 March 1965; Komer and Haynes to McGeorge Bundy, 30 March 1965; Clifford Alexander to Bundy, Johnson Papers, NSF, Vol. II (7/64–6/66), Country File: Africa, Box 76, Africa-General Memos and Misc. [1 of 2] folder; Haynes to White, 30 August 1965, Johnson Papers, CF, Box 6, CO 1–1 Africa (1964–1965) folder, LBJL. Given this evidence, further research into the demise of the ANLCA might be in order to ascertain the role of the Johnson administration.

11. USIA, "Racial Prejudice Mars the American Image," 17 October 1962, Record Group 306, Office of Research, Box 10, "R" Reports, 1960–1963, NA.

12. "Address by Donald M. Wilson, Deputy Director, U.S. Information Agency to the Women's National Democratic Club, Washington, D.C., Monday, June 10, 1963," RG 59, Williams Papers, Subject Files, Box 16, Civil Rights folder, NA. For brief summaries of the events in Birmingham and Oxford, see Sitkoff, *Struggle for Black Equality,* 124, 129–149.

13. "Media Comment on the Mississippi Crisis," n.d., Papers of John F. Kennedy, President's Office Files (POF), Departments and Agencies, Box 91, USIA 7/62–12/62 file, John F. Kennedy Library (JFKL).

14. "London Log," *West Africa* (18 February 1961): 192; USIA, "The Role and Trend of Public Opinion in Africa—1961," 16 February 1962, RG 306, Office of Research, Box 7, "R" Reports, 1960–1963, NA; Murrow to Kennedy, 7 March 1963, Kennedy Papers, POF, Departments and Agencies, Box 91, USIA 3/63 folder, JFKL; USIA, "African Students in the U.S.: I. Basic Attitudes and Aspirations, and Reactions to U.S. Experiences," November 1963, RG 306, Office of Research, Box 18, "R" Reports, 1960–1963, NA.

15. See the previously cited works by Mahoney, Noer, Lyons, and Thomas.

16. Thomas L. Hughes to Rusk, 15 May 1964, Johnson Papers, NSF, Vol. I (2/64–6/64), Country File: Africa, Box 76, Africa-General Memos and Misc. file, LBJL.

17. G. Mennen Williams to Ambassadors and Certain Principal Officers, 10 May 1965, Johnson Papers, NSF, Vol. II (7/64–6/65), Country File: Africa, Box 76, Africa-General Memos and Misc. [2 of 2] file, LBJL; Williams to Ambassador at Large, 6 July 1965, Harriman Papers, Box 429, Africa, General, 1963–1967 file, LC; M. Bundy to Johnson, 8 March 1965, Johnson Papers, NSF, Vol. II (7/64–6/65), Country File: Africa, Box 76, Africa-General Memos and Misc. [1 of 2] file, LBJL.

18. Administrative History of the Department of State, 1968, Johnson Papers, Spe-

cial Files, Administrative Histories, Administrative History of the Department of State, Box 2, Chapter V: Africa, Secs. A and B, LBJL.

19. Remarks by Carl T. Rowan, "Fourth Regional Operations Conference," Lima, Peru, 10 October 1961, Kennedy Papers, POF, Departments and Agencies, Box 88, State 10/61–12/61 file, JFKL; Rollie White to Mr. Abernethy, RG 59, Williams Papers, Subject Files, Box 16, U.S. Civil Rights and Foreign Policy-General file, NA.

20. Thomas Sorenson to Heads of Elements and USIS Posts, 6 April 1964, Papers of Leonard Marks, Box 27, USIA Media Priorities file; Administrative History of USIA, 1968, Johnson Papers, Special Files, Administrative History of USIA, Box 1, Vol. I: Administrative History [2 of 2], LBJL.

21. Thomas Sorenson to Heads of Elements and USIS Posts, 6 April 1964, Marks Papers, Box 27, USIA Media Priorities file, LBJL.

22. Sidney Fine to Williams, 14 June 1963; Rollie H. White to Mr. Abernethy, 19 July 1963, RG 59, Williams Papers, Subject Files, Box 16, U.S. Civil Rights and Foreign Policy-General file; Civil Rights file, NA.

23. Administrative History of USIA, 1968, Johnson Papers, Special Files, Administrative History of USIA, Box 1, Vol. I: Administrative History [1 of 2], LBJL; Donald Culverson, "The U.S. Information Agency in Africa," *TransAfrica Forum* (Winter 1989): 61–80.

24. "Tuskegee Institute: A Successful Experiment in Self-Help," 15 June 1962, RG 306, Office of Research, Box 9, "R" Reports, 1960–1963, NA; "More Than Equality," enclosed in Leonard Marks to President Johnson, 13 September 1965, Marks Papers, Box 34, White House Library, 1965 file, LBJL.

25. "The Negro American: A Progress Report," 1961, Marks Papers, Box 12, loose publication, LBJL.

26. "America's New Civil Rights Act," 1964, Marks Papers, Box 10, loose publication, LBJL.

27. Carl Rowan to President Johnson, 8 April 1965; Murrow to President Johnson, 17 January 1964, Johnson Papers, WHCF, SF, FG 296, Box 314, FG 296–USIA (1/1/65–6/1/65) file, LBJL.

28. Robert Dyer MacCann, *The People's Films: A Political History of U.S. Government Motion Pictures,* 188, 192.

29. Carl Rowan to President Johnson, 5 June 1964, Johnson Papers, WHCF, CF, Box 44, FO Foreign Affairs (1964–1965) file, LBJL.

30. "Summary of Discussions and Conclusions, Addis Ababa Conference, May 22–26, 1965," enclosed in Alfred Wellons to Dept. of State, 2 June 1965, Harriman Papers, Box 545, African Chiefs of Mission, May 23–29, 1965 file, LC; Rick Haynes to M. Bundy, 5 June 1965, Johnson Papers, NSF, Vol. II (7/64–6/65), Country File: Africa, Box 76, Africa-General Memos and Misc. [2 of 2] file, LBJL.

31. "Racial Issues in the US: Some Policy and Program Indications of Research," 14 March 1966, RG 306, Office of Research, Special Reports, 1964–1982, Box 2, S-3–66 file, NA.

32. "Report to the Director from Lawrence H. Rogers II: USIA-Tropical Africa, April 15, 1967," Marks Papers, Box 28, Report: VOA Operations in Africa file, LBJL.

33. "Reactions to U.S. Race Relations and General Opinion of the U.S.," 12 April 1968, RG 306, Office of Research, Special Reports, 1964–1982, Box 4, S-20–68 file, NA.

34. G. Mennen Williams to Compliance Officers, 17 July 1961, RG 59, Williams Papers, Administrative-Office Files, Box 3, EEE 2.-Reports file, NA; "Government Employee Survey," c. 1961, Kennedy Papers, White House Staff Files: Harris Wofford, Box 14, Subcabinet Group on Civil Rights, Government Employment Survey file, JFKL.

35. Harriman to Ted Sorenson and Archibald Cox, 30 September 1960, Papers of W. Averell Harriman, Box 405, Africa Trip, 1960: Memoranda of Conversations file, Library of Congress (LC); "Task Force on Sub-Sahara Africa: Questions," and "Task Force on Sub-Sahara Africa: Answers . . . Edward R. Dudley," mid-December 1960, Papers of Edward R. Dudley, Box 1, Folder 13, Amistad Research Center (ARC); Task Force on State Department Field Operations," "Recruitment of Negroes Into the Foreign Service," 27 December 1960: Task Force on State Department Operations Overseas and In Washington, "Report to the Honorable John F. Kennedy," 31 December 1960, Part Five" Recruitment of Negroes and Other Minority Groups into the Foreign Service; Task Force on Africa, "Report to the Honorable John F. Kennedy," 31 December 1960, Papers of James C. Thompson, Box 1, Task Force Reports, 1960, State Department Recruitment of Negroes, 12/27/60 file; State Department Operations-Copy 5, 12/31/60 file; Africa, 12/31/60, Part VI and Appendices file, JFKL.

36. Oral History of William J. Crockett, 20–22 June 1990, FAOHP; Roger Jones, Memorandum, 7 January 1960 (sic—1961), Papers of Roger Jones, Box 16, State Department, Memoranda, 1960–1962 file; Kennedy to Bowles, 26 January 1961, Kennedy Papers, WHCF, SF, Box 122, FG 105–Department of State, 1-1-61–2-28–61 file, JFKL.

37. Johnson to Kennedy, 15 April 1961, Johnson Papers, Vice Presidential Papers, Vice Presidential Security Files: Vice Presidential Travel, Box 1, Vice President's Trip to Africa and Europe file; "Strengthened African Program," c. 1965, Johnson Papers, NSF, Vol. III (5/65–3/66), Country File: Africa, Box 76, Africa-General file, LBJL.

38. Rusk to Kenneth Clark, 24 July 1961, Papers of Kenneth Clark, Professional File, Subject File, Box 101, State Department, Committee on Foreign Affairs Personnel, Correspondence and Memoranda, 1961 (1 of 3) file, LC; "Conference on Equal Employment Opportunity," 16 August 1961, RG 59, Williams Papers, Administrative-Office, Box 3, EEO 3.-Meetings file, NA.

39. Bowles to Frederick Dutton, 6 October 1961, Kennedy Papers, NSF, Departments and Agencies, Box 285, Department of State, General, 10/1/61–10/6/61 file, JFKL.

40. Richard Fox to Mr. Abernethy, 18 March 1964, RG 59, Records of EOE, Box 2, EEO, 1964–1965 file, NA. The two ambassadors were Clifton Wharton in Norway and Mercer Cook in Niger (both appointed in 1961). The two deputy assistant secretaries were Chester C. Carter (Congressional Relations) and Samuel Westerfield (Economic Affairs).

41. Oral History of Richard K. Fox, 8 March 1989, FAOHP; "A Training Program in Foreign Affairs: A Career With A Future," pamphlet produced by Howard University, late 1963 or early 1964, Clark Papers, Subject File, Professional File, Box 46, EEO Conferences, Federal Government, 1961–1964 file; "Summary of FASP Achievements (Current as of March, 1967)," Clark Papers, Subject File, Metropolitan Applied Research Center File, Box 375, Foreign Affairs Scholars Program, Howard University, Meeting, 16 December 1965 file, LC.

42. "Negro Officer Employment in the Department of State," attached to Eddie Williams to Idar Rimestad and Jules Bassin, 26 May 1967, provided to author from Personal Papers of Ronald D. Palmer.

43. Harriman to Sorenson and Cox, 30 September 1960, Harriman Papers, Box 405, Africa Trip, 1960: Memoranda of Conversations file, LC.

44. Dutton, "Minimal Civil Rights Program Within the Executive Branch," n.d., Kennedy Papers, WHCF, SF, Box 358, HU 1-20-61–5-10-61 file; Clinton to Ralph Dungan, 1 May 1963, Kennedy Papers, POF, SF, Box 97, Civil Rights-General 7/15/63–8/31/63 file; Eugene L. Krizek to Richard Maguire, 12 May 1961, Kennedy Papers, WHCF, SF, Box 388, IT 47–8/A file, JFKL. Ulric (Rick) St. Clair Haynes was the eventual choice for the NSC position.

45. "Brief for the Appointment of Edward R. Dudley to be American Ambassador to Nigeria," 17 June 1963; John T. Abernethy to Terry Scanlon, 14 October 1963; "Third Deputy Assistant Secretary of State for African Affairs, Responsible for Economic Matters," n.d., RG 59, Williams Papers, Subject File, Box 19, Personnel: untitled folder (for first two documents); Personnel: Candidates for 3rd Deputy Assistant Secretary of State for African Affairs folder, NA.

46. John Macy to Mr. Sherman, 12 January 1965, Macy Files, Box 705, Ambassadorial-Negro Candidates file; "Afghanistan," n.d., Johnson Papers, WHCF, Box 12, FO 2 Diplomatic-Consular Relations, 12/8/65–6/15/66 file; Macy to President Johnson, 3 May 1966, Macy Files, Box 703, Presidential Memos-Ambassador 1965–1966 file; Macy to Johnson, 27 September 1968, Macy Files, Box 644, Williams, Franklin H., D-Calif. file, LBJL.

47. Valenti to the President, 1 July 1964; Valenti to M. Bundy, 6 July 1964; Rusk to the President, 10 June 1964, Johnson Papers, WHCF, Box 13, FO 2/CO 192–CO 203 file (for first two documents); WHCF, CF, Box 45, FO 2/CO 201 file, LBJL.

48. William Attwood, *The Reds and the Blacks: A Personal Adventure*, 46–47.

49. Edward L. Sherman to John Macy, 27 September 1965, Macy Files, Box 693, State Department-General-1965 file; Ramsey Clark to President Johnson, 7 January 1965, Johnson Papers, WHCF, Box 8, PE 2 12/21/64–3/2/65 file, LBJL.

50. Fox to Crockett, 12 October 1964; Haynes to Williams, 19 October 1964, RG 59, Records of EOE, Box 1, AF '65, State Department-Negro Employment file, NA.

51. "Excerpts from Rusk's Testimony on Civil Rights," *New York Times* (11 July 1963): 16; " 'I'd demonstrate if were colored,' Secretary Dean Rusk Tells Thurmond," *Baltimore Afro-American* (20 July 1963): 3; Oral History of Dean Rusk, Rusk EE, p. 13, Richard B. Russell Memorial Library, University of Georgia; Oral History of William J. Crockett, 20–22 June 1990; Oral History of Herman Pollack, 5 December 1990, FAOHP; Lee White to President Kennedy, 17 December 1962, Kennedy Papers, WHCF, SF, Box 360, HU 2 12–26–62 - 6–20–63 file, JFKL.

52. Rusk, *As I Saw It*, 526–527; Walt Rostow to President Johnson, 22 May 1968, Johnson Papers, WHCF, Box 9, FO 2 Diplomatic-Consular Relations (12/13/67–6/10/68) file, LBJL.

53. Oral History of Katie Louchheim, 14 April 1969, LBJL; Henry Serrano Villard, *Affairs at State*, 156–157.

54. Idris Rossell, "Equal Employment Opportunity—Too Much or Not Enough?" *Foreign Service Journal* (January 1969): 12.

55. Thomas J. Schoenbaum, *Waging War and Peace: Dean Rusk in the Truman, Kennedy, and Johnson Years*, 277–279; *United States Chiefs of Mission*, 286; Kenneth Clark to Frederick C. Mosher, 24 July 1963, Clark Papers, Subject File, Professional File, Box 101, State Department, Committee on Foreign Affairs Personnel, Correspondence and Memoranda, 1963–1964, n.d. (3 of 3) file, LC.

56. Frederick Dutton to Frank Reeves, 25, 27 March and 17 April 1961; Dutton to Harris Wofford, 19 July 1961, Kennedy Papers, WHCF, SF, Box 124, FG 105 1-1-61–5-31-61 file; Box 360, HU 2, 7-1-61–7-24-61 file, JFKL.

57. Untitled and undated notes by Mercer Cook, Papers of Mercer Cook, Box 5, Folder 27, Moorland-Spingarn Research Center (M-SRC); Cook to President Johnson, 7 August 1965, attached to Cook to W. Averell Harriman, 14 August 1965, Papers of W. Averell Harriman, Box 429, Africa, General, 1963–1967 file, LC.

58. Williams to Marvin Wachman, 18 September 1966; Williams to Hugh Smythe, 18 September 1966; Williams to Moyer, 9 December 1966; Williams to Fox, 6 December 1966, Papers of Franklin H. Williams, Box 1, Official-General 1966 file; Box 1,

Department of State, Field 1966 file; Box 1, White House 1966–1967 file; Box 1, Department of State, Field 1966 file, LBJL.

59. Skinner to Smythe, 15 June 1967, Papers of Elliott Skinner, Box 1, Correspondence, 1966–1967 file, LBJL.

60. Skinner to Smythe, 15 June 1967; Skinner to Smythe, 18 May 1967; Skinner to Smythe, 13 March 1968; Skinner to Williams, 5 March 1968, Skinner Papers, Box 1, Correspondence, 1966–1967 file (first two letters); Correspondence, 1968–1969, Papers file; Williams Papers, Box 1, Department of State, Field, 1968 file, LBJL; Skinner to Smythe, 2 February 1968, Papers of Hugh Smythe, Foreign Service File, Ambassadorial File-Malta-Office File, January-May 1968 file, LC.

61. Smythe to John M. Steeves, 13 February 1968, Smythe Papers, Foreign Service File, Ambassadorial File-Malta-Office File, January–May 1968 file, LC.

62. Smythe to Eddie Williams, 28 February 1968; Smythe to Elliott Skinner, 4 October 1968; Smythe to Franklin Williams, 17 June 1968, Papers of Hugh Smythe, Box 5, Correspondence, 1968: W-Z file; Box 4, Correspondence, 1968: S [2 of2] file; Box 5, Correspondence, 1968: W-Z file, LBJL.

63. Oral History with Patricia Roberts Harris, 19 May 1969, LBJL.

64. Carl T. Rowan, *Breaking the Barriers: A Memoir,* 173–176, 209.

65. Richard K. Fox, 15 July 1994, interview with author; Oral History of Richard K. Fox, 8 March 1989, FAOHP.

66. Terence A. Todman, 13 June 1995, interview with author, FAOHP.

67. "Negro Employment in the Department of State."

68. "Task Force on Sub-Sahara Africa: Answers . . . Edward R. Dudley," 1960, Dudley Papers, Box 1, Folder 13, ARC.

Notes to Chapter 8

1. R. Peter Straus, "Is the State Department Color-Blind?" *Saturday Review* (2 January 1971): 12–13, 62.

2. "American Blacks Seeking to Influence the African Policy of U.S.," *New York Times* (13 February 1972): 5; "Excerpts from Dr. Smythe's Charter Day Address," *The Atlanta University Bulletin* (March 1973): 6–8.

3. "Black Envoys Seek More Non-Africa Posts," *New York Times* (13 August 1974): D:4.

4. Alvin E. White, "Showdown in Foggy Bottom for Black Ambassadors," *Sepia* (August 1976): 16–23; Memorandum, "EEO Briefing," 14 August 1976, Papers of Barbara Watson, Box 24, US Dept. of State-Bur. of Sec. and Consular Affairs-Employment-Minorities, 1973, 1976 file, Schomburg Center for Research in Black Culture.

5. Pat Patterson, "Blacks in the Foreign Service," *Black Enterprise* (February 1978): 41–43, 47–48; Lisa Peterson, "The State Department—Still Pale and Male?" *Encore American & Worldwide News* (15 January 1979): 16–17.

6. Michael Beaubien, "Making Waves in Foreign Policy," *Black Enterprise* (April 1982): 38–42.

7. D. Michael Cheers, "Why Aren't There More Blacks in Foreign Service?" *Ebony* (May 1983): 89–90, 92.

8. "Report on Minority Progress: Still 'Distressing,' " *New York Times* (28 June 1983): B:6.

9. "Shultz wants more blacks in 'role model' positions," *State* (October 1986): 18; "Spiers: Foreign Service needs more blacks," *State* (November 1986): 4.

10. "Foreign Service's Painful Passage to Looking More Like America," *Washington Post* (21 April 1994): A29.

11. Bruce Shapiro, "A House Divided: Racism at the State Department," *The Nation* (12 February 1996): 11–16.

12. "Black diplomats win compensation," *The Miami Herald* (6 April 1996): 6A.

13. Terence A. Todman, interview with author, 13, 27 June 1995, FAOHP.

14. Dr. Horace Dawson, interview with author, 18 July 1995, FAOHP.

15. John E. Reinhardt, response to author, 28 June 1994.

16. Richard K. Fox, interview with author, 15 July 1994, FAOHP.

Bibliography

Primary Sources

Archival Sources

Manuscript Collections

Amistad Research Center, Tulane University, New Orleans, LA
  Papers of Edward R. Dudley
  Papers of Giles Hubert

Dwight D. Eisenhower Presidential Library, Abilene, KS
  Papers of John Foster Dulles
  Dwight D. Eisenhower, Papers as President (Ann Whitman File)
  Dwight D. Eisenhower, Papers as President, White House Central Files, 1953–1961
  Papers of Bryce Harlow
  Papers of Christian Herter
  Papers of Katherine Howard
  Papers of C.D. Jackson
  Papers of E. Frederick Morrow, Pre-Accession, Administrative Office, Special Projects Group, Records, 1952–1963
  Records of the Republican National Committee
  White House Office, Office of the Special Assistant for Executive Appointments, 1952–1961
  White House Office, Office of the Special Assistant for National Security Affairs, 1953–1961

John F. Kennedy Presidential Library, Boston, MA
  Papers of Roger Jones
  Papers of John F. Kennedy, President's Office Files, 1961–1963
  Papers of John F. Kennedy, White House Central Files, 1961–1963
  Papers of John F. Kennedy, White House Staff Files: Harris Wofford

Papers of James C. Thompson
Records of the Democratic National Committee

Library of Congress Manuscripts Division, Washington, D.C.
Papers of Kenneth Clark
Papers of W.E.B. Du Bois (microfilm edition)
Papers of W. Averell Harriman
Papers of Rayford Logan
Papers of the NAACP
Papers of NAACP, Washington Bureau
Papers of A. Philip Randolph
Papers of Hugh Smythe
Papers of Arthur Spingarn
Papers of the United Negro College Fund (microfiche edition)

Lyndon Baines Johnson Presidential Library, Austin, TX
John Macy Files
Papers of Lyndon B. Johnson, National Security File, 1963–1969
Papers of Lyndon B. Johnson, Special Files, 1927–1973: Administrative Histories
Papers of Lyndon B. Johnson, Vice Presidential Papers, 1961–1963
Papers of Lyndon B. Johnson, White House Central Files, 1963–1969
Papers of Leonard Marks
Papers of Elliott Skinner
Papers of Hugh Smythe
Papers of Franklin H. Williams

MIT Libraries, Institute Archives and Special Collections, MIT, Cambridge, MA
Max Franklin Millikan Papers

Moorland-Spingarn Research Center, Howard University, Washington, D.C.
Papers of Mercer Cook
Papers of John W. Davis
Papers of Rayford Logan

Mugar Memorial Library, Special Collections, Boston University, Boston, MA
Papers of Clifton Wharton Sr.
Papers of the American Committee on Africa (microfilm edition)

Schomburg Center for Research in Black Culture, New York, NY
Papers of Lester Walton
Papers of Barbara Watson

Seeley G. Mudd Manuscript Library, Princeton University, Princeton, NJ
Papers of John Foster Dulles

Harry S. Truman Presidential Library, Independence, MO
Papers of Dean Acheson
Papers of George Elsey
Papers of Philleo Nash
Papers of David Niles
Papers of Howland H. Sargeant

Papers of Harry S. Truman, Papers as President of the United States
Records of the President's Committee on Civil Rights

University Research Libraries, Department of Special Collections, UCLA, Los Angeles, CA
Papers of Ralph Bunche

Yale University Library, New Haven, CT
Papers of Chester Bowles
Papers of Anson Phelps Stokes

Other Manuscripts

Personal Papers of Ronald Palmer (in possession of Ronald Palmer)

Oral Histories and Interviews

Foreign Affairs Oral History Program, Lauinger Library, Georgetown University, Washington, D.C.
William J. Crockett
Horace Dawson (interview with author)
Edward R. Dudley (interview with author)
Richard K. Fox, 1989
Richard K. Fox, 1994 (interview with author)
Ronald Palmer (interview with author)
Herman Pollack
Terence A. Todman (interview with author)

Richard B. Russell Memorial Library, University of Georgia, Athens, GA
Oral History of Dean Rusk

Other Interviews
John E. Reinhardt (written reponse to interview questions)

Harry S. Truman Presidential Library, Independence, MO
Kenneth Birkhead
William H. Hastie

Lyndon B. Johnson Presidential Library
Patricia Roberts Harris
Katie Louchheim

Government Documents

National Archives, Washington, D.C.
Record Group 43. Records of U.S. Participation in International Conferences, Commissions, and Expositions
Records Relating to U.S. Participation in the Brussels Universal and International Exhibition of 1958
Record Group 59. General Records of the Department of State

Decimal File, 1945–1959
 Papers of G. Mennen Williams
 Records of the Assistant Secretary of State for Near Eastern, South Asian, and
   African Affairs, 1946–1951
 Records of the Assistant Secretary of State for Public Affairs, 1947–1950
 Records of the Bureau of Near Eastern, South Asian, and African Affairs: Office
   Files of Assistant Secretary of State George C. McGhee, 1945–1953
 Records Relating to Equal Opportunity Employment and Minority Employment in
   the Department of State, 1943–1966
 Records Relating to International Information Activities, 1938–1953

Record Group 306 . Records of the United States Information Agency

USIA, Historical Collection, Washington, D.C.

Exhibits and Fairs (Brussels, 1958)

Government Publications

Congressional Record. Washington: Government Printing Office, various years.
Department of State. Foreign Relations of the United States, 1945–1963. Washington:
   Government Printing Office, 1967–1988.
Department of State. "Black American Chiefs of Mission." Washington: Department of
   State, March 1993.
Department of State. United States Chiefs of Mission, 1778–1982. Washington: Depart-
   ment of State, 1982.
Department of State. "A Chronology of Key Negro Appointments in the Department of
   State and the Foreign Service, 1869–1969." Washington: Department of State, 1969.
Department of State. "The Truth About America." Washington: Department of State, 1947.
Public Papers of the Presidents of the United States: Harry S. Truman. Washington:
   Government Printing Office, 1963.
President's Committee on Civil Rights. "To Secure These Rights." Washington: Gov-
   ernment Printing Office, 1947.

Newspapers and Journals

The African
Afro-American (Baltimore)
AMSAC Newsletter
Chicago Defender
The Crisis
Department of State Newsletter
Ebony
Foreign Service Journal
Harlem Quarterly
Jet
London Times
Miami Herald
Negro Digest
Negro History Bulletin
New Africa

New York Age
New York Amsterdam News
New York Times
New York Times Magazine
Norfolk Journal and Guide
Pittsburgh Courier
Race Relations
The Saturday Review of Literature
U.S. News & World Report
Washington Post
West Africa

Secondary Sources

Books

Anderson, J.W. *Eisenhower, Brownell and the Congress: The Tangled Origins of the Civil Rights Bill of 1956–1957*. Birmingham: University of Alabama Press, 1964.
Attwood, William. *The Reds and The Blacks: A Personal Adventure*. New York: Harper and Row, 1967.
Bardolph, Richard. *The Negro Vanguard*. New York: Rinehart and Company, 1959.
Barrett, Edward W. *Truth is Our Weapon*. New York: Funk and Wagnalls, 1953.
Berman, Daniel M. *A Bill Becomes Law: The Civil Rights Act of 1960*. New York: Macmillan, 1962.
Bernstein, Irving. *Promises Kept: John F. Kennedy's New Frontier*. New York: Oxford University Press, 1991.
Borstelmann, Thomas. *Apartheid's Reluctant Uncle: The United States and South Africa in the Early Cold War*. New York: Oxford University Press, 1993.
Bowles, Chester. *Promises to Keep: My Years in Public Life, 1941–1969*. New York: Harper and Row, 1971.
Brauer, Carl M. *John F. Kennedy and the Second Reconstruction*. New York: Columbia University Press, 1977.
Burk, Robert F. *The Eisenhower Administration and Black Civil Rights*. Knoxville: University of Tennessee Press, 1984.
Calkin, Homer L. *Women in the Department of State: Their Role in American Foreign Affairs*. Washington: Department of State, 1978.
Carson, Clayborne. *In Struggle: A History of SNCC*. Cambridge: Cambridge University Press, 1981.
Curtis, Susan. *The First Black Actress on the Great White Way*. Columbia: University of Missouri Press, forthcoming
Davis, John A., ed. *Africa from the Point of View of American Negro Scholars*. Paris: Présence africaine, 1958.
Davis, John A. and James K. Baker, eds. *Southern Africa in Transition*. New York: Frederick A. Praeger, 1966.
DeConde, Alexander. *Ethnicity, Race and American Foreign Policy: A History*. Boston: Northeastern University Press, 1992.
De León, Arnoldo. *They Called Them Greasers: Anglo Attitudes Toward Mexicans in Texas, 1821–1900*. Austin: University of Texas Press, 1983.
Dower, John. *War Without Mercy: Race and Power in the Pacific War*. New York: Pantheon, 1986.

Drinnon, Richard. *Facing West: The Metaphysics of Indian Hating and Empire Building.* New York: Schocken Books, 1990.

Du Bois, W.E.B. *Color and Democracy: Colonies and Peace.* New York: Harcourt, Brace, 1945.

Dulles, Foster Rhea. *The Civil Rights Commission, 1957–1965.* East Lansing: Michigan State University Press, 1968.

Duram, James C. *A Moderate Among Extremists: Dwight D. Eisenhower and the School Desegregation Crisis.* Chicago: University of Chicago Press, 1981.

Garrow, David J. *Bearing the Cross: Martin Luther King, Jr., and the Southern Christian Leadership Conference.* New York: William Morrow, 1986.

Garvey, Amy Jacques. *Garvey and Garveyism.* New York: Macmillan, 1968.

Geiss, Immanuel. *The Pan-African Movement.* London: Methuen, 1974.

Haddow, Robert H. *Pavilions of Plenty: Exhibiting American Culture Abroad in the 1950s.* Washington: Smithsonian Institution Press, 1997.

Harris, Joseph E. *African-American Reactions to War in Ethiopia, 1936–1941.* Baton Rouge: Louisiana State University Press, 1994.

Harvey, James. C. *Black Civil Rights During the Johnson Administration.* Jackson: University and College Press of Mississippi, 1973.

Henry, Charles P., ed. *Ralph Bunche: Selected Speeches and Writings.* Ann Arbor: University of Michigan Press, 1995.

Hickey, Dennis, and Kenneth C. Wylie. *An Enchanting Darkness: The American Vision of Africa in the Twentieth Century.* East Lansing: Michigan State University Press, 1993.

Hietala, Thomas R. *Manifest Destiny: Anxious Aggrandizement in Late Jacksonian America.* Ithaca: Cornell University Press, 1985.

Hixson, Walter L. *Parting the Curtain: Propaganda, Culture, and the Cold War, 1945–1961.* New York: St. Martin's Press, 1997.

Horne, Gerald. *Black and Red: W.E.B. Du Bois and the Afro-American Response to the Cold War, 1944–1963.* Albany: State University of New York Press, 1986.

Horsman, Reginald. *Race and Manifest Destiny: The Origins of American Racial Anglo-Saxonism.* Cambridge: Harvard University Press, 1981.

Hunt, Michael H. *Ideology and U.S. Foreign Policy.* New Haven: Yale University Press, 1987.

Johnson, John J. *A Hemisphere Apart: The Foundations of United States Policy toward Latin America.* Baltimore: Johns Hopkins University Press, 1990.

Lauren, Paul Gordon. *Power and Prejudice: The Politics and Diplomacy of Racial Discrimination.* Boulder, CO: Westview Press, 1988.

Lewis, David. *King: A Biography.* Urbana: University of Illinois Press, 1978.

Logan, Rayford W., ed. *What the Negro Wants.* Chapel Hill: University of North Carolina Press, 1944.

———. *The Negro and the Post-War World.* Washington, DC: The Minorities Publishers, 1945.

Lynch, Hollis. *Black American Radicals and the Liberation of Africa: The Council on African Affairs, 1937–1955.* Ithaca, NY: Africana Studies and Research Center, Cornell University, 1978.

MacCann, Robert Dyer. *The People's Films: A Political History of U.S. Government Motion Pictures.* New York: Hastings House, 1973.

Mahoney, Richard D. *JFK: Ordeal in Africa.* New York: Oxford University Press, 1983.

Mann, Peggy. *Ralph Bunche: UN Peacemaker.* New York: Coward, McCann, and Geoghegan, 1975.

McCoy, Donald R., and Richard T. Ruetten. *Quest and Response: Minority Rights and the Truman Administration.* Lawrence: University of Kansas Press, 1973.

McGhee, George C. *Envoy to the Middle World: Adventures in Diplomacy.* New York: Harper and Row, 1983.

Miller, Jake C. *The Black Presence in American Foreign Affairs.* Washington, DC: University Press of America, 1978.

Morrow, E. Frederic. *A Black Man in the White House.* New York: Coward-McCann, 1963.

Morrow, John H. *First American Ambassador to Guinea.* New Brunswick, NJ: Rutgers University Press, 1968.

Noer, Thomas J. *Cold War and Black Liberation: The United States and White Rule in Africa, 1948–1968.* Columbia: University of Missouri Press, 1985.

O'Reilly, Kenneth. *Black Americans: The FBI Files.* New York: Carroll and Graf, 1994.

Padmore, George. *Pan-Africanism or Communism.* New York: Anchor Books, 1972.

Plummer, Brenda Gayle. *Rising Wind: Black Americans and U.S. Foreign Affairs, 1935–1960.* Chapel Hill: University of North Carolina Press, 1996.

Polenberg, Richard. *One Nation Divisible: Class, Race, and Ethnicity in the United States Since 1938.* New York: Penguin, 1981.

Redding, Saunders. *An American in India: A Personal Report on the Indian Dilemma and the Nature of Her Conflicts.* New York: Bobbs-Merrill, 1954.

Rivlin, Benjamin, ed. *Ralph Bunche: The Man and His Times.* New York: Holmes and Meier, 1990.

Rowan, Carl T. *The Pitiful and the Proud.* New York: Random House, 1956.

———. *Breaking the Barriers: A Memoir.* Boston: Little, Brown, 1991.

Rusk, Dean (as told to Richard Rusk). *As I Saw It,* ed. Daniel S. Papp. New York: W.W. Norton, 1990.

Rydell, Robert W. *World of Fairs: The Century-of-Progress Expositions.* Chicago: University of Chicago Press, 1993.

Schaffer, Howard B. *Chester Bowles: New Dealer in the Cold War.* Cambridge: Harvard University Press, 1993.

Schoenbaum, Thomas J. *Waging Peace and War: Dean Rusk in the Truman, Kennedy, and Johnson Years.* New York: Simon and Schuster, 1988.

Schulzinger, Robert D. *The Making of the Diplomatic Mind: The Training, Outlook, and Style of United States Foreign Service Officers, 1908–1931.* Middletown, CT: Wesleyan University Press, 1975.

Scott, William R. *The Sons of Sheba's Race: African-Americans and the Italo-Ethiopian War, 1935–1941.* Bloomington: Indiana University Press, 1993.

Simmons, Charles A. *The African American Press: With Special Reference to Four Newspapers, 1827–1965.* Jefferson, NC: McFarland, 1998.

Sitkoff, Harvard. *The Struggle for Black Equality, 1954–1980.* New York: Hill and Wang, 1981.

Sorenson, Thomas C. *The Word War: The Story of American Propaganda.* New York: Harper and Row, 1968.

Staniland, Martin. *American Intellectuals and African Nationalists, 1955–1970.* New Haven: Yale University Press, 1991.

Steigman, Andrew L. *The Foreign Service of the United States: First Line of Defense.* Boulder, CO: Westview Press, 1985.

Stein, Judith. *The World of Marcus Garvey.* Baton Rouge: Louisiana State University Press, 1986.

Stern, Mark. *Calculating Visions: Kennedy, Johnson, and Civil Rights.* New Brunswick, NJ: Rutgers University Press, 1992.

Sundquist, James L. *Politics and Power: The Eisenhower, Kennedy, and Johnson Years.* Washington, DC: The Brookings Institution, 1968.

Takaki, Ronald. *Iron Cages: Race and Culture in Nineteenth Century America.* New York: Knopf, 1990.

Urquhart, Brian. *Ralph Bunche: An American Life.* New York: Norton, 1993.

Villard, Henry Serrano. *Affairs at State.* New York: Thomas Y. Crowell, 1965.

Vincent, Theodore G. *Black Power and the Garvey Movement.* San Francisco: Ramparts Press, 1972.

Von Eschen, Penny M. *Race Against Empire: Black Americans and Anticolonialism, 1937–1957.* Ithaca: Cornell University Press, 1996.

Weil, Martin. *A Pretty Good Club: The Founding Fathers of the U.S. Foreign Service.* New York: W.W. Norton, 1978.

Weisbord, Robert G. *Ebony Kinship: Africa, Africans, and the Afro-American.* Westport, CT: Greenwood, 1973.

Westheider, James E. *Fighting on Two Fronts: African Americans and the Vietnam War.* New York: New York University Press, 1997.

Weston, Rubin Francis. *Racism and U.S. Imperialism: The Influence of Racial Assumptions on American Foreign Policy, 1893–1946.* Columbia: University of South Carolina Press, 1972.

White, Walter. *A Rising Wind.* New York: Doubleday, 1945.

Wieck, Randolph. *Ignorance Abroad: American Educational and Cultural Foreign Policy and the Office of Assistant Secretary of State.* Westport, CT: Praeger, 1992.

Articles

Anderson, Carol. "From Hope to Disillusion: African Americans, the United Nations, and the Struggle for Human Rights, 1944–1947." *Diplomatic History* 20:4 (Fall 1996): 531–563.

Beaubien, Michael. "Making Waves in Foreign Policy." *Black Enterprise* (April 1982): 38–42.

Berman, William C. "Civil Rights and Civil Liberties." In *The Truman Period as a Research Field,* ed. Richard S. Kirkendall. Columbia: University of Missouri Press, 1967.

Brantley, Daniel. "Black Americans as Participants in the Foreign Service." *The Crisis* 93:9 (November 1986): 32–33.

Calkin, Homer L. "A Reminiscence: Being Black in the Foreign Service." *Department of State Newsletter* (February 1978): 25–28.

Caprio, Gene. "View of America." *Foreign Service Journal* (July 1952):20–21, 53.

Cheers, D. Michael. "Why Aren't There More Blacks In Foreign Service?" *Ebony* (May 1983): 89–90, 92.

Culverson, Donald. "The U.S. Information Agency in Africa." *TransAfrica Forum* (Winter 1989): 61–80.

Dalfiume, Richard M. "The 'Forgotten Years' of the Negro Revolution." *Journal of American History* 55:1 (June 1968): 90–106.

Davis, John A. "Black Americans and United States Policy Toward Africa." *Journal of International Affairs* 23:2 (1969): 236–249.

Dudziak, Mary L. "Desegregation as a Cold War Imperative." *Stanford Law Review* 41 (November 1988): 61–120.

———. "Josephine Baker, Racial Protest, and the Cold War." *Journal of American History* 81 (September 1994): 543–570.

———. "The Little Rock Crisis and Foreign Affairs: Race, Resistance, and the Image of American Democracy." *Southern California Law Review* 70 (September 1997): 1641–1716.

Gatewood, Willard B. Jr. "Black Americans and the Quest for Empire, 1893–1903." *Journal of Southern History* 38 (November 1972): 545–566.

———. "Black Americans and the Boer War, 1899–1902." *South Atlantic Quarterly* 75 (Spring 1976): 226–244.

Hanson, Earl P. "The United States Invades Africa." *Harper's Magazine* (February 1947): 170–177.

Hero, Alfred O. "American Negroes and U.S. Foreign Policy, 1937–1967." *Journal of Conflict Resolution* 8 (June 1969): 220–251.

Isaacs, Harold R. "World Affairs and U.S. Race Relations: A Note on Little Rock." *Public Opinion Quarterly* (Fall 1958): 364–370.

Krenn, Michael L. " 'Outstanding Negroes' and 'Appropriate Countries': Some Facts, Figures, and Thoughts on Black U.S. Ambassadors, 1949–1988." *Diplomatic History* 14 (Winter 1990): 131–141.

———. " 'Unfinished Business': Segregation and U.S. Diplomacy at the 1958 World's Fair." *Diplomatic History* 20:4 (Fall 1996): 591–612.

———. "Edward R. Dudley." In *Notable U.S. Ambassadors Since 1775: A Biographical Dictionary*, ed. Cathal J. Nolan. Westport, CT: Greenwood, 1997, 88–93.

———. "Clifton Wharton, Sr." In *Notable U.S. Ambassadors Since 1775: A Biographical Dictionary*, ed. Cathal J. Nolan. Westport, CT: Greenwood, 1997, 365–369.

Lawson, Steven F. "Civil Rights." In *Exploring the Johnson Years*, ed. Robert A. Divine. Austin: University of Texas Press, 1981, 93–125.

Levy, Peter B. "Blacks and the Vietnam War." In *The Legacy: The Vietnam War in the American Imagination*, ed. D. Michael Shafer. Boston: Beacon Press, 1990, 209–232.

Logan, Frenise A. "Racism and Indian-U.S. Relations, 1947–1953." *Pacific Historical Review* 54 (February 1985): 71–79.

Logan, Rayford W. "Discrimination: Weakness of Our African Policy." *Current History* (January 1962): 28–35, 48.

Lyons, Terrence. "Keeping Africa Off the Agenda." In *Lyndon Johnson Confronts the World: American Foreign Policy, 1963–1968*, ed. Warren I. Cohen and Nancy Bernkopf Tucker. Cambridge: Cambridge University Press, 1994, 245–278.

Martin, Ralph G. "So You Want To Be a Diplomat." *New Republic* (October 27, 1947): 17–19.

Mayer, Michael S. "With Much Deliberation and Some Speed: Eisenhower and the *Brown* Decision." *Journal of Southern History* 52 (February 1986): 43–76.

McGhee, George C. "United States Interests in Africa." *Department of State Bulletin* 22:572 (July 19, 1950): 1001.

Noer, Thomas J. "New Frontiers and Old Priorities in Africa." In *Kennedy's Quest for Victory: American Foreign Policy, 1961–1963*, ed. Thomas G. Paterson. New York: Oxford University Press, 1989, 253–283.

Patterson, Pat. "Blacks in the Foreign Service." *Black Enterprise* (February 1978): 41–43, 47–48.

Peterson, Lisa. "The State Department—Still Pale and Male?" *Encore American & Worldwide News* (15 January 1979): 16–17.

Plummer, Brenda Gayle. "The Afro-American Response to the Occupation of Haiti, 1915–1934." *Phylon* 43 (Spring 1982): 125–143.

Roark, James L. "American Black Leaders: The Response to Colonialism and the Cold War, 1943–1953." *African Historical Studies* 4:2 (1971): 253–270.

Rogers, Ben F. "William E.B. DuBois, Marcus Garvey, and Pan-Africa." *Journal of Negro History* 40 (April 1955): 154–165.

Ross, Red. "Black Americans and Italo-Ethiopian Relief, 1935–1936." *Ethiopia Observer* 15:2 (1972): 122–131.

Rowan, Carl T. "New Frontiers in Race Relations." *Interracial Review* 34 (October 1961): 259–262.

Scott, William R. "Black Nationalism and the Italo-Ethiopian Conflict, 1934–1936." *Journal of Negro History* 63 (April 1978): 118–134.

Shapiro, Bruce. "A House Divided: Racism at the State Department." *The Nation* (12 February 1996): 11–16.

Solomon, Mark. "Black Critics of Colonialism and the Cold War." In *Cold War Critics: Alternatives to American Foreign Policy in the Truman Years*, ed. Thomas G. Paterson. Chicago: Quadrangle, 1971, 205–213.

Straus, R. Peter. "Is the State Department Color-Blind?" *Saturday Review* (2 January 1971): 12–13, 62.

Thomas, Gerald E. "The Black Revolt: The United States and Africa in the 1960s." In *The Diplomacy of the Crucial Decade: American Foreign Relations in the 1960s*, ed. Diane B. Kunz. New York: Columbia University Press, 1994, 320–360.

Washburn, S.L. "Thinking About Race." *Annual Report of the Smithsonian Institution* (Washington: Government Printing Office, 1946): 363–378.

Weisbord, Robert G. "Black America and the Italian-Ethiopian Crisis: An Episode in Pan-Negroism." *Historian* 34:2 (1972): 93–104.

Wesley, Charles H. "International Aspects of the Negro's Status in the United States." *The Negro History Bulletin* (February 1948): 118.

White, Alvin E. "Showdown in Foggy Bottom for Black Ambassadors." *Sepia* (August 1976): 16–23.

Zimmerman, Jonathan. "Beyond Double Consciousness: Black Peace Corps Volunteer in Africa, 1961–1971." *The Journal of American History* (December 1995): 999–1028.

Index

About the Author

Michael L. Krenn is an associate professor of history at the University of Miami, where he has taught since 1985. He received his Ph.D. from Rutgers University in 1985, studying under the guidance of Lloyd C. Gardner. His first book, *U.S. Policy Toward Economic Nationalism in Latin America, 1917–1929,* was published in 1990; his second, *The Chains of Interdependence: U.S. Policy Toward Central America, 1945–1954,* in 1996. His articles have appeared in *Diplomatic History, The SHAFR Newsletter, SECOLAS Annals, Radical History Review,* and *Nature, Society and Thought.* He is currently at work on a study of American art and propaganda during the Cold War.